CW01333090

The Lost Years: Life as a Far Eastern POW

The Lost Years: Life as a Far Eastern POW

**Roger Rothwell
Edited by Chris Rothwell**

Pen & Sword
MILITARY
AN IMPRINT OF PEN & SWORD BOOKS LTD.
YORKSHIRE – PHILADELPHIA

First published in Great Britain in 2024 by
Pen & Sword Military
An imprint of
Pen & Sword Books Ltd
Yorkshire - Philadelphia

Copyright © Chris Rothwell, 2024

ISBN 978 1 03610 482 5

The right of Chris Rothwell to be identified as the Author of this work has been asserted by him in accordance with the Copyright, Designs and Patents Act 1988.

A CIP catalogue record for this book is available from the British Library.

All rights reserved. No part of this book may be reproduced or transmitted in any form or by any means, electronic or mechanical, including photocopying, recording or by any information storage and retrieval system, without permission from the Publisher in writing.

Typeset in INDIA by IMPEC eSolutions
Printed and bound in England by CPI (UK) Ltd.

Pen & Sword Books Ltd. incorporates the Imprints of Pen & Sword Archaeology, Atlas, Aviation, Battleground, Discovery, Family History, History, Maritime, Military, Naval, Politics, Railways, Select, Transport, True Crime, Fiction, Frontline Books, Leo Cooper, Praetorian Press, Seaforth Publishing, Wharncliffe and White Owl.

For a complete list of Pen & Sword titles please contact

PEN & SWORD BOOKS LIMITED
47 Church Street, Barnsley, South Yorkshire, S70 2AS, England
E-mail: enquiries@pen-and-sword.co.uk
Website: www.pen-and-sword.co.uk

or

PEN AND SWORD BOOKS
1950 Lawrence Rd, Havertown, PA 19083, USA
E-mail: uspen-and-sword@casematepublishers.com
Website: www.penandswordbooks.com

Contents

Foreword		vii
Chapter 1	Awakening	1
Chapter 2	Prelude	8
Chapter 3	Initiation	17
Chapter 4	Intermission	26
Chapter 5	Aldershot	33
Chapter 6	Fulfilment	42
Chapter 7	Baptism of Fire	47
Chapter 8	Blitz	56
Chapter 9	Outward Bound	71
Chapter 10	Hong Kong	80
Chapter 11	Diehards	86
Chapter 12	Command Headquarters	94
Chapter 13	Courtland	102
Chapter 14	Storm Clouds	109
Chapter 15	The Battle for Hong Kong	117
Chapter 16	Capitulation	127
Chapter 17	Humiliation	137
Chapter 18	Shamshuipo	144
Chapter 19	Valley of the Shadow	155
Chapter 20	Argyle Street	165
Chapter 21	Stormy Weather	174
Chapter 22	Hungry Days	185
Chapter 23	Bowen Road	196
Chapter 24	Return to Shamshuipo	207
Chapter 25	Towards Freedom	216
Chapter 26	Journey's End	225

Foreword

Roger Rothwell (or Pops as we knew him growing up) was the archetypal grandfather. Gin and tonic in hand, he was full of stories of his experiences in the war, before and after capture. My brother and I listened, sometimes incredulously, to tales of heroism and horror. Editing this book has brought these stories to life, filled with details he never shared with us as children.

After the events depicted in this book and his eventual release from prison, Roger went back to education. He devoted much of his life to improving the lives of the young people he had the pleasure of teaching.

Terry Tozer, an ex-pupil of Pops and the man who has helped me publish this book, describes his memories of Mr Rothwell (as he knew him).

Roger Rothwell became headmaster at Rye Secondary Modern School in 1957. He swiftly began the change that banished the negative, loosely disciplined atmosphere to positivity and progress.

Mr Rothwell was a man who instantly commanded respect. Not from fear, as some teachers seemed to think necessary, but we certainly would not challenge his authority.

We were the failures of the 11+ system and, before Mr Rothwell, were treated as such. The mood became one of new ideas and performances of Shakespeare upon his arrival. I still remember the shock when Mr Rothwell took our maths class during a teacher's absence. Mathematics was transformed from mental torture to suddenly being interesting.

After Rye Grammar, Roger became headmaster at Tideway School in Newhaven, and upon retirement from teaching, became a Justice of the Peace at the Sussex Bench and, after this, was still working, well into his seventies, as Town Clerk of Newhaven.

We knew Pops had written a book about his war experiences, capture and eventual release from a Japanese prison in Hong Kong. In its lever-arch file, the manuscript sat on the shelf in Pops' office for many years. As children, we had also glimpsed the scrapbook he kept secret from his captors, which he presented as a gift to Daisy, my grandmother, upon his return. Some pages from this scrapbook have been reproduced here.

Since my father, Tim (Roger's son), died suddenly at the end of 2022, it emerged he had been thinking of publishing this book. I have carried on this work in memory of my father, Tim, and Pops.

What rings out from the pages is a man who, although he suffered indescribable hardship, never lost his sense of humour and never gave up hope that he would see Daisy again.

Roger was a devoted husband to Daisy, father to Tim and Gill, and Grandfather to me, Alex and Kate. He passed away after a long illness in 2007 at the age of 89, having lived the fullest and most extraordinary of lives.

Chris Rothwell, July 2023

Chapter 1

Awakening

Roger stirred uneasily, uncomfortably. The concrete floor beneath the old rice sack that formed his mattress had numbed his hip, sending a tingle of pins and needles down his thigh, and he turned onto his back to ease the pressure.

He looked dimly around him through half-opened eyes at the now familiar sight of his sixty companions who shared the hut. Some, like him, were rousing from their sleep. Others more fortunate were snoring in a variety of keys. These sounds, mingling with those of coughing and the occasional groan from the sick, were part of the usual pattern of the daily life to which he had become accustomed. All were packed so closely together as to leave no appreciable space between them. Each jealously guarded his territorial boundaries.

A few, more enterprising than the others, had contrived various ingenious ways of raising themselves off the floor. They used contraptions of spars of wood with crossed ends joined by poles, over which they had slung sacking retrieved clandestinely on a Monday morning when the lorry delivered the week's supply of rice. Others had devised hammocks suspended from the wooden roof of the hut.

In the half-light of the early morning, he looked across the hut where his friend Jack Poole had perched a bottle of bean oil on a jury-rigged shelf. He saw a large black rat scramble along the horizontal support of the weather-boarding which formed the wall. It reared itself up towards the neck of the bottle, attracted by the smell of the rancid oil.

Roger shouted and hurled his clogs (shaped pieces of flat wood with webbing loops which served him as sandals) at the creature, which gave a terrified squeak and disappeared.

The clogs had missed the rat but had awakened Jack, who enquired in unprintable terms what was afoot. Roger did not enlighten him. After all, a bottle of oil was a precious possession when no form of fat had been available for nearly two years. Despite its unpalatable taste, it was useful for frying the meagre rice ration. It helped it go down a little more quickly. It contributed towards the battle against the malnutrition they all suffered. Jack, like so many others, had already had dysentery.

2   The Lost Years: Life as a Far Eastern POW

Roger reckoned, quite mistakenly as it turned out, that he was now immune from further attacks.

The encounter with the rat had roused him sufficiently to let him take stock of his situation. He was accommodated with some 500 or so of his comrades in the prison camp in Hong Kong, where they had surrendered on Christmas Day in 1941 following a merciless battle which had commenced with the attack on the colony with no formal declaration of war on December 8th, 1941.

The date was August 24th, 1942 – his second wedding anniversary. He put his hand under the bundle of clothing that served as a pillow and drew a photograph of a very pretty young girl in a knitted Fair Isle jumper. Daisy, the childhood sweetheart he had married a few short months before he had been drafted abroad and with whom the total extent of his married life had been no more than a few short weeks in London under the ferocious air raids of the Autumn of 1940.

He had to keep the photograph well hidden since a Japanese sentry had grabbed it and started to march off with it. He had snatched it back and had thrown it to his neighbour, who had passed it down and across the hut to the others as in a rugger match in a series of bewildering moves until it was safely concealed at the far end under a pile of bedding. Consequently, the frustrated sentry had given him the statutory beating for his resistance but had been unable to retrieve the photograph, which had remained well concealed along with other keepsakes ever since.

The photograph was his most important and treasured possession, representing the hope that one day – God only knew when – he would hold its subject once again to him. This had given him the reason for living without which so many had perished.

Whether she was safe and well, he did not know since he had received no word from her or from anyone else during the long months of his captivity. Likely enough, she also would not know if he had survived the battle or, if so, whether he was, by this time, alive or dead. His captors delighted in giving horrific details of starvation and carnage in England resulting from the German bombing and blockade. Although no one believed them, there was always the possibility that it might be so.

Roger kissed the photograph gently and put it back in its hiding place.

Then he felt the tickle of an insect crawling across his face. Although he knew the folly of so doing, he slapped instinctively at it with his hand. He was rewarded by the revolting stench of the blood of the bloated bed bug, which had been successfully foraging for food from his companions all night.

The bugs lived in the wooden roof of the hut during the day and dropped down at night to feed. Roger knew that when he got up in the morning, he would find a black line of them clustered along the seams of the sacking. This would entail a visit to the nest of soldier ants at the corner of the camp and the satisfaction of watching the little creatures marching off in triumph, each gripping a struggling bed bug between its tiny jaws.

By now, he was thoroughly awake and able to take stock of his situation.

First, he must make a trip to the latrine at the end of the camp. This would be his fifth night visit since an exclusive diet of rice kept the kidneys in excellent operative order and forced everyone into a constant safari to and fro along the rough earth path between the huts. This would not be without some difficulty since the beriberi, which had swollen his legs to twice their normal size, also produced sharp stabs of pain through the soles of his feet, a condition known to them all as "electric feet". It caused those suffering from the complaint to walk with a stagger and the knees slightly bent, which helped to ease the pain a little.

He slipped his feet into the webbing straps of the clogs and put on his fundoshi - a strip of cloth about two feet long with a length of string at one end. This was tied around the midriff from behind, leaving the fabric dangling down at the back. It was then pulled up between the legs and behind the string so that it hung down in front like a little skirt and made a modest, if somewhat basic, article of clothing.

As he went down between the line of huts, he heard the guttural challenge of the sentry and the unmistakable sound of the bolt pushing a bullet into the breach of the rifle. Without delay, he shouted "Benjo!" - the Japanese for toilet and one of the only two words he knew. The other was "Ni" - the word for "two", which he had to call out as his number at the morning counting parade. In common with most of his comrades, he made it a point of honour not to learn the language, even though it would have been handy when encountering a sentry in circumstances requiring an explanation.

On his way back to the hut, he exchanged greetings with his fellow prisoners, who were obliged to stand on guard at the door of each hut. If any inmates escaped during his one hour of duty, those on guard would doubtless be shot.

This was a most unwelcome chore carried out following a strictly monitored rota. It was not so bad from October to December following the summer monsoon. It became most unpleasant during the early part of the year when, by European standards, the night temperature of around 40 degrees Fahrenheit might not seem all that low, the thinness of their blood resulting from their diet made it seem unbearably cold. From April onwards, there was a good chance of getting soaked by the torrential rain and the difficult task of drying oneself before crawling back into bed.

Roger had completed his stint of duty the previous night and would not be required to go on duty for another ten days.

Back on his bed, he contemplated the immediate future and wondered what the day would bring forth. No doubt, like so many of the hundreds that preceded it, it would be one of unrelieved monotony unless some new drama were to unfold. Terrible though some of these had proved, they at least provided something new to talk about when all the personal anecdotes of one's past life had long since been exhausted.

The first thing would be the morning muster, when all five hundred would stand in line according to their regiment or unit and bellow the Japanese word for their number.

How long this would last depended on the mood of Colonel Tokanaga, the camp commandant, the "Fat Pig" as he was known to his reluctant guests. And to "Panama Pete" Inouye, the interpreter who gained great satisfaction from hurling insults and threats at the prisoners in a strong American accent. Panama Pete had spent several obviously unhappy years in San Francisco before the war and frequently referred to them: "When I was in the States, youse guys kick me round plenty. Now, I kick you round plenty too!".

The odd clout from a sentry was a matter of almost daily routine. However, on one occasion, when he was on duty outside the hut one chilly night in February, Roger was wearing a naval greatcoat a kindly naval commander lent to him to keep out the cold. A passing sentry who had had a brush with the commander the previous day mistook Roger for his proposed victim and removed his two front teeth with the butt of his rifle. After which, he drew in his breath with a sharp hiss and a slight bow in the true spirit of Bushido, the Japanese code of honourable conduct.

But a brush with Panama Pete was an entirely different matter and something to be avoided at all costs. He had been known to kick a man to death, an incident which had been duly noted along with many others to be submitted as evidence in the unlikely event of his being brought before a war crimes tribunal at some time in the distant and uncertain future if ever they survived to tell the tale.

By now, Roger was back in his tattered sleeping bag - a relic from far-off happy days at many summer Boy Scout camps. It was very much the worse for wear, having been hung on a barbed-wire fence by well-meaning comrades after they had immersed it in a bucket of water for ten days. This after a bad attack of dysentery combined with malaria, nearly finishing him off in Shamshuipo Camp two months after his captivity. This treatment had produced a thousand little snags through which the feathers peeped out and had cost him many hours of patience and only partly successful labour to repair.

He was not certain of the time – his watch had long ago been sold to a Japanese sentry through the good offices of an RASC lieutenant who had learned some basic Japanese and acted as a go-between with the camp guards. As a result, he and his partner were able to run a most profitable business on the commission arising from the transactions. These enabled them to live comfortably compared to the remainder of their less enterprising companions. By the time everything of value in the camp had thus been sold, the ingenious couple had amassed a sufficiency either of Military Yen or of quantities of such goodies as rice bran, soya beans, oil or the coveted oblong cakes of hard brown sugar.

Though he disapproved of making personal profit from the hardships of one's companions, Roger had to admit that it was helpful to have this means of overcoming a crisis in times of desperate need. The watch sale had been a blessing when it was essential to get sugar for his sick hut mate, Major Jack Wood, to replace the energy lost from an attack of dysentery. Although the yield of Military Yen had been very meagre, and he had calculated that at the current exchange rate of four Yen to the pound sterling, the sugar had cost something like twenty-five pounds per pound.

After roll call, he proposed a session with the little group, which included General Maltby, a Colonel and several others of less exalted rank to whom he was teaching French. However, he was aware this could well be frustrated by his selection for a working party either to clean out latrines in the Japanese officers' quarters below the camp or to be marched out to cut grass on the hillside to be dried and used for fuel in the camp kitchen.

Of the two, he much preferred the latter as it got him out beyond the barbed wire and electric fence and on to the slope of the hill from which he could look out on the remainder of the world and feel almost free for a couple of hours despite the presence of the armed guard.

On the last trip, however, he had picked up a bundle of grass which had housed a black and yellow bamboo snake which, luckily, had been as surprised and scared as he was and had disappeared with speed in the opposite direction without any further argument. He hoped that this would not happen again. One did not willingly cross swords with bamboo snakes.

However, cleaning out Japanese Headquarters had its compensations, as there was always the chance of picking up some unconsidered trifle that might be useful in the camp. This was not without its dangers since concealing contraband about one's person when dressed only in a fundoshi presented difficulties. However skilful a thief one had become, the penalties for getting caught were severe.

6   The Lost Years: Life as a Far Eastern POW

On one occasion, when he had picked up a metal scouring pad which would be invaluable in removing the rust from the old milk powder tin which served him as both cup and plate, he had at first concealed it securely in the lowest part of his fundoshi. Finding its contact with the more sensitive parts of his person uncomfortable, he had transferred it to his armpit but, on his return to the camp, had been nudged by the next in line and had dropped the pad from its hiding place right at the feet of the Sergeant of the guard who was inspecting the returning working party.

This resulted in his being made to stand with a bowl of water held above his head for several hours and receiving a clout from his guard each time the water slopped over the rim of the bowl. In the end, the pain in his arms was so intense that he spilt the water deliberately since the beating at least relieved his tortured muscles for a few moments and was less painful.

Under the skilful guidance of members of the Royal Signals, his companions collected sufficient components to make a most effective radio, which had been buried in an old biscuit tin between two huts. The radio had been tuned to Radio New Delhi, from where a daily bulletin of news was received and relayed in whispers throughout the camp by word of mouth. This process inevitably led to the wildest distortions of the truth at the end of the line.

The radio was an all-mains affair receiving power from an underground cable attached to the electric fence. It worked with excellent efficiency for more than a year.

The news was received via an earphone whose connection with the set was by a wire from the biscuit tin attached to two nails in the hut's wall over which hung an old coat. The duty man for the day would lie at his bed space with his head on the hand which concealed the earpiece, relaying the news to his neighbour in whispers.

Not that the news that it brought was of much encouragement to them. Things were going very badly for the Allies. Very little progress was being made in the Pacific. In Africa, the earlier successes against the Italians had been repulsed. The Germans, under Rommel, had pushed the Eighth Army back to within striking distance of Egypt and the Suez Canal and were besieging Tobruk. Only a few days before, August 20th, news had come of an assault by British and Canadian forces on Dieppe, and, even accepting the optimistic account from the B.B.C., it was clear that, whatever its purpose, the attack had been defended with heavy casualties. The Japanese propaganda sheet, the 'Hong Kong Times News', gleefully reported total disaster and the annihilation of the attackers. It would be a long time, indeed years, before they could hope for release. Roger, resolving not to get depressed on this particular day, put such matters from his mind and addressed himself to the issues of more immediate concern.

His thoughts turned inevitably to the most pressing problem of all - food. This was a perpetual topic of conversation among them. Many hours were spent happily planning the gargantuan meals consumed after their release. Fierce arguments would arise from a discussion of the relative merits of Sirloin as opposed to rump steak or the menu to be selected at the next visit to Simpson's in the Strand (if it were still there at the end of the war), and they live to patronise it.

They were perpetually hungry - not as one is in pleasant anticipation of a good meal at the end of a day's work when says: "Gosh, I am hungry - I could murder a steak and kidney pie", but with a dull, ever-present ache that could only be staunched for an hour or so by the daily ration of rice and mug of watery vegetable - as often as not boiled chrysanthemum leaves and stalks which had a strange aromatic flavour. These leaves were preferable to boiled lettuce with its slimy tastelessness or stewed daikon, which no amount of cooking could soften and which looked like a parsnip but which, like the lettuce, was entirely without flavour.

Roger had been elected as the dispenser of these delicacies for his hut - an extremely sensitive task. Critical eyes watched every portion to ensure that no one received a couple of grains more than anyone else. This was not easy, especially given the wide assortment of receptacles and the nature of the container from which he had to dispense it - a round metal can which, in more prosperous days, had formed the bottom half of an oil drum and, inevitably at the end of the distribution any shortfall had to be borne by the distributor. Whereas any surplus had to be shared out as accurately as possible. He had at first been flattered by his election, thinking that it was a sign of general trust in his integrity. He rapidly learned that it was only because no-one else wanted the thankless task.

Recalled to the present reality, he became aware that the hut was now astir and the time for the morning roll call was at hand. Roger scrambled up, adjusted his fundoshi, ensured his possessions were as secure from search as possible, and set off for the parade ground.

Another day had begun.

Chapter 2

Prelude

The start of the war had found Roger in the school's staffroom in Thornton Heath, where he had been teaching since September of the previous year when he had graduated and qualified at London University. The job of teaching reading and basic arithmetic to seven and eight-year-olds was not quite what he had envisaged for himself. Still, work had not been easy to find when the country had just emerged from the recession of the early 1930s. He counted himself lucky to have found an appointment of any kind.

It was 9 a.m. on Sunday, 3rd September 1939, and he had been recalled by telegram to report to the school at the earliest possible time two days previously.

The children had been summoned to school and assembled in the playground to be issued with their completed identity labels and gas masks, each in its little cardboard box and hung around their necks by a piece of string, checked and tested to ensure it fitted properly. It was generally assumed that the outbreak of war would be accompanied by a massive air raid and gas attacks on the capital. It was essential for the children to be able to fit and adjust the evil-smelling things without delay.

He had spent the latter part of the previous summer term with his colleagues and others at a local hall assembling the masks. These consisted of a circular metal canister to which a rubber face-piece was attached by a wide elastic band of such strength that it required an almost super-human effort to slip it over the canister and on to the base of the mask. It had been just his luck to be at the end of the assembly line where this final process took place, and his fingers had suffered accordingly.

Given the apparent inevitability of the outbreak of war following the invasion of Poland by the German Army on September 1st, the planned evacuation of children from the capital into safe areas had begun the following day.

Like all good plans, the evacuation arrangements were simple. The movement from London was to be a radial one, with all schools in the south-east of the capital moving to the southeast, the south of London to the south, the north of London to the north and so on.

Those on the city's outskirts moved farthest away while the inner areas moved to the inner fringes of the reception areas some twenty miles from the centre. The children and their teachers were to be carried by train from the station nearest their school so that there would be no inconvenient crossings of the city centre and no intermediate changes of train to be made. Under the circumstances, delays might result in congestion and a massive loss of life.

It was all as simple as ABC, and schools had received detailed instructions in large envelopes double-sealed with wax before the end of the summer term. The contents of these envelopes were duly noted by the teaching staff, and the information was conveyed to the parents.

Incredibly, the only information not to be divulged was the destination of the potential evacuees. This was sealed in a separate envelope, not to be opened by the headmaster until ten minutes after the departure of the train.

It was 10 o'clock, and the labels were all affixed to the most prominent part of the youngsters' anatomies.

Five minutes later, a fresh set of instructions in new sealed envelopes arrived. All the labels were removed, fresh ones written, and instructions issued to the swarm of anxious parents thronging the school gates and peering through the iron railings of the playground.

The whole exercise had been complicated by half of the children whose names had been entered on the register of children to be evacuated not arriving at the school. Additionally, a not inconsiderable number whose parents had initially refused the offer of evacuation but had changed their minds at the last moment were now thronging round their teachers, demanding labels and adding to a steadily developing chaos.

However, by 10.55, the last child had been ushered out from the playground with instructions to report to Thornton Heath station at 10.45 the following day. Roger and his colleagues retreated to the staff room for a well-earned cup of coffee.

Five minutes later, they were listening to the voice of the Prime Minister, Neville Chamberlain, over the wireless, saying in sombre tones, *"and I have to tell you now that no such assurance has been received and that, in consequence, this country is at war with Germany"*.

Almost instantaneously, the stunned silence that followed was interrupted by the wailing of the first air raid warning of the war. Looking through the staff room window, staff were horrified to see a swarm of planes sweeping across the sky. The knowledge that all their pupils were in the streets on their way home struck terror into their hearts. Clearly, the theory that the declaration of war would be followed immediately by massive air strikes was about to be proved correct.

As was to happen so often during the next ten months, this was the first of a series of false alarms. The teachers breathed sighs of relief, took a last look around the familiar room, which many were never to see again, and went their ways. Meanwhile, the planes returned to the nearby Hendon Aerodrome, from which they had been scrambled just before the sounding of the alarm.

Roger returned to his lodgings in Carew Road, where his landlady, the kindly and ageing Mrs Holton, who mothered him as if he had been her own son, greeted him with tears, coffee and homemade buns. He sat down to write to the War Office. He was informing them that as a former member of the University of London Officer Training Corps who had attained the distinction of achieving his Certificate 'A', albeit of failing Certificate 'B', he wished, given his expertise in military matters, to volunteer himself in the service of his King and Country as a commissioned officer.

At 11 o'clock the following day, he found himself in a train pulling out of Thornton Heath Station precisely on schedule, leaving behind on the platform a host of distressed and dewy-eyed mothers who, although they had been specifically asked not to, had not unreasonably come to kiss and wave their little ones goodbye.

The children, many of whom were travelling by train for the first time in their young lives, clearly regarded the whole operation as an exciting adventure. Roger was hard put to it for a while to keep them on their seats.

When the first excitement had died away, however, they quietened down and occupied themselves in huffing on the carriage's windows and drawing pin men with their fingers in the resulting condensation.

Precisely ten minutes after the train had left, the headmaster - a stickler for protocol - had opened the remaining envelope according to his instructions and announced that their destination would be Shoreham by Sea.

Roger found this a little odd since the principal reason for the school's evacuation in the first place had been its proximity to Croydon Aerodrome. That morning, all the Imperial Airways planes from Croydon had also been transferred to Shoreham for their safety. He wondered for the first time, but by no means the last, if the operation would be quite as efficient as he had supposed.

However, other thoughts took precedence over considering the vagaries of the bureaucratic mind, and he settled down to establish his priorities for future action.

There would be an immediate response from the War Office to his offer of enlistment, which would undoubtedly be followed by early service overseas. The first priority, therefore, must be to ask Daisy to marry him. They had been sweethearts for more than seven years when he was 15 and she 12. Although no formal declaration had ever been made, it had always been an unspoken understanding between them that they would get married one day. However, his mother had warned that there should be no thought of marriage until he was earning at least five pounds per week.

On his teacher's salary of three pounds ten shillings, the likelihood of attaining such wealth had seemed so remote as to make this prospect seem depressingly distant.

But the outbreak of war must surely render such a barrier invalid, and he resolved to take the plunge at the earliest opportunity. Warmed by this, the miles passed happily away, and by now, the train was puffing its way through Hove. It was time to marshal the now subdued children and check their gasmasks, brown paper parcels and bags in preparation for their arrival at their new home.

The train disgorged its cargo onto a piece of waste ground behind Shoreham station, and the children were lined up along a broken flint wall on the far side. They were by now silent and a little apprehensive. Sisters grasped smaller brothers firmly by the hand and fought back the tears which, later, were to flow much more freely.

At one end of the field, behind trestle tables loaded with tea urns, lemonade, bags of oranges and chocolate, were ranged the good ladies of the local Women's Voluntary Service who had spent many months in careful preparation for this great day.

On the opposite side, facing the children, stood many other ladies who, having volunteered to accommodate evacuees, had come to take their pick of the bunch. After all, the remuneration for their hospitality was to be ten shillings per head per week for a single child and eight shillings and sixpence each if more than one was to be housed. Clearly, no one was to become rich from this exercise, and the careful Shoreham housewives were scarcely to be blamed for trying to strike the best deal they could.

There then followed a scene which reminded Roger irresistibly of a slave traders' market. One by one, the selected children were inspected, taken by the hand, and led away to the ladies at the end table to be registered and docketed before disappearing, each grasping his little bundle of possessions and bag of chocolate and sweets.

The first to disappear were the prettiest, cleanest and best dressed of the little girls and boys, some of whom were separated from brothers and sisters and wept bitterly in consequence.

In vain did the teachers protest that it was essential to know details of the homes to which their pupils were being led away since their advice concerning the children's home backgrounds and parentage was vital if disastrous placement mistakes were to be avoided. However, the good souls in charge of the operation were in complete control. All would be well, they said. There were no such things as bad homes in Shoreham. Each one had been carefully vetted, and there was no cause for alarm.

Their pleas were useless; the ladies had worked on this for many months. They knew exactly what they were doing, all would be well, and the interfering teachers would be much better employed in drinking another cup of tea and, really, given that most of the children had by now disappeared, leaving only the scruffiest and less attractive little boys to be distributed more or less indiscriminately later on, this did seem to be the only possible course of action to take.

Sipping his tea, Roger surveyed the future gloomily and resolved to take advantage of the inevitable chaos of the early stages of the operation and get himself back home to Daisy and his proposed plan of action as soon as was practicable.

Accordingly, having settled comfortably into the billet in Hebe Road to which he had been allocated, he caught an early train the following day.

That evening, he proposed to Daisy and was accepted, no further reference to the importance of his future weekly income having been made and, indeed, his mother having gone so far as to lend him her own engagement ring to clinch the deal until such time as her future daughter-in-law could choose her own.

His future happiness thus secured, he sped back to Shoreham on his motorcycle and reported for duty to Dan Holman, the headmaster, without his absence being noticed. The Roman maxim *'Carpe Diem'* had clearly paid dividends.

However, the days following this highly satisfactory development fully justified his worst fears. Many of the children had disappeared into the blue, and several days were to elapse before they were all located, and little town maps had been drawn to establish their whereabouts.

Even this brought little relief since many of the placements were clearly inappropriate and much diplomacy had to be exercised in resolving the problems thus arising, as well as coping with a torrent of complaints from foster-parents who were discovering that looking after someone else's children was not as simple as they had at first supposed.

For the reimbursement of ten shillings per week, the foster parent was expected not only to provide food and laundry costs but also had to endure the inconvenience and expense of unaccustomed scratches on furniture, mud on carpets, stains on table cloths and wet beds which, as the children became more emotionally disturbed as a result of their isolation from home, were an increasingly common occurrence.

For many of them, there were also problems arising from diets unfamiliar to the youngsters, many of whom from the poorer homes rebelled against the meals provided by their kindly and well-meaning hosts and demanded fish and chips. The more affluent complained of the food's lack of variety and quality.

To cope with these problems, the teaching staff organised a rota of home visits every weekday evening, often as late as ten o'clock, making home visits and listening to lengthy tales of woe.

Most of the foster parents made great efforts to be tolerant and cooperative, but there were those who, often not unreasonably, felt themselves approaching the end of their tethers. The principal among these was Mrs Barton, who had selected three children from a good home background and who waylaid him as he went through the town, on his way to the shop and even into the bar of the Green Man. He had crept there unknown to the Headmaster, who objected to his teachers being seen in public houses to drown his sorrows in company with his like-minded colleagues and to compare gloomy notes on future prospects.

What bothered Mrs Barton most was the unfavourable comparisons with their home accommodation, meals and entertainment. They said the bed all three shared was too hard, and they were tired of beans on toast. Mum and Dad used to take them to the cinema at least once a week, their pocket money had run out, and she couldn't be expected to give them any on the miserable allowance she got from the government, now could she? Mrs Barton felt put upon, as she termed it, and on his twice-weekly visit, Roger was treated to long lectures on the inadequacy of the remuneration, the unreasonable demands of the three and the inaccuracy of the complaints to their parents made in a letter home which she had intercepted.

"Now, young man," she would say, "just you come upstairs and lie on that bed and tell me if that is not as clean and as comfortable as your own!" and Roger would follow her meekly up the narrow staircase into the tiny dark room with its minute window, and lie obediently on the hard lumpy mattress, pronouncing it to be all that she had said it was and mentally resolving to arrange a transfer for the unfortunate trio as soon as it could be arranged. Courage was not his strong point, especially when dealing with the likes of Mrs B.

But by no means was Mrs Barton typical, nor had all the prospective foster parents joined in the competitive scramble for the most attractive children and never, indeed, through all his time at Shoreham did he come across a single case of absolute neglect. On the contrary, kindness, patience and tolerance under challenging circumstances were the norm.

Among the foster parents on his visiting list was Mrs Campbell, the mother of Sir Malcolm Campbell, the racing driver. She was a lovely old lady and had explicitly asked for a little boy from a deprived background. Roger had had no hesitation in recommending his Billy Sanders as qualifying without fear of contradiction for this distinction.

Billy came from a home with almost daily violence and constant neglect. He was grubby, ill-clad, rebellious and possessed a vocabulary that would have credited the proverbial fishwife. Roger made the choice with no bit of trepidation. Mrs Campbell would have a problem on her hands, but then she had asked for it.

On his first visit to her house – a charming bungalow set in a beautiful garden – he was greeted by a little boy dressed in a new suit and with a shining clean face proudly holding a brand new bicycle who greeted him politely with a cheerful grin. It was a transformed Billy Sanders who had clearly landed on his feet.

Not that Mrs Campbell spoiled him. On the contrary, she insisted on good table manners, curbed his language, trained him in good habits and tried to improve his speech. Above all, she loved, cared for, and stood between him and probing teachers bent on unearthing possible misdemeanours.

On one occasion, soon after she had taken possession of Billy, Roger, detecting a note of hesitation in her response to his enquiry as to whether Billy was behaving himself, boldly stood his ground and demanded a complete and truthful exposition of what had gone wrong in the Campbell household since his last visit.

With great reluctance and having demanded a firm assurance that no punitive action would follow her report, she revealed that Billy, who had never seen a refrigerator in his life, had "done his little business on one of my best willow pattern plates and frozen it, but you did promise that you would not punish him!"

If ever there was a saint, Mrs Campbell was undoubtedly one, and she was not alone in deserving canonisation.

Although not called upon to exercise tolerance on such a scale, other foster parents faced situations they had not envisaged when answering the call for the accommodation of evacuees and did their honest best to cope with them. Those with a family of their own often found it difficult to integrate the newcomer with their other children, who either demanded preferential treatment or resented the extraordinary tolerance extended to the stranger.

The most significant cause of difficulty was the weekend visit by the child's parents. These visits inevitably had a disturbing effect that took days to overcome and frequently caused disputes between the two groups of parents and an abrupt return of the child to Thornton Heath.

Some of the host parents complained that the visitors arrived without sustenance and expected to be entertained at their expense, and others that the emotional scenes at the arrival and departure were more than they were prepared to tolerate.

This, and the long period of stalemate in the war situation with no sign of aggression by the enemy, resulted in a steady drift back to Croydon so that only one-third evacuated initially remained in Shoreham by the end of December. These represented only one-fifth of the whole school population, 700 having taken no part in the evacuation exercise in the first place and having been left to wander the streets without educational provision of any kind.

The effect of all this on the children's education was catastrophic. The only suitable accommodation was the local school, which had to be shared between the rightful occupants and the invaders who took possession in the mornings, leaving the place to the Shoreham children in the afternoons.

The afternoons were spent either in the local Baptists' Hall when it was wet or on fine days, and mercifully - the weather that autumn was unusually kind - in rambles over the hills or along the seashore trying as far as possible to supplement the bare bones of the morning's teaching, a fossil picked up on the beach providing a welcome bonus or a rabbit's burrow on the Downs.

Not that the whole of the session could be devoted to academic pursuits since a great deal of time had to be spent in issuing books, stationery and pencil stubs, which had to be kept separate from those of the locals and collected up and stowed away at the end of the morning. Consequently, practically every other topic had to be sacrificed to teach the 3 Rs with no time to spare for anything else.

Wet days were a nightmare. Early experiments in dividing the tiny hall into ten sections for the separate instruction of the various age groups were abandoned at a very early stage, the resultant babble making anything like coherent teaching a total farce, and the teaching staff adopted the only possible alternative of taking it in turns to keep the whole group of 400 youngsters sitting or squatting on the floor entertained by stories, drama and music.

These dreadful afternoons seemed endless and usually finished with bad tempers and recriminations.

Roger sighed at the arrival of the call to arms from the War Office, which seemed strangely reluctant to use his services. However, the long-awaited letter arrived at the beginning of October, summoning him to report to the recruiting centre at the Imperial Institute in London. In the very hall in which he had taken his final examinations, he was stripped, pummelled, subjected to embarrassing assaults on the more intimate parts of his person and finally pronounced fit to serve his country.

He was also informed that the awarding of automatic commissions to former officer cadets had ceased the previous day. He would, consequently, be enlisted as a private into the Royal Fusiliers and must await call-up with the rest of his age group; so much for his dreams of military glory.

He took his two shillings pay for his first day's service in the army and returned to Shoreham, where he purchased a silver Royal Fusiliers lapel badge for his fiancée to wear with pride as proof that her man was not a conscript.

As the weeks dragged on, and more and more afternoons were spent in the Baptists' Hall, the drift of children back to Croydon increased. The growing escalation of juvenile crime there made it clear that since the expected attacks on the capital had not materialised, there was an urgent need to make proper provision for those youngsters. Plans were made to reopen the school in Thornton Heath at the beginning of the Spring Term.

As far as Roger was concerned, however, the ordeal was over. His calling-up papers arrived requiring him to report, not to the Royal Fusiliers as he had assumed, but to the Queen's Royal Regiment at Stoughton Barracks in Guildford on January 15th, 1940. He purchased another lapel badge, this time Paschal Lamb, the emblem of the "Mutton Lancers" (as the Queen's were called), for Daisy to wear in place of the exploding grenade insignia of the Fusiliers.

The sequel to the evacuation to Shoreham was terrible in the extreme. In August, the Germans settled down to bombing London in earnest. In their attempt to eliminate the Royal Air Force in preparation for the planned invasion, a heavy raid on Shoreham aerodrome claimed the lives of forty remaining evacuees. A belated decision was made to relocate them to Aldershot (of all places) for their safety. It was not until several more had been killed there that sixty children - all that remained out of the original eight hundred who had left Thornton Heath on that memorable day in September - were sent for safety to Ilfracombe.

When Roger returned to the school in December 1940 on his embarkation leave to say goodbye to his former colleagues, he found that the casualty list among the children had been tragically high. One wing of the school had been destroyed by a direct hit, and the playground where he had helped muster the youngsters fifteen months previously consisted of three large bomb craters. All the staff not called up were back on duty except two lucky ones looking after the remaining evacuees - all sixty in Ilfracombe.

With a guilty feeling of relief, he reported back for duty to his regiment and his last few remaining days with Daisy, now his wife, before embarking for Hong Kong.

Chapter 3

Initiation

January 15th, 1940 was a freezing, dismal day which found Roger standing on the platform of Tonbridge Station, giving a bravely smiling Daisy a final kiss and hug before the train bore him away to Guildford. On arrival, a truck was waiting to carry him and a small group of fellow recruits to the grim arched brick gateway of Stoughton Barracks on the outskirts of the town.

Here they were greeted by Sergeant Fox, who, in common with most of his kind, affected a profound contempt for the pallid and round-shouldered civilians forming a ragged line before him.

"Oh dear, oh dear, oh dear," he said, "what have we got here?" and, like jesting Pilate, who would not stay for an answer, went on: "Well, we shall have to smarten you up a little, shan't we? Stand up straight, for goodness' sake, get those heads up, stand in a line, get those shoulders back. I've got to make soldiers of you, God help me. I may break your hearts, but you won't break mine; I can tell you that. By the time I've finished with you, your own mothers won't know you," and much more in the same strain.

Following these words of welcome, they were ushered away to a hut which, although shabby, was immaculately clean with a floor scrubbed white and furnished with iron bed frames devoid of either bedding or even a base. Roger wondered how their bodies would be supported if they were ever allowed to go to bed.

He was soon to find out. When they had deposited their bags and cases on the floor, they were led away to a vast, corrugated iron building where, from behind long trestle tables, they were issued with battle dress, shirts, boots, greatcoat, forage cap and various webbing straps accoutrements of whose purpose they could only guess.

At a separate table, Roger was handed a little brown book entitled A.B.64. The book had blank pages on which his pay and details of his future military career would be recorded, and from which he learned that he was no longer Mr Roger Rothwell, but *6464659, Private Rothwell R.S.*

He was also presented with two brown discs, one circular and the other hexagonal in shape, together with a piece of string with which to fasten these around his neck. "These here are your identity discs," he was informed. "You wear them all the time, and you never, ever, take them off, no matter what". With these, he received the gloomy news that, in the event of his untimely end, the circular one would accompany him to his grave and the other be sent to his next of kin.

Encouraged by this information and loaded with these new possessions, they staggered back to their hut under the hostile gaze of Sergeant Fox, who, when they had dumped them beside their bed spaces, commanded: "Now away at the double to get your boards and pally arses".

Mystified by these strange instructions and speculating what sort of posterior a pally arse betokened, they trotted back to the equipment store, receiving three long planks of wood and a canvas sack. Summoning up all his courage, Roger asked: "Please, Sir, what are we to do with these?"

Sergeant Fox regarded him with incredulity - clearly, he had got a right one here. "Look, sonny Jim, my name is Sergeant Fox, and you call me Sergeant, not Sir - that's for RSMs and officers of which you will never be one. So, remember. The boards are for you to put on your bed to kip on, my lad."

Not to be deterred by the scorn in the Sergeant's voice, Roger persisted: "But aren't we going to have a mattress?"

"You've got it in your hand, sonny," replied Sergeant Fox.

Roger looked blank; the others, equally ignorant but content to let him bear the weight of the Sergeant's sarcasm, awaited the solution to the mystery.

"That there," explained the Sergeant, taking the sack from Roger's hand, "is what is known as a pally arse - you stuff it up with straw, and you puts it on your boards, and you lies on it, now for God's sake stop asking daft questions and go over there to draw your straw and mind you don't spill any on the floor or I'll be having you."

The recruits did as they were bidden and returned to the hut with their bed boards and bloated palliasses, which they fitted onto the bed frames. They started to unpack their belongings and stow them away in the wooden lockers beside their beds under the interested scrutiny of the Sergeant.

"What have you got there, sonny?" enquired Sergeant Fox as Roger unpacked pyjamas and a dressing gown. "You are in the army now, lad, not in the ruddy Grand Hotel. Things like that are for civvy street and officers, which you are not. Put them away, boy and don't let me catch you wearing la-di-da gear like that, or you'll find me chasing you all round the parade ground in them."

The Sergeant left them alone, and they sat gloomily on their bed boards, contemplating their future after this inauspicious start to their military careers. Roger would have given a great deal to be back at Shoreham and even more to be at home with Daisy, from whom he seemed to have been parted for a lifetime. He even remembered Mrs Barton with something even approaching nostalgia.

Platoon No. 5, of which he was now a member, was a motley collection of thirty chaps of his own age representing a complete range of social, financial and academic backgrounds.

Frank was a professional footballer who had played for Torquay United, Jimmy was a solicitor, Maurice a racing driver, George a gravedigger by profession, whilst Gordon and his twin brother had inherited millions from their stock-broker father and, all in all, they represented the most unlikely group of future warriors as one could wish to meet.

No wonder Sergeant Fox had regarded them with dismay. He had just eight weeks to mould them into a fighting infantry unit capable of upholding the regiment's reputation, which he was so proud of. Nevertheless, he had done it before with material no more promising than the shower that had now been visited upon him, and he would do it again or die in the attempt, or they would.

He was well-equipped for the job, being small, wiry and tough with a stubble of red hair, which boded ill for any recalcitrant recruit. He had a stock of standard jibes without which no self-respecting Sergeant could prosper.

"Am I hurting you?" he would enquire from the rear of his chosen victim. "No, Sergeant," would come the reply from the luckless rookie who stood smartly to attention expecting the worst. "Well, I ought to be, lad. I'm standing on your hair. Get it cut!"

He had a fund of these gems of wit and, later in his military career, Roger, having heard them repeated by numerous other NCOs, came to the conclusion that somewhere in the army files marked "Top Secret," there must be a little book entitled "Merry sayings for Sergeants," which those qualifying for promotion must learn by heart before sewing onto their sleeves the coveted stripes which endowed them with their power over lesser mortals such as he.

"Now, lads," he said, "is there any of you who can play a musical instrument?"

Roger, who by that time should have known better but thought there might just be a possibility of transfer to the more sheltered life of the Army School of Music at Kneller Hall, volunteered the information that he could play the violin.

Sergeant Fox could scarcely believe his luck - he had found a sucker who had fallen for the oldest one in the book.

"Good lad," he chuckled. "So you can double away to the Sergeants' mess and shift the piano - at the double - move!". The luckless Roger trotted off, mentally kicking himself for his stupidity, only to find that the Sergeants' mess had never been blessed with any musical instrument other than a mouth organ. So he first learned the three cardinal rules that every experienced soldier should observe: "Never volunteer for anything". The two others whose value he was to learn later are "time spent in reconnaissance is never wasted" and "never advance until you have prepared your lines of retreat".

The days which followed their reception into His Majesty's Forces kept them all fully occupied and found them at the end of each day to do anything other than collapse onto their beds of straw for an hour or so. There was, in any case, not much entertainment on offer except to swill beer in the NAAFI, where spirits were not available to 'Other Ranks' like himself.

It was forbidden to leave the barracks to find more congenial entertainment in the town, which was, in any case, too far away to reach on foot after a long day on the parade ground, even if one had the time or the money to do so.

Then there was what was euphemistically described as the "Interior Economy". This covered a wide variety of activities ranging from scrubbing out the "ablutions" to practising the art of folding blankets and arranging kit on the bed in the manner prescribed, an essential skill if one was to avoid "jankers" - punishment fatigues - at the morning hut inspection.

There were floors to be swept, bed frames to be dusted, and lockers to be cleaned, polished and kept in immaculate order with their contents. Woe betides him whose kit was found wanting in this respect.

Maintenance of equipment and clothing was another chore that took up any spare time in the evenings after one had recovered from the day's labours. Belts and gaiters must be smothered in green *Blanco* - a name which Roger found a curious misnomer, buttons, cap and epaulette badges to be polished with *Brasso* until they sparkled. It was a foolish recruit who neglected to ensure that the back of the badge or button was burnished to the same extent as the front, for, of a certainty, Sergeant Fox would sniff it out on parade with dire consequences for the luckless offender.

But the boots made the greatest demands on their spare time. These must first be smothered in blacking, which was then impressed into the leather of the toecaps with the handle of a toothbrush which had been heated in the flame of the candle with which every prudent soldier provided himself. This operation could last up to half an hour until the first faint trace of a shine began to show through the dull black surface. This signalled a new form of attack consisting of spitting on an old piece of rag dipped in the wax and rubbing it round in tiny circles lubricated by the frequent application of spittle until a clear hard mirror-like shine emerged. There must be no trace of blemish or surplus blacking around the edges of the sole, which might later be inadvertently transferred to a Blancoed gaiter. It was a foolish recruit who then succumbed to the temptation to secure additional gloss by an additional rub with a duster, as this would inevitably cloud the finished toecap and require further recourse to blacking and ragging.

The finished boots were wrapped reverently in a clean, soft duster and placed for safety underneath the bed to await the morning inspection and the coveted grunt of approval from Sergeant Fox.

Their day began at 6 a.m. with a *Reveille*, and after immersion in cold water in the ablutions, beds were arranged, blankets folded, articles of clothing and kit laid out according to a pre-ordained model of which they were all given a copy, and minutely checked to ensure perfection in every respect in preparation for the morning inspection. Next, breakfast - an ample meal of bread, bacon and 'pozzy' - the affectionate term for the coloured concoction which passed for jam in His Britannic Majesty's Forces.

The dreaded inspection completed, they were out on the parade ground, a vast sanded area which no recruit was allowed to cross on pain of instant reprisal. Here, they marched and counter-marched, shouting at the top of their voices the numbers which marked the various stages of the manoeuvre that they were being called upon to perform: "Up, two three, Salute two three, down two three." They slow marched, quick marched and double marched. They moved to the right in threes, about turned. They dressed by the right and dressed by the left. They sloped arms, ordered arms and presented arms. They stood at ease and easy whilst Sergeant Fox, his voice a little hoarse from his shouting in competition with his colleagues engaged in identical activities on other parts of the parade ground, addressed his charges in colourful terms, explaining the shortcomings he had observed during the exercise.

"I've seen some showers in my time," he would say, "but never, never in all my army service have I seen such a collection of pregnant penguins as you lot. For God's sake, keep in step, get those shoulders back, hands down the seam of your trousers, toes ten inches apart and keep those heads up."

All this tirade they would bear with fortitude and in silence. It would have been a bold and foolish recruit to discuss the matter with Sergeant Fox.

Drill parade would be followed by an hour of physical training in the gym. There was a more relaxed atmosphere here, under the care of gymnastic specialists. They enjoyed the challenges afforded by the vaulting horse, the parallel bars and the climbing ropes, although the physical exertion was no less than it had been on the parade ground.

Great emphasis was placed on the coordination of mind and body, culminating in the most difficult of all – rhythmic jumping: "feet together, apart together, together, feet together, apart together, together, arms bend up, arms bend forward, arms bend sideways, arms bend down" all at the same time, and it was with a sense of real achievement that Roger finally mastered the complex manoeuvre and mentally resolved to inflict it on his pupils should he ever survive to return to civvy street and the school P.E. lesson.

By this time, they were hungry and exhausted and were glad to rush to the cookhouse to savour what it offered.

On his first visit, Roger had been impressed by the variety in the week's menu inscribed in chalk on a blackboard:

Monday – Vienna Steaks, Tuesday – Beef Olives, Wednesday – Rissoles, Thursday – Meat Balls in Gravy.

He soon found that they all consisted of the same ingredients and provided identical flavours, the menu varying only by the inclusion on Friday of macaroni cheese – which he hated – and which not even the army cooks could make to taste like rissoles. On Saturday, there was stew and, with luck, roast beef on Sunday.

Years later, in his Japanese prison camp, he was to remember these despised meals with nostalgia, and his mouth would water with the memory of those delicious repasts; a plate of macaroni cheese would have been paradise itself.

The afternoons were devoted to more academic studies, including weapon care and construction. They learned the names of the different parts – the stock, the breech, the magazine into which they inserted five rounds of blank ammunition, the bolt, and the piling swivel. They stripped and reassembled the automatic Bren Gun, of which only one was available to the platoon and shared with Number 13 and 15 Platoons. As a special concession, they were allowed to handle the Boyes anti-tank rifle for whose destructive accounts were given and which had a tremendous reputation of frequently shattering the shoulder of the operator unfortunate enough to be required to fire it unless the butt was sufficiently snugly placed there.

It had a curious bulbous contraption known as the "flash eliminator" affixed to the end of the barrel, which, it was alleged, obscured the flash from the gaze of the enemy when fired at night and which Sergeant Fox described as the "flash illuminator". No one, to his knowledge, had ever actually fired the thing. Still, later, when used in battle against Nazi tanks, it was utterly ineffective. However, its evil reputation for recoil had been fully justified.

Then there was the bayonet, which Sergeant Fox described as the "soldier's best friend", for which there was a special drill for attaching it to the business end of the rifle. "You holds the 'ipe between your knees, and when I says 'Bayonets', you don't do nothing, but when I says 'fix', you whips it out, and you whops it on" and much time was spent in whipping and whopping until even Sergeant Fox was satisfied.

"Whipping" it from its leather scabbard, which was suspended from the webbing belt on the right-hand side by transferring the left hand across the body to grasp the hilt, was, in fact, an operation requiring some skill as, inevitably, it stuck fast with the result that it was "whopped" on a fraction of a second later than the remainder of the squad and thus invited critical comment from the Sergeant.

The drill for its use was also laid down with precision: "When I says 'Bayonets ready' you holds them so," pushing the rifle with its gleaming appendage forward in a most aggressive manner – "and when I says 'At the enemy in front Charge' you gives the Indian Love Call and you sticks it in his guts and you gives it a twist when it is in him or else you'll never get it out, and some other sod will have his up your arse before you can look round."

Thus instructed, they would charge across the parade ground, uttering wild and savage cries, and plunge the points of their bayonets into the vast bags of straw dangling from their gibbets and immediately dodging away since the sack would swing back revengefully and knock them head over heels with their feet in the air to the delight of their comrades and the fury of Sergeant Fox.

Unfortunately, the weapon's manipulation before firing consisted of a series of movements designed by the drill regulations to end with the rifle tucked into the right shoulder. Having completed the manoeuvre, Roger was obliged to transfer it surreptitiously to the left before firing, as he could never fire from his right shoulder.

He became pretty skilful at achieving this without detection and thus risking the wrath of Sergeant Fox, who was more usually intent on checking that the legs in the recumbent position were spread at the correct angle with the inner sides of the feet pressed firmly and most uncomfortably against the ground.

Apart from the risks attached to this subterfuge, Roger enjoyed firing practice most of all. He was quite a good shot, and this not only earned him the approval of Sergeant Fox and was, after all, the reason he had joined the army, and from the point of view of one's personal survival, seemed a more acceptable way of disposing of one's enemy in the unfortunate event of this becoming necessary than by sticking a steel blade into his anatomy at close quarters.

Worst of all, however, were the night exercises, which required them to lie out in the gorse and bracken for hours at a time with no real clue as to what was afoot or what was required of them. It so happened that January and February of 1940 were freezing. They would lie miserably in the snow, chilled to the bone, awaiting the decision by whoever was in charge and who presumably knew what it was all about that the exercise had reached a satisfactory conclusion and that they could get back to barracks and a mug of cocoa.

Presumably, because it was thought that weaning the recruits away from the comforts, outlook and habits of civilian life might undo the careful work of moulding them into hardened soldiers, no home leave was allowed for the first six weeks of the course. Roger kept a detailed tally of the days which separated him from his 48 hours of weekend leave and a blissful reunion with Daisy.

However, at the end of the fourth week of the course, by which time they had acquired an acceptable military bearing that would not disgrace their uniform or cap badge, they were allowed to sally forth into the town.

Daisy made the long journey to Guildford after work on a Friday evening. Roger, who had discovered a method of leaving and re-entering the barracks by a route that avoided reporting to the guard room at the gate, went down to Guildford Station to meet her and escort her to the nearby bed and breakfast accommodation reserved for her.

The following morning, armed with a day pass, he reported to the guard room for permission to leave the barracks and into the street where Daisy awaited him.

But the guard Sergeant who had been eyeing this pretty young girl with lascivious approval and had been waiting for a bit of fun to while away the hours of duty demanded if the young lady was waiting for him.

Roger, still not yet wise to the ways of wily Sergeants, was foolish enough to tell him she was. "Well, well," said the Sergeant, "we must be smart for her, mustn't we? Just look at those buttons," he said, "not properly clean, are they? Back you go, lad and get them polished."

Roger returned disconsolately to the barrack room and, after waiting two or three minutes without touching the buttons on which he had lavished much labour with *Brasso* and the button stick the previous day, returned to the guard room. "That's better," said the Sergeant, "nice and shiny they are now, but I wonder if they have been sewed on properly," and, with a deft flick of his wrist, snatched a button from the greatcoat and threw it on the floor. "There we are," he said, "as I thought. Can't have that, can we? Get back and sew it on properly, lad. We mustn't keep the young lady waiting, must we?". Roger, inwardly fuming but not daring to rise to the bait so carefully laid for him, returned once more to borrow a coat from Frank, who was about his size and, after a decent interval, went back to the gate where Daisy, blue with the cold, was contemplating physical assault on the wicked Sergeant.

Guildford, in wartime on a cold winter's day, was not exactly brimming with opportunities for pleasure and relaxation. After lunch in the Angel, the couple stayed by the fire there for as long as the management could reasonably tolerate before transferring to the cinema across the road where, in the back row, they sat through the programme three times until the place closed. When it came to an end, neither could have said what the films had been about.

By evil chance, on the Sunday of her visit, No. 5 Platoon was scheduled for a church parade, and so Daisy was obliged to trail along behind the marching column and succeeded in joining him and holding his hand at the back of the Garrison church with the connivance of Sergeant Fox who, after all, proved for the first time that he was human.

At last, the long-awaited weekend leave was only three days away, but all was not well with Roger. A high temperature, a throbbing headache and dizziness told him something serious was brewing. By Thursday, he was feeling miserably ill, but he knew that a report to the sick bay would assuredly rob him of the weekend leave for which he had waited so long, and he resolved to stick it out.

A bright red rash appeared on his chest and face on Friday morning. He prayed it would not be noticed on parade since he had decided to get home or die in the attempt.

After pay parade, at the end of which they were to be free to go their ways, his friend Jimmy, who lived in the town, took him down in his car to Guildford Station and put him on the train for home.

They were never to see each other again.

Chapter 4

Intermission

How he reached home after leaving Jimmy at Guildford Station, he never knew. Somehow he must have changed trains at Tonbridge for Tunbridge Wells and, from there, by bus to Eridge. He had no coherent memory of this. He only became aware of his surroundings when he found himself in the armchair by the fire at home at the School House with Daisy weeping over him and stroking his close-cropped hair.

He had made it, was home, and nothing else mattered.

His condition was greatly aggravated by his determination to carry on, complicated by the Medical Officer's decision to give all recruits their anti-tetanus and typhoid injections at the beginning of the week. Tetanus was no real problem, but TAB (typhoid anti-bacillus) was a different matter and resulted in a swollen and excruciating arm and a high temperature for which those affected were rewarded by 48 hours of light duties.

In their case, these light duties had been interpreted by authority as a prolonged period of 'spud bashing' (the peeling of a mountain of potatoes for the cookhouse), a chore generally reserved for the Jankers squad. Others had been called upon to whitewash the large square blocks of coal, which formed a low wall holding back the main coal stack. Neither of these activities had done much to alleviate the discomfort of the swollen arms. But, compared with rifle drill, route marches and physical training did constitute a recreational occupation in the eyes of those responsible for such decisions.

None of this had improved his developing condition, and he was lucky to have reached home without a total collapse.

His doctor, who had been summoned after his arrival home, took a pessimistic view of the situation. He diagnosed a severe attack of German measles and a suspected return of the heart murmur caused in happier days by strain following a seven-mile cross-country race around Richmond Park when he was at the university. The doctor also diagnosed acute anaemia, hinting darkly that if this should prove to be of the pernicious variety, then things were bleak indeed. Roger's military career would end abruptly, culminating in a discharge from the army.

Neither Daisy nor he knew what to hope for on this score. Much as they would have welcomed such a development, the prospect of his becoming a permanent semi-invalid was even more unattractive. However, blood samples were taken, and he was told that no further action could be taken until these had been checked. They hoped fervently that this would take a very long time.

However, after two weeks of good nursing and loving care, his health improved rapidly, and he could enjoy the good fortune that had befallen him. Had he not persevered, he would most certainly have had a wretched time in the military hospital instead of enjoying good home cooking and the companionship of his girl. This was suffering that he could endure without any difficulty at all.

But all good things must come to an end. The test results arrived and proved negative; the heart murmur had disappeared, and the doctor apologetically pronounced him fit and capable of rejoining his unit at Guildford. There was no escaping from this verdict, and so, with a heavy heart, he took a fond farewell of a tearful Daisy. He started his motorbike and headed for Stoughton Barracks by road.

Here he found that there had been significant changes since his absence. The bed-boards and palliasses had disappeared and had been replaced by wire springs and horse-hair mattresses so that the new recruits lived in previously unimagined luxury. He took great delight in recounting to them the horrors suffered by their predecessors.

The new draft had arrived a few days previously, and he was still in the same state of shock where he had found himself two months before. In light of his previous training, he concluded that they were spineless as a platoon compared with the stalwart souls of the previous lot.

He felt rather lonely and isolated since their common adversity had already welded the rest into a mutually protective group. He sensed that the intrusion of the stranger was unwelcome. He thought nostalgically of his vanished friends, Jimmy, Maurice, Frank Gordon and especially of the grave-digger, George, who had been a universal favourite. He used to delight them all with salacious tales of his marital relationship.

"I used to come home on a Friday night when I had got my wages and put half a crown on the mantelpiece. She never said anything but knew what I meant, so she went straight upstairs after supper. It was a good life," he would say regretfully, "a bloody sight better than this."

Strangely enough, however, apart from George, there was very little discussion of their relationships with the opposite sex between them. This phenomenon was attributed to a dark theory, universally believed by all 'Other Ranks', that bromide was regularly introduced into the tea urn to curb their sexual desires. Marital relations weren't even discussed in prison, where his comrades had been denied female companionship for nearly four years.

He did miss the comradeship in the old Number 14 Platoon despite, or perhaps because of, the wide range of the social, cultural and financial backgrounds from which they came. There had never been any attempt to put on 'side', and the wide differences in their economic status seemed to present no barriers between them. He remembered Gordon the millionaire suggesting to George, the gravedigger, that it was his turn to buy him a half a pint, which George had complied with without demur.

They were a good crowd, and Roger made strenuous efforts to get himself drafted to wherever they had been sent so they could be reunited.

But this was all to no avail. He had not completed his initial training course, and they had. Although he had been only two weeks short of the end, he must start over again from the beginning, and that was the end of the matter. He had no alternative but to accept this, but it was a bitter pill.

He was never to see any of them again. After additional training, they were sent to join their regiment in France. At the beginning of June, they had formed part of the rearguard action during the retreat to Dunkirk. They had been ordered to make a suicidal charge across an open field towards the canal bank where the German machine gunners were waiting for them.

Of the whole of No. 14 Platoon, only two had survived.

Although his new companions initially tended to resent his intrusion into their midst, they soon found advantages to be gained from his previous experience. He knew the quickest way to arrange the bed space for inspection and how to burnish boots to an acceptable gloss and a dozen other tricks of the trade to make life less unbearable. He gradually became a sort of father confessor, a role to which his professional training suited him.

Nevertheless, he was obliged to go through the basic drill all over again and shout out with the others the numbers of the various stages of the drill movements he had found so irksome during his initial training period.

His experience in these matters did not increase his popularity with the others since it caused him to be more proficient than they were during the early stages of their training. Sergeant Fox would single him out to stand in front of the squad to demonstrate the correct way to perform the various manoeuvres.

"Now just come out in front, professor," he would say, "and show these dozy men how to stand to attention. Now just watch him – see, toes ten inches apart, back straight, hands down the seams of the trousers. Now, you lot, if he can do it, so can you!"

As the days passed and their own expertise equalled and frequently surpassed his own, he became more readily acceptable to them. Like his former unit, they began to mould themselves into a coherent group, although never with the same quiet and unspoken bond between them that had existed in his old platoon.

As usual with such groups, banter and leg-pulling were commonplace and were engineered and received with good humour. On one occasion, though, things nearly went badly wrong.

Tony, who had discovered the secret exit from the barracks and was wont to return late at night somewhat the worse for wear when they were all asleep and put himself noisily to bed, was adjudged by a secret tribunal to be worthy of being taught a lesson.

The mattresses on which they slept consisted of V-shaped pieces of wire hooked together and fastened to the iron bed frame by strong coil springs, which only a superhuman effort could detach.

After Tony had departed for one of his evening jaunts, the springs were detached from one end and fixed back to the frame by thin string. When he returned well after midnight, he lurched into the hut. He threw himself onto the bed, which promptly collapsed and deposited him onto the floor.

The following day a dreadful sight met their eyes. The pieces of wire released from the tension which had held them in place had become detached from each other and lay in a confused pile of small V-shaped pieces of wire on the floor.

Desperate attempts to piece them together in time for the morning inspection were useless, and the situation seemed hopeless. However, to his eternal credit, Tony, an accomplished actor, confronted the Platoon Commander on his arrival at the hut door with a limp and woeful expression.

"Permission to register a complaint, Sir," he said while they all held their breath, thinking he would get revenge by shopping the lot of them.

"Permission granted," replied the Officer. "What is the problem?"

"This bed, Sir," said Tony, his face a mask of innocence, "has always been defective and very uncomfortable, but I haven't reported it, Sir, because I didn't want to make trouble, but now it has collapsed and, as you see, Sir, I have injured my leg." He hopped convincingly over towards the debris to reveal the extent of the disaster.

The platoon commander made a cursory inspection of the damaged bed and, not noticing the pieces of string still attached to the springs, said, "Very well. Sergeant

Fox, get this mess taken away and a new bedspring issued," and he passed on down the hut for the remainder of the inspection.

Sergeant Fox paused by the bed, picked up a piece of string from the end of a spring, put it in his pocket, gave his recruits an inscrutable look and followed the officer thoughtfully down the hut.

In the army, one did not let one's comrades down however much they deserved it, nor did a Sergeant betray his platoon to an officer. However, that morning's whole drill parade was carried out at the double without either a pause or a word of the bed incident being mentioned. At the end of the torture, he surveyed his exhausted and perspiring recruits with an air of quiet satisfaction. "Well, now we have all had our little bit of fun, haven't we?" he said. "Right turn. Dismiss."

Sergeant Fox was a resourceful man. Having discovered Roger had been a teacher and having addressed him that thenceforth as "professor", he found that the lessons on topics such as the care of gas masks, the dismantling and reassembly of the Bren Gun, the construction of Molotov Cocktails, the properties and odour of mustard, phosgene and chlorine gases (which tended to tax his vocabulary to its limits) could more conveniently be entrusted to Roger, leaving him to conserve his energies for more congenial matters.

"Right, now, professor," he would say when his audience had assembled, "you can take over for a bit and see how you get on." He would then disappear into the ablutions for a quiet smoke while the lesson proceeded.

On one such occasion, Roger was horrified to see the Commanding Officer approaching and clearly about to take an interest in the proceedings.

"Where is the Sergeant?" inquired the CO.

"He was called away suddenly, Sir," said Roger, remembering with gratitude the splendid reaction of Sergeant Fox to the incident of the bed, "and he asked me to carry on, Sir, in case he should be delayed."

"I see," said the CO. "But what do you know about it?"

"I have done this part of the course already," replied Roger with perfect truth, and he explained how this had come about.

"I see," said the officer, "well, carry on then." Roger did while the CO stood and listened to the remainder of the lesson, even telling him to continue after a pale-faced and anxious Sergeant Fox returned after his smoke.

The Sergeant's gratitude was profound. "Well done, professor," he said, "one of these days, we shall see you with a stripe up."

Although flattering, this prophecy of promotion to the exalted rank of Lance Corporal was not as welcome as intended. The appointment of Lance Jack, as they were styled, was an unenviable one. He was close enough to the men to be regarded with suspicion and hostility as "one of them" but with insufficient status to be accorded the respect due to a proper Non-Commissioned Officer.

Roger hoped fervently that the prophecy would not be fulfilled. He had discovered that the rank of Private had distinct advantages. He was not required to take any initiative or responsibility, make any decisions or do anything other than obey orders.

Financially, also, he was in a very comfortable position. A generous Education Authority made up his 14 shillings a week pay to his full teaching salary. So, with a weekly income of £3.10s, where his only expenses were what he cared to spend in the NAAFI, he was in the plutocrat class.

About a week after the incident with the Commanding Officer, he was summoned to appear at Company Headquarters. This command filled him with apprehension. No one was "sent for" unless there was trouble brewing. He cast over in his mind which misdemeanours the establishment might have uncovered.

In the office, he found himself confronted with the CO and three other officers whom he had never seen before. After giving his smartest salute, name, rank and number, he was stood at ease, physically, although by no means mentally.

He then answered questions about his background and career.

This recital completed, his attention was directed to a large sand tray, the like of which he had never seen before, arranged attractively with model hills, trees and hedgerows.

"Supposing you were under fire from behind that hill, and you had a platoon of infantry with you, what would you do?" he was asked.

He examined the set-up with no real idea what this was about or what answer was expected of him. Remembering parallel situations from his Scouting 'Wide Games', "I expect it would be wrong, Sir," he said, "but I think I should get some of the chaps to kick up a bit of a shindy from in front here and get the others to make their way round to the back of the hill and surprise them from behind." The officer grunted: "Alright," he said, "that's all. You can fall out."

Roger saluted, did his best about-turn, which, mercifully, he got right for once, and returned to his hut, wondering what all that had been about. At least he was not on a 'charge' and had escaped the ordeal unscathed, which was something to be thankful for.

He later consulted Sergeant Fox as to what it all might betoken. "Can't say," replied that worthy. "Officers get up to all sorts of tricks. But," with a sudden flash of inspiration, "it could be that your Lance Jack's stripe is on the way, old son."

Nothing more was said about the incident; it had vanished from his mind. Only a week remained before his next home leave, and this pleasing prospect occupied all his thoughts.

At the beginning of the week, he was out on a route march when a dispatch rider on a motorcycle drew up at the head of the column.

"Have you got a Private Rothwell here?" he asked. "Fall out, professor," said Sergeant Fox. "What's up?" he demanded of the despatch rider.

"How should I know?" came the answer. "He's wanted at Headquarters, that's all I know. Come on, get on behind. It won't be very comfortable." Roger climbed up on the bare metal carrier of the motorcycle.

The dispatch rider had been right. It was one of the most uncomfortable journeys of his life, made all the worse by a sickening fear of what might be awaiting him at the other end of the journey. Immediately he thought that some tragedy had occurred at home and mentally prayed that all was well with Daisy.

They arrived at the barracks, and he was told by the dispatch rider to report to the Regimental Sergeant major's office. Weak at the knees, he stood to attention in front of the junior officers worthy of whom everyone stood in awe.

"Private Rothwell?" inquired the RSM. "Sir!" answered Roger. "Get your kit packed, lad," he was told, "and get yourself over to Aldershot and report to Malplaquet Barracks on Queen's Parade in Farnborough."

"Why is that, Sir?" enquired a relieved Roger - at least there had been no catastrophe at home.

"You're to go to the 170 Machine Gun Officer Cadet Unit," said the Sergeant Major, "they're going to try and make an officer of you, so look lively!"

Chapter 5

Aldershot

Riding over the Hog's Back on his motorcycle that sunny April afternoon, Roger pondered over the strange and sudden turn of events taking him to Aldershot. How this had all come about, he did not know. Possibly, it was because his service in the Officer Training Corps at College, discounted at the time of his enlistment, had now caught up with him. Or perhaps his encounter with the Commanding Officer and his subsequent mysterious interview with what he now perceived to have been some sort of selection board had had this unexpected result. Or whether it was a combination of all three, he was never to discover.

One thing was sure. If it had not been for the attack of German measles and the perseverance in sticking things out during that terrible week, Roger would now be somewhere in France with his friends of No.5 Platoon instead of heading for Aldershot and the possibility of a commission. He reflected on how one's fate can be decided by such an apparently insignificant event.

His first reaction on hearing the news from the Sergeant Major had been acute frustration since it effectively cancelled the weekend leave, which he had looked forward to for so long. He guessed how disappointed Daisy would be, but then one was no longer master of one's fate in these strange times, and he was sure she would be happy to receive the news even though it meant a lost weekend.

Nevertheless, life at the Officer Cadet Training Unit would undoubtedly be much more civilised than at Guildford. He warmed at the thought that leave might be much easier to obtain.

By now, he had reached Aldershot and was going up the long road by Queen's Parade towards Farnborough and Malplaquet Barracks, where the next phase of his life awaited him.

Malplaquet was the centre of a group of three gaunt barrack blocks ranged along the top end of Queen's Parade, a vast area of grassy land fringed by trees and stretching away for nearly half a mile to Wellington Barracks in Aldershot.

At the guard room, he found himself with a large group of recruits like himself. Some of them seemed older, and he guessed that these were men whose service in the army was more significant than his.

Standing close to him was a young round-faced lad of about his own age wearing the same bewildered look as he guessed must be on his own face. A Sergeant appeared, a gaunt and forbidding-looking character to whom Roger took an instant dislike.

"My name is Sergeant Fraser," he said, "and I've got the job of licking you lot into shape. Now line up proper and give your name, rank, unit and religion to my mate at the table over there."

Roger and his companion followed the remainder and approached the table.

"Name?" asked the Sergeant, running his finger down a list.

"Percy Powell," replied his new companion.

"Percy, eh?" said the Sergeant. "Now, there's a fine name for a cadet. And what is your religion, Percy?"

"I am a Plymouth Brother, Sergeant", replied Percy.

"Plymouth Brother, Plymouth Brother?" said the Sergeant. "Never heard of them - are you pulling my leg Percy, my lad?"

"Certainly not, Sergeant," he replied, "it is an ancient and greatly respected faith."

"Well, well," said the Sergeant, clearly enjoying himself and turning to the clerk sitting by his side and recording the details.

"Put him down as RC, George, and if I find you're having me on, lad," he said, "I'll have you!"

Percy stood his ground. "I am not pulling your leg, Sergeant, and I would much rather you did not put me down as a Roman Catholic, if you don't mind."

The Sergeant could scarcely believe his ears. Here was a young whipper-snapper, a newcomer, arguing the toss as soon as he arrived. "But you see, I do bloody well mind," he snarled. "I'll put you down how I want to, my lad, and you'd better watch your step, or you and me is going to fall out. Next!"

Roger stepped forward: "6464659, Private Rothwell, The Queen's Regiment, C of E, Sergeant."

This declaration of his faith was near enough to the truth. Although he had no sectarian affiliations, you can't go wrong with C of E, even though it meant regular church parades. He would have given the same reply even if he had been a Jehovah's Witness or a Moslem. He did not have Percy Powell's faith or courage, and he perceived that things being as they were, he would be wise not to make himself conspicuous.

Nevertheless, he admired the courage of his new acquaintance, which was greatly enhanced the same evening when they were turning in just before 'Lights Out'. To their astonishment, Percy knelt quietly beside his bed and, with his hands over his eyes, was obviously saying his prayers. Roger's respect and admiration for this young man grew even greater.

There was dead silence in the barrack room. This was something beyond their experience, but to their eternal credit, no one commented or raised a titter. They all respected cold courage when they saw it. The same quiet little ceremony took place every night throughout the five months of the course. The whole hut lapsed into silence until he had finished, and no one ever referred to the matter, nor did they even discuss it among themselves.

The cadets, now equipped with their white cap bands and shoulder tapes, the badge of their new rank, settled down to their new life together. They came from a wide assortment of units, many from established machine gun regiments like the Hampshires, the Devons, the Middlesex and Northumberland Fusiliers, the 'Diehards' and the 'Dirty Shirts' as they were called. This gave them a slight edge over the others from infantry regiments like his own. Since the 170 Octu was a Vickers Machine Gun unit, all their weapons training concerned this.

The Vickers was a relic from the First World War. It was a clumsy and ill-tempered weapon with a reputation for frequently going wrong. An essential part of the training involved reciting the long series of 'stoppages' to which it was prone and quickly taking the necessary remedial action.

The Vickers consisted of a heavy metal tripod onto which the gun was secured by a stout metal pin. The weapon was of .303 calibre, and the barrel was encased in a corrugated metal jacket that had to be filled with water to keep it cool. Failure to do so made the barrel bulge with the heat and the whole thing inoperable. They were told this was a major crime, as gun barrels were in very short supply and a precious commodity.

The Vickers required a team of three to operate it. Number One sat on the ground behind the gun, his hands grasping the handles on either side and his thumbs on the thumbpiece in the centre. In action, he was required to pull a handle on the right-hand side of the gun, known as the cocking piece. This was pulled twice – once to push the first bullet into the breech and the second time to commence firing. It then continued to fire as long as the thumbpiece was pressed, delivering its lethal load at 250 rounds per minute.

The sequence of actions required to overcome any stoppage invariably ended with removing the lock which controlled the breech and closing the flat metal plate under which it was housed. The drill for this manoeuvre was for Number One to call out as soon as the remedial action was completed.

"Lock in, cover down!", which every machine gunner worth his salt was wont to translate into "Cock in, lover down!"

The role of Number Two was to feed the webbing belt holding the ammunition into the slot on the right-hand side and ensure that it entered at an angle of precisely 90 degrees since any variation inevitably led to a significant stoppage and rendered him highly unpopular with all concerned.

Number Three operated lying down on the left-hand side of the range finder. They calculated the angle of elevation or depression required to ensure that the bullets reached their target according to their distance away and the slope of the ground.

Although he became adept at handling the gun and dealing with the long list of stoppages, at no time did Roger ever actually fire it with live ammunition. Although they would never be required to use it, they continued, unabated, to drill with the rifle, and much time was still spent in this apparently pointless activity.

The only weapon they were told nothing about and given no chance to use was the .38 revolver, which would be their only personal weapon in action. They found this a little odd.

If he had had any illusions that life at the Octu would be less strenuous or less exacting than at Guildford, Roger was very swiftly to be disabused of these. The regime of life was infinitely more rigidly controlled than previously, and he often found himself longing for the halcyon days at Stoughton Barracks.

Worst of all was the guard-mounting parade conducted by the Regimental Sergeant Major, 'Dusty' Miller. He was a monumental figure of a man topping six feet six inches in height and as erect as a flagpole. He was a Coldstream Guardsman and determined that the cadets under his care should all attain the standards of appearance, smartness and discipline to which his regiment was accustomed. By the end of the course, he had all but succeeded.

He would stalk down the line, his eagle eye searching out and invariably finding some blemish in his chosen victim's posture, dress or appearance. He invariably addressed his charges as 'Gentlemen' as required on parade by regulations. Still, he had the knack of making the expression sound more offensive than the most withering term of abuse.

"You are a filthy gentleman, Sir. A disgusting gentleman, Sir," he would say, removing the poor fellow's cap badge or grubby shoulder tape or examining his fingers still stained with the remnants of Brasso or blacking. Pointing out the shortcoming with profound scorn, he would deliver a withering lecture on the need for discipline and a soldierly appearance. The remainder of the parade stood rigid and silent, thanking their Maker that they had escaped notice.

The regulations required that army boots had thirteen metal studs, no more no less, in each sole. Failing all else, the unfortunate chosen for attention would lift his foot like a horse being shod. Dusty would count the studs and record the defaulter's name for later attention if any were absent.

A favourite ploy was to stand before the squad and look down the line with half-closed eyes. "Is there any gentleman here who thinks he's clean? If there is, let him take two paces forward." Any right-minded cadet would have felt himself to be worthy of certification for the loony bin to have accepted the challenge. Occasionally, someone was stupid or provoked enough to take him on while the rest of the parade, content to wallow in their filth, sat back mentally, though not physically, to enjoy the pantomime.

Dusty would then go over him with the finest of tooth-combs, scraping the back of a button or badge, turning out a pocket to detect fluff or any unauthorised substance inside, or running his finger-nail along the inner seam to locate any lingering dust or grime. He never failed to find or comment on some deficiency in the most withering terms.

And yet, strangely enough, there was never a cadet who disliked him. On the contrary, everyone had an unspoken affection and respect for this remarkable man, who, although he verbally abused them, always did so with the hint of a twinkle in his eye, which even he could not disguise. He wanted to be proud of his cadets and for them to be proud of themselves. He was also scrupulously fair when it really mattered, and Roger had reason to be grateful for this.

One of the great burdens of anxiety they all had to bear was the correct rolling and wearing of the gas cape, which had to be worn on guard-mounting parade. The cape was carried across the shoulders and must be rolled immaculately after the fashion of a Swiss Roll according to the specified width and thickness dimensions. It was secured by two tapes fastened in such a way that the slightest tug on them released the cape, which then fell its entire length from the shoulder to the ankle, enveloping the whole body and shielding it from the effects of mustard or any other noxious gas or substance designed to afflict the body.

The ever-present fear of the cadet on guard-mounting parade was that one or other of the tapes would not have been secured sufficiently tightly and would allow the cape to unroll itself unbidden with the most unpleasant consequences culminating, usually in a punishment parade where everything was done at the double and which each lasted for an hour by Dusty Smith's watch.

As a consequence of this hazard, wily cadets planning to beat the system would roll their capes to perfection and fasten the tapes so that they would not release them when they were pulled and thus never needed to be adjusted. Being wise to such an unauthorised and totally illegal practice, the inspecting officer would occasionally pass along the rear of the rank and give the end of the tape a tweak to ensure that regulations had been correctly observed.

It so happened, on one memorable occasion, that Dusty himself, passing behind a rigid Roger, gave one of the tapes a pull to check that he had not offended in this way and passed on before he had noticed that, in consequence, one side of the cape had become unrolled and had fallen down his back. The adjutant, following behind, pounced on the defective item and, in consequence, Roger's name was taken for report as improperly dressed on guard-mounting parade.

Much as he would have liked to do so, any word of protest or explanation on parade would have been regarded as an offence, besides which the defective cape would have paled into insignificance. One did not argue on parade.

The following day at the Company Commander's office, where he was summoned to answer to the charge of being improperly dressed, he was astonished to see the Regimental Sergeant Major come in and request permission to speak. This granted, he stood smartly to attention and said: "This cadet, Sir, is not at fault, Sir. It was my fault, Sir. His cape was in good order, Sir, until I touched it. Request that the charge be withdrawn, Sir!"

Whereupon Roger was dismissed without a stain on his hitherto unblemished character but with renewed respect for this remarkable man who had taken the trouble to ensure that one of his cadets was not wrongly accused.

Although parades and weapons drills occupied a substantial part of their daily programme, many other activities were designed to increase efficiency.

One which pleased him more than any was driving instruction. He learned how to handle a 15-hundredweight truck and to manoeuvre it over difficult terrain.

On one memorable occasion, his instructor, unfamiliar with the terrain, directed him up a sloping track through the heather and between tall silver birch trees. Suddenly, the path ended in a vertical drop some ten feet deep, and the truck sailed through the air, landing on all four wheels, which splayed outwards from their axles most grotesquely and interestingly. They had climbed a ramp designed for tank manoeuvres, and the truck, not being used to such treatment, had responded in the only way it knew.

Motorcycle training was much more enjoyable; he was thoroughly at home, having taken part in reliability trials and long-distance rallies since passing his driving test. In this, his expertise was rewarded by his being appointed as an assistant instructor. He also became the official dispatch rider on the various tactical exercises which became an increasingly important part of the course. This suited him down to the ground as riding around the pleasant Hampshire countryside was preferred to route marching or being thrown around in the back of open trucks.

Then there were lectures to attend on tactics, army law as outlined in King's Regulations and in the handling of men, where he found the home-spun psychology of Sergeant Fraser much more entertaining than his college lecturers and, indeed, much more practical and down to earth.

"There comes a time in the life of every British soldier, gentlemen," explained the Sergeant, who had now become much more human and less objectionable than on their first encounter, "when he takes off his cap, and he puts down his rifle, and he lays down his pack, and he says, in a manner of speaking and if you don't mind my saying so, gentlemen, 'Bugger!'"

Roger was never to forget this advice, nor could he count the numerous occasions when he metaphorically reached this condition during his military career.

Gradually, as the weeks went by, they began to see the relevance and value of the harsh regime to which they were subjected and far more severe than in the old days at Stoughton Barracks. They now understood the importance of an instant response to a command and the need for unquestioning discipline, which would stand them and their men in good stead when the chips were down. They had been through the hoop themselves. They knew what it was to be exhausted, tired and discouraged yet carry on without complaint. Above all, they understood the limits to which men could be pushed. Roger ceased to regret that he had not been given an instant commission as he had expected at his enlistment. He had had an experience which, although unpleasant at the time, was an excellent investment for the future.

Probably their greatest anxiety was the possibility of the dreaded RTU - returned to unit - which was the fate of the unfortunate cadet who failed to make the grade and, as the weeks went by, quite a few of these drifted away whence they had come and were never seen again.

It was not so much the indignity of having been found wanting as the hostile reception they were likely to get from their former regiment who had judged them worthy of promotion. Each one fervently prayed that he would not be the next on the list.

As far as leave was concerned, he fared no better than he had at Guildford; indeed, there was to be no weekend leave at all until the end of the course, a depressing five months distant. However, it was possible to obtain a day pass which entitled the bearer to be absent from the barracks from 9 a.m. until midnight on a Sunday unless he was scheduled for church parade.

This arrangement allowed Daisy to come up by train on a Saturday evening, stay at a bed and breakfast in Farnborough, and give them the whole Sunday together. They would go out on the motorcycle to the country, have a picnic and get back to the old happy routine of life for a brief spell until it was time to make their way back to Wanborough Station, where he would stand on the bridge and watch the tail light of the train disappear into the twilight before disconsolately making his way back to the barracks.

Provided he had saved enough from his petrol ration of two gallons per month to make the 70-mile journey home to Eridge, he could slip home on a Sunday morning, leave the machine home, and return by the last train. This had the disadvantage of having to repeat the exercise in reverse on a subsequent weekend to get the bike back to Aldershot in readiness for Daisy's next visit. There was never enough petrol for the double journey.

Returning by road late on a Sunday night presented some difficulty since blackout regulations required that the headlamp be encased in a black metal box with two or three narrow slits in front, which allowed only the faintest glimmer of light to fall on the road immediately in front.

As the sunny days of spring wore on, it seemed that the war had ceased to exist for all practical purposes. Any air-raid warning was invariably a false alarm. On the Western Front in France, there was practically no hostile activity other than a few reconnaissance forays in the no-man's-land in front of the Maginot Line. This stretched along the French frontier with Germany as far north as the border with Belgium. At this point, the line stopped abruptly since it was calculated that no offensive action could penetrate the hilly forested region of the Ardennes and that, in any case, Belgium was neutral and seemed likely to remain so.

The Maginot, an extensive network of inter-communicating tunnels and artillery emplacements, faced the correspondingly equipped Siegfried Line a few kilometres to the east, creating a sort of military stalemate. It seemed as though the violent assaults they had envisaged nine months earlier would never happen. There even appeared to be a possibility that the war would end, as T.S. Eliot would have put it, "Not with a bang but a whimper."

They were soon to be rudely disabused. On May 10th, the German tanks, in great numbers, poured through neutral Holland and Belgium accompanied by unrelenting air attacks sweeping to the north of the now useless Maginot Line and into France. From where, the defending forces, with their training in conventional warfare, could not stand against this 'Blitzkrieg' and their movements hampered by the hordes of refugees pouring westward.

Contrary to the experts' expectations, the Panzer tanks had also moved through the forested German Ardennes, which they had believed would form a natural defence against armour. They had, in fact, provided excellent cover from aerial reconnaissance and had allowed them to muster their invincible forces unobserved.

French and British troops fought with the utmost bravery. However, a pincer movement from north and south designed to cut off the enemy's advanced forces and starve them of the essential fuel and ammunition supplies necessary for their continued advance ended in failure. The German attack swept westward towards Paris and northward to the sea, pinning the British troops into an ever-decreasing pocket between them and the coast.

In early June, France capitulated, and Hitler triumphantly rode down the Champs Elysees.

With the Germans in control of all the Channel ports, with the exception of Dunkirk, 350,000 British troops found themselves trapped against the sea, with a seemingly impossible evacuation the only hope of survival.

It was then that the miracle of Dunkirk occurred. A flat calm sea and a temporary halt in the German advance made it possible for a vast armada of little ships to lift the bulk of the stranded troops back across the Channel. They left all their transport, guns and equipment to the enemy, destroying as much of it as possible.

The rearguard, of which his old regiment formed part, holding off the German advance to allow as many of their comrades as possible to escape, suffered frightful casualties. Those left stranded on the beaches were led away to the prison camps where they were to stay for the next five years.

The war had begun in real earnest, and nothing would be the same again.

Chapter 6

Fulfilment

His first contact with the reality of war came during the second week of June, towards the end of the evacuation from Dunkirk. He and a group of cadets were drafted to a reception camp near Camberley to care for the survivors.

What he saw in this hastily erected tented camp was to remain in his memory for the rest of his life. Here were two or three hundred dishevelled and dispirited men, clearly exhausted with ragged and torn uniforms, some with injuries roughly bandaged with field dressings just as they had come off the rescuing boats.

They came from a confused variety of units, infantry, sappers and artillerymen, all mixed up with only one thing in common - they wanted to rest and sleep and forget what they had seen and suffered. Some were in small, disciplined groups under the control of their officers or NCOs. Others merely lay about on the grass, their rifles scattered around them, seemingly unwilling or incapable of conforming to any request to stand in line or get themselves organised and appeared to be totally demoralised.

These men had seen sights and endured hardships beyond all imagination. They had lain among the dunes, scraping pathetic little shelters in the sand in a fruitless attempt to escape from the constant bombing and machine-gunning of the Luftwaffe. They had seen comrades dying of their wounds or blown to pieces by their sides. They had stood waist-deep in the sea, their rifles either abandoned or held above their heads. They ducked under the water as the planes dived on them before scrambling into tiny fishing boats, eventually to be ferried to the larger transports lying off in deeper water, where some had drowned. For many, this ordeal had lasted for five or six days without respite or relief.

They all shared one wish to get away and get home as soon as possible and resented any attempt to organise or control them. Roger was vividly reminded of Sergeant Fraser's lecture on the handling of men. These were the men of whom he had spoken. They had taken off their caps, dropped their rifles, laid down their packs and said, quite literally: "Bugger!"

Shocked as he was to see men in this distressing state and concerned as he was to give them what help and reassurance he could, he could not escape the thought that, but for the lucky accident of his illness, he himself would either be one of these, or on his way to a German prison camp. He was to find later that he would most probably have been dead along with the remainder of No.5 Platoon.

After feeding them, helping to clean them up and issuing them with what kit was available for distribution, the first task was establishing their identities and units before organising their transport and travel warrants to send them off on their way back to their headquarters for rest and home leave.

It took two whole days after the last man had departed. It was safe to assume that no fresh evacuees would arrive to clear up the litter, collect discarded clothing, items of kit, abandoned ammunition and rifles from the grass, and close the camp.

He found this experience depressing in the extreme. Clearly, things were in a very bad way. If the Germans were to follow up their victory with an immediate invasion, as seemed more than possible, the survival prospects were indeed gloomy. For the first time, he began to consider the possibility that the war could be lost.

These fears appeared to be well-justified by the authorities' urgent measures (which seemed to be verging on panic). All signposts were destroyed, and the names of railway stations, village signs, and even the names on village halls were removed to confuse the enemy when it landed. However, he guessed that an invasion force might, just possibly, have been supplied with maps before they set off for England.

All large open spaces which might provide landing grounds for planes and gliders were strewn with obstacles of every kind - spare farm machinery and concrete blocks. Wires were strung between stout poles to frustrate and hinder the airborne landings, which would probably be the forerunner of the main invasion.

On the radio, the new Prime Minister, Winston Churchill, made powerful rallying speeches promising that the people "*would fight on the beaches and in the streets...they would never surrender*". Every able-bodied man not of military age was organised into local defence groups, forming the Home Guard or "Dads' Army", as they were affectionately called. In the early stages, most of these had no weapons or ammunition. They drilled with broom handles and, in place of rifles, armed themselves with pitchforks, scythes or whatever piece of potentially offensive piece of ironmongery came to hand. They learned how to make Molotov cocktails and were trained in methods of fouling the tracks of armoured vehicles to put them out of action.

It was, indeed, a very anxious time.

Much of the training programme at the Octu was temporarily suspended. The cadets were sent off to Crowthorne to dig trenches and tank traps to form some sort of line of defence to delay an enemy advance, if only for a few hours.

Looking at the pathetic results of his handiwork at the end of a hard day's labour, Roger could not feel much confidence that it would be of any avail against an attack of the type which had overthrown France in less than six weeks against experienced and well-equipped forces. Their work afforded them little consolation or prospect that what they were doing could in any way improve the situation. They gloomily munched their way through the wads of cake and drank their mugs of tea from the snack bar provided by the Salvation Army. The Salvation Army were always on the scene when needed to supply the troops with whatever help they could. Help which was greatly appreciated only because the 'char' was of a better quality and the 'wads' more toothsome than those provided by the NAAFI.

It now seemed unlikely that their course, due to finish towards the end of September, would ever be completed. They speculated whether they would be formed into a composite fighting unit or returned to their original regiments for the battles ahead.

Quite apart from these considerations, Roger felt deep concern as to what might happen to Daisy should their worst fears be realised. It seemed crystal clear to him that they should arrange their marriage as soon as possible.

Then, at least, they would have belonged to each other, however brief the time might be, and, in the event of his death, she would receive some support as an army widow.

Not that this would be, in any way, a marriage of convenience. They were deeply in love with each other and had been ever since childhood. Their dearest wish was to be married and have a family of their own. Her next visit to Aldershot was timed for the following weekend, and so, sitting in a field by Wanborough Station on a beautiful and peaceful summer evening, they fixed the date for their wedding.

Despite all their fears, however, there appeared to be no immediate follow-up to the German victory. It became clear that the Germans were pausing to reorganise in preparation for their attack on Britain. The Germans would need command of the air and the sea since the navy was still at full strength and the air force, although seriously weakened by its losses during the German advance into France and in its attempt to protect the troops stranded on the beaches of Dunkirk, was still a force to be reckoned with.

Everyone awaited the next move with apprehension.

It was not long in coming. One afternoon during the second week in June, a lone plane bearing French markings circled the barracks as if to land at Farnborough airfield.

They watched it with only casual interest. Following the fall of France, many French planes based in the yet unoccupied part of the country were escaping to England to carry on the fight, and several of these had landed at Farnborough.

The plane circled once more over Queen's Parade and then, diving down, dropped a giant bomb into the centre of Wellington Barracks, at the opposite end of Queen's Parade, before climbing away steeply and disappearing into the sun.

The bomb had caused considerable destruction, falling onto the parade ground where a squad was doing a punishment drill, killing them all.

Two days later, on a sunny Saturday afternoon, the air-raid siren sounded when they were all sitting outside their hut at the edge of Queen's Parade. They moved into the slit trenches under the trees purely as a matter of following routine regulations. The Commanding Officer, unaccustomed to obeying his own orders, stood out in the field and waved his cane into the air as a flight of ten or twelve planes swept in over the trees. "Good chaps," he said, "don't know what we would do without them."

The next moment, he was diving headlong into the trench as the bombers with the iron crosses of Germany under their wings swept over at little more than roof-top height. They wheeled around to the left, and almost at once, everyone was deafened by colossal explosions as their bomb loads cratered the airfield, destroying both the runway and the planes parked there. Planes which had not had time to take off before the attack. The next phase of the attack, to immobilise first the airfields and then the Air Force in preparation for the planned invasion, had begun.

Regarding their wedding date, Roger discovered that such an event constituted grounds for 'compassionate leave', entitling one to 48 hours of bliss provided it was taken at the weekend and did not interfere with training. Accordingly, the date was brought forward from the week's leave to which he would be entitled when he was commissioned to August 24th. Even this earlier date seemed quite far enough away given the steadily increasing hostility of the enemy, whose raids on airfields and installations were becoming a daily event.

As far as Roger was concerned, approval of his application for leave would be only a matter of routine, and he put his written request into the company office without further thought or anxiety. He was most surprised to receive a summons to appear before the Company Commander the following day.

"This leave application of yours," said the Captain, "I assume you have the Commanding Officer's permission to get married."

Roger was thunderstruck. "Certainly not," he said, "my fiancee and I have agreed on the date, and I have her parents' blessing."

"I have no doubt you have," came the reply, "but the fact is that nobody can get married without the approval of the CO."

"What do you suggest I should do then, Sir?" Roger asked. "Well, the only thing you can do," he answered, "is to request an interview with him. I will arrange it if you like."

Roger disconsolately agreed, and two or three days later, which seemed an eternity to him, he appeared before the Commanding Officer, ready to do battle if necessary. He and Daisy were going to get married, and nothing and nobody was going to stop them, even if it cost him his commission.

The CO received him courteously enough. "This young lady," he said, "I should very much like to meet her. Is she able to come to Aldershot in the near future?"

"She can come any weekend you choose," said Roger, mentally wrestling with the problem of how he would break the news to her.

"Very well," said the CO. "Bring her to the lounge bar in the Queen's Hotel at eight o'clock this Saturday."

Roger departed in an agony of apprehension. He wondered if the CO would examine her shoes and fingernails and see if she was correctly dressed. It was ten to one that if he explained the situation to her, she would flatly refuse to come, and he could not blame her if she did. After all, it would be as if she were on one of Dusty Miller's guard-mounting parades.

Miserably he took the coward's way out and asked her to come up without mentioning anything about his interviews or the CO's instructions.

When he met her at North Camp Station, he suggested they might drop into the "Queen's" the following evening for a drink. Daisy was puzzled. Their time together was precious and not to be wasted in public houses, however select they might be, but Roger stuck to his guns.

Chapter 7

Baptism of Fire

The great air raid of September 15th, afterwards known as 'Battle of Britain Day', had marked the Germans' last serious attempt to eliminate the RAF. Had they succeeded, they would undoubtedly have gone ahead with their plans to invade Britain, but the young fighter pilots - 'The Few', as Prime Minister Churchill called them - had held their ground. Despite enormous casualties in both men and planes, 'The Few' had inflicted so much damage on the enemy that they were forced to postpone and, later, abandon their strategy of destroying the RAF in head-on combat. Every available German bomber had been committed to the battle on September 15th, and although Hitler did not know it, every British fighter plane had also been deployed, and no reserves were available. To use the words of the Duke of Wellington after the battle of Waterloo, it had been "a damned nice thing".

Adolf Hitler now began to be concerned with other matters. Given his losses and the need to conserve his strength for a more important project, namely the invasion and conquest of Russia, he resolved, against the advice of his military advisers, to put off his conquest of Britain until after he had removed the threat from the east. Hitler decided to limit his attack on Britain to destroy our cities and centres of industry (taking care not to eliminate the latter completely since he hoped to use these to increase the prosperity of the Greater Reich).

This decision was to lose him the war.

In view of his enormous losses resulting from the massive daylight raids, Hitler decided that his objective should be to bomb by night, minimising his losses while causing the maximum terror to the civilian population.

Night raids on the capital had begun in the second week of September. Now they had increased in both tempo and severity. Between September 7th and the beginning of November, London had suffered no fewer than fifty-seven consecutive nights of bombing. The attacks increased in intensity as the weeks went by. By mid-November, more than 13,000 tons of high explosive and 12,000 incendiary bombs had fallen on the city and its suburbs.

Other industrial centres and cities also received their share of attention. On the night of November 14th, such destruction rained down on the city of Coventry that a new word, 'Coventrated', entered the English language to describe the utter devastation of a town. In one night alone, 60,000 of the total 70,000 buildings in the city, including its cathedral, had been destroyed or severely damaged, and more than 1,800 of its citizens had been killed or wounded.

The gloves were off with a vengeance.

Roger began to doubt his wisdom in opting for Middlesex, with its main barracks at Mill Hill in North London. It was not without some misgivings that he travelled up to London on September 28th and reported for duty at Inglis Barracks.

As no accommodation was available there, he was billeted in Bittacy Hill Park, opposite the entrance to the barracks, in a private house where the proprietor, although not averse to receiving a substantial payment for lodging him, made it abundantly clear that, although she conceived it to be her contribution to the war effort, it was nevertheless a most annoying inconvenience. Roger spent as little time as possible in the house.

The first few weeks of his time at Mill Hill were spent learning the complex art of controlling the movement of large numbers of recruits on the parade ground. This was to be done without marching them off into the wide blue yonder by a wrong word of command. He was tasked with explaining to his platoon of recruits the mysteries of the Vickers machine gun, and, in all of this, he became more and more grateful for his sufferings at Guildford and Aldershot, which helped him understand and sympathise with the problems of the men under his control, and to establish the sort of relationship which ensured their cooperation.

The incessant nightly air raids also occupied a good deal of his time either on bomb or fire watch. One night when he was on duty as Orderly Officer, he received a telephone call from the Sergeant at the lower guard room at the bottom of Bittacy Hill. "There's a bloody great thing in the sky over Hendon, Sir, and it is floating this way. I don't like the look of it at all, Sir."

Roger went outside and saw a large parachute mine of the sort that had cratered the Tunbridge Wells Road suspended only a few hundred feet above Golders Green and, as the Sergeant had said, drifting towards the barracks. Clearly, something must be done since the devastation would be horrific if it came to earth in the barracks.

In something approaching blind panic, he rushed back to the Commanding Officer's quarters and shook him awake.

"What the bloody hell is going on?" he demanded.

"There's a damned great parachute land mine floating towards the barracks, Sir. What do you want me to do?"

The Colonel opened a sleepy eye: "Then tell the bloody thing to go away. We don't want it here," he said, turning over and returning to sleep. The land mine floated clear of the barracks and landed harmlessly with an enormous explosion in fields half a mile away. Roger went sheepishly back to duty, hoping no one noticed his panic.

At this time, London was under continuous attack, and not a night passed without sounding the air raid warning at dusk, followed by the roar of the bombers and the explosions either of bombs or of anti-aircraft fire.

Clear moonlit nights were the worst. The black shapes of the planes could be seen silhouetted against the night sky or picked out in the pencil of light from the searchlights reaching out beyond the grotesque sausage-like shapes of the barrage balloons.

The principal danger was the jagged shrapnel fragments from anti-aircraft fire, which rained down on them and made a steel helmet their best friend. However, some were less fortunate than others. His friend Cheesewright, who had joined him from Aldershot, was bombed out of no fewer than five billets during his stay at Mill Hill. Returning a little the worse for wear after an evening in the West End, it was he who was surprised to find a large hole where the pathway to his billet should have been. He clambered out and was even more alarmed to be able to go straight upstairs from the entrance hall without opening the door.

He woke the following day to the sound of laughter and found himself on display to a crowd of delighted spectators. The whole of the front wall of the house had disappeared into the crater, leaving his bed teetering on the brink of the abyss.

By the middle of October, Roger was adjudged capable of doing something useful for his living. He found himself in a convoy of lorries with his new platoon heading through the shattered East End of London bound for Purfleet.

At that time, the possibility of invasion was still very real. One of the means of striking at the heart of the capital by mass seaplane landings on the lower reaches of the river was thought to be a strong possibility. Accordingly, it was decided to build a string of machine gun posts along the river eastwards from Blackwall Reach, extending towards Tilbury. Consequently, their days were spent filling countless sandbags and constructing ramshackle defence posts.

In the main, the posts were built near the entrances to docks where the platform by the lock gates afforded an excellent field of fire along the river and were accessible along the dockside.

There were disadvantages, however. Although the bulk of air attacks took place at night, small strikes by squadrons of Stuka bombers during the day were quite frequent. These planes were greatly feared, not only because of the accuracy of their attacks but also due to the terrifying screech thought to be made by sirens attached to their wings as they dived down to release their bombs onto their target.

The Docklands was a favourite target for these raiders, who often followed the line of the river to avoid interception. On one occasion, this nearly caused Roger and his squad to be drowned.

They were walking in single file along the dockside between King George V and the Albert Docks, a dismal sight with the masts and funnels of sunken ships poking up out of the water, when, without warning, a string of Stukas swept down the length of the dock and deposited four bombs straight down the centre. This had thrown an enormous wave over him and his platoon, which were flat on their faces on the paved quayside and left them gasping like stranded fish when the flood receded.

A few days later, on a Monday morning, they were at work at the terminal of the Northern Outfall sewer - a very insalubrious place - where the outpourings from the toilets of north-eastern London discharged themselves, untreated, into the Thames.

Although shipping of every sort had, by this time, ceased to use the Port of London, there was a little tug which used to set forth from the outfall every Monday, towing a string of barges loaded with such of the solid material as could be dredged from it, and deposited its unsavoury cargo at the river's mouth.

As they were working at the far end of the little wooden pier which stuck out into the river, a flight of Stukas arrived and began circling around, like seagulls, searching for a suitable target. Suddenly, the leader peeled off and, with an ear-splitting screech, dived head-first at the string of barges. One after another, the planes dived down, machine guns blazing and releasing their bomb loads until the whole convoy of barges was destroyed. Knowing their contents, everyone fell flat and covered themselves with whatever they could find to protect themselves from the inevitable rain of pollution about to descend on them.

Roger and his men picked themselves up and searched for a bath.

But not everything was a disaster. The most westerly of the pill-boxes in their area was on the side of the LMS Wharf in Blackwall Reach. Here there had been a cheese warehouse which had been hit first by incendiaries, followed, as was usual, by high-explosive bombs so that, to get to their work site, they had to wade ankle-deep through a rotting Welsh Rarebit.

Next to the warehouse were the remains of a store belonging to Keiller's provision merchants. This also had been completely destroyed by high explosives and was a vast heap of rubble, the walls having fallen inwards on the contents.

One morning, when they were at work, a very smart-looking civilian with a clipboard under his arm appeared and announced that he was from the Ministry of Food. He told them he inspected damaged warehouses to arrange salvage or condemn their contents.

He looked perfunctorily at Keiller's and the cheese warehouses, scribbled some notes on his clipboard and prepared to leave.

"Can anything be salvaged?" asked Roger,

"Good God, no," replied the man from the Ministry. "It's a complete write-off."

"So," asked Roger, "if we find anything worth eating, will that be looting?"

"If I have condemned it," replied the official with dignity, "it's not fit for human consumption. Of course, it would not be looting, but you would be very unwise to try and eat it."

They waited until he was well out of the way and then went to work with pick and shovel on the debris. Before long, beneath the rubble appeared an Aladdin's Cave of tinned sausages, butter, corned beef and other goodies the like and quantity of which they had not seen for many months.

For some weeks afterwards, Roger's platoon was very well-fed indeed.

They had a lucky escape a little later when they had moved on to the Prince Regent's Wharf just down the river to build another pill-box there. The wharf was a tiny affair and housed a timber yard, a bitumen factory and a petrol storage depot.

Just after they left to return to Purfleet that evening, an incendiary bomb raid reduced the entire wharf to total devastation. When they arrived the following day, it was as though they had landed on the surface of the moon. Nothing remained but heaps of twisted metal and charred wood. Survival in those days was very much a matter of luck.

As well as their daytime work of building pill boxes, they had to spend the nights on stand-to in their own platoon areas, arriving there just before midnight.

The platoon had been allocated a three-and-a-half mile stretch along the river bank eastwards from Ford's factory at Dagenham, where he had his platoon headquarters on the lower deck of the two-tier pier. This curved into the river for several hundred yards and then back to the bank, enclosing a substantial stretch of water between it and the land. The headquarters itself was on the curve of the lower deck with a view of nearly two miles down the river. On the top deck above, they had mounted a gun position with as fine a field of fire as anyone could wish.

It was a honey of a position except for the fact that it was a favourite target for the Luftwaffe on their nightly visit to the capital. However, they noticed that the bombs never fell on the main body of the factory, and they drew their own conclusions from this.

The headquarters was well placed within easy reach of the factory paint shop, where the night foreman was generous with his mugs of tea. Roger made it his business to establish a good relationship with him.

One night, soon after arrival, he poked his head into the paint shop door to bid the foreman good evening. "I've just got the kettle on the boil, Sir. Care for a cup now?"

"No thanks," replied Roger, "I'll just get the chaps organised, and I'll be back. Keep it hot for me!"

He set off along the quay and had just reached the pier when there was the scream of a bomb coming down at close quarters; the shorter the scream, the closer the bomb was - a lesson they had all learned from personal experience. He threw himself flat on his face whilst the bomb burst about a hundred yards behind him. He raced back to the paint shop, but it was no longer there. Neither was the foreman. The paint shop had had a direct hit.

Part of his nightly routine was to set off along the river bank to visit the three machine gun posts in their sandbag pill-boxes. As far as he could see, these formed the only part of that part of the river defence against the German invasion.

The men in the pillboxes had a miserable time sitting and staring out into the cold darkness and taking turns to sleep. He felt sorry for them and himself since a seven-mile walk along the river bank to and from the positions was something he found somewhat less than enjoyable.

One night when he arrived at the end post, he found the entire gun crew fast asleep and, waking them up a little brusquely, he enquired of the Number One sitting behind the gun if the weapon was half-loaded as required. "Yes, Sir," replied the sleepy lad.

"And have you pressed the thumb piece?" Roger persisted.

"No, Sir!" the gunner replied.

"And why the hell not?" asked Roger.

"Because the gun will go off if I do," came the reply.

"Of course, it won't," snarled Roger. "Go on, press the bloody thing and get the pressure off the spring."

The Number One shrugged his shoulders as if to say, "Well, I told you so!" and pressed the thumb piece.

Before Roger could kick the gun out of his grasp, he had fired a dozen rounds across the river into Erith on the opposite bank. The weapon had been fully loaded.

Roger bought the local newspaper for the next few days to see if anyone had died in Erith that night.

Another problem which bothered them at Ford's was the attention of Stuka dive-bombers which, if a raid took place in daylight, developed a nasty habit of diving down onto the pier and either machine-gunning it or dropping their bombs around it – mercifully mainly into the water. The gun crew on the top deck of the pier became very frustrated by these attentions but, owing to the limited angles of elevation, could not fire back at the diving planes. The Section Corporal complained bitterly to Roger. "If I could only get a tripod jury-rigged so I could get the gun pointing up in the air, I could have a go at them," he said.

Roger was impressed by this proposal and, after discussing it with someone in the machine shop, was presented with an ideal purpose-built gadget that allowed the gun to point up practically vertically into the air.

Two days later, at daylight, just before they were coming off duty, a couple of Stukas came diving down on them. Roger heard the machine gun's chatter from the pier's top deck.

He never really knew what happened to the plane, but the triumphant Number One claimed it had gone head-first into the Thames in a great plume of water. Whether the story was true, it was undoubtedly worth arguing, and he phoned the Company Commander at Purfleet.

"We've shot down a Stuka, Sir."

"You've done what?" came the astonished reply.

"A Stuka, Sir. We've shot it down." And he explained how this miracle had come about.

"Report to me as soon as you get back," replied the Company Commander, "and bring the gun with you."

Roger's journey back to Purfleet was a very happy one. He had a mental image of a table laden with medals from which he would be invited to take his pick; perhaps the VC would be too much to expect. Still, he would be happy to settle for a DSO or, at any rate, an MC.

When he returned to the Company Commander's office, there were no medals, however, only a very tight-lipped Captain.

"Strip the gun," he said, "and show me the barrel."

Roger did as he was told. The barrel had a prominent bulge at one end. He had forgotten about the water jacket and why one should never tilt the gun higher than its prescribed angle of elevation. The barrel was ruined, and he only got a severe choking off for his pains. Time spent in reconnaissance, he reminded himself, is never wasted.

This lesson would be dramatically brought home to him a few nights later. All the pill-boxes along the river were identified by a code number, his headquarters at

Ford's factory being Number Nine. However, building additional posts caused these numbers to be amended occasionally.

Having completely forgotten this, he called up his trucks to take them to their posts, and, it getting on for midnight and he being still very sleepy, climbed into the leading truck and gave the order "Number nine" to the driver.

"Don't you mean Number twelve?" asked the driver.

"No, I don't," replied Roger, rather bad-tempered.

"When I say nine, I mean nine. I don't mean twelve. Now get on with it!" The driver was too good a soldier to argue with an officer, and they set off. Roger dozed off. He had a long night ahead of him, and the chance of a half-hour's sleep was not to be missed.

He woke up with a start. All hell was being let loose around him, and he saw that he was in a strange place. Three or four gas holders were ablaze, and fire engines were shrieking around him. As he tried to get his bearings, three high-explosive bombs blasted the burning gasometers.

"Where the hell are we?" he shouted to his driver.

"Beckton Gasworks, Sir," he replied imperturbably.

"What the devil are we doing here, for God's sake?" Roger demanded.

"This is number nine, Sir. Beckton Gasworks, Sir. Like what you said, Sir."

Then Roger remembered that the numbers of the posts had been changed two days previously. He had dropped a clanger of significant proportions. Ford's, which had been Number 9, was, indeed, now Number 12, as the driver had said. Beckton, a favourite target for the night-bombers, had been changed from 6 to 9.

"Get the hell out of this as fast as you can!" he shouted to the driver above the crazy din surrounding them. The driver backed his vehicle around and made for the entrance to the works, a narrow road between two tall warehouses.

At this moment, the whole world seemed to go mad as a bomb landed right in the middle of the road with an enormous explosion. The two warehouse walls collapsed in towards each other, completely blocking the way out. Roger and his driver got to work with a pick and shovel.

Luckily, the other trucks had turned off and had gone to Dagenham, where his Sergeant had taken charge of the Platoon and got things organised, ignoring, as every good Sergeant should, his Platoon Commander's curious conduct.

It was six o'clock in the morning when he, at last, telephoned his Company Headquarters in Purfleet. "Number Four Platoon in position, Sir," he reported.

"I should bloody well hope so!" came the reply - "and where the hell have you been?"

The company commander did not seem pleased with Roger's reasons, and he learned another lesson; experience can be an expensive commodity. Ruefully he concluded that he could have lost his own life and that of his driver by his own carelessness and that, despite his training, he still had a great deal to learn.

Towards the middle of November, his company was replaced, and thankfully, he returned to Mill Hill and the life of the depot. He was not at all sorry to leave Purfleet, where the accommodation was spartan, to say the least, and where the rusty corrugated iron roof of his quarters offered little resistance to the showers of shrapnel which frequently rattled on and, sometimes, through it.

Best of all, his month's tour of duty there, where opportunities of writing to Daisy had been very limited, now entitled him to a weekend's leave. Joyfully, he made his way back by train to Eridge.

Chapter 8

Blitz

On his way south from London Bridge Station, Roger had ample opportunity to see the damage done to that part of the city from three months of continuous bombing. Wherever one looked, there were roofless houses, heaps of rubble, the empty shells of churches, their spires still standing as if to point an accusing finger up into the sky from which destruction had rained down upon them.

By some miracle, St. Paul's Cathedral, standing in a sea of surrounding devastation, still seemed to be unharmed, its great dome dominating the ruins at its feet, giving a reassurance that all would be well in the end.

He wondered how it had been possible for people to survive this rain of terror and still go cheerfully about their daily business with a grin and a joke.

When he arrived home, he was faced with a demand from a resolute Daisy that she should accompany him back to Mill Hill. The danger, she said, was probably no worse than she was already experiencing in 'Bomb Alley', the primary flight path for the bombers heading for London and where there were many more aerial dogfights during daylight hours and just as many jettisoned bomb loads at night as there were at Mill Hill.

Along with other volunteers from the village, she took her share of fire-watching. She had spent many a chilly night, a blanket around her shoulders, peering into the darkness to note the position of explosions and keeping a sharp lookout in case there should be a parachute landing. This was either a precursor to an invasion or, as sometimes happened, from the crew of a damaged enemy bomber or one of our own night fighters.

Although he was reluctant to expose her to any additional danger, Roger was obliged to admit that she was such exposed.

"I would just like you to meet some of the chaps," he said, "and I have asked my pal Bert Veitch if he would be best man, and I should like you to see him and see if you agree he would be suitable."

This slight prevarication succeeded, and at eight o'clock to the minute, they went into the bar where the faithful Bert was waiting. The Colonel was standing at one end, and after a while, he strolled over.

"Ah, Rothwell," he said, "nice to see you here. Won't you introduce me to the young lady?"

Suddenly all Roger's anxieties disappeared. Daisy could hold her own in any company, provided she did not feel she was under inspection.

"Very glad to meet you, my dear," said the Colonel, and for the next ten minutes, Roger might as well not have been there. The two chatted away as if they had known each other all their lives, and eventually, the CO wished them goodnight and went.

"What a nice man your Commanding Officer is," said Daisy, "he was really charming". Roger said nothing. He was too busy praying.

Two days later, he received a summons to the CO's office. "Lovely girl, your fiancee," he said, "you're a lucky fellow - wish I was a bit younger; I'd give you a run for your money!" "I am sure you would, Sir," said Roger, "but what about your permission for me to marry her?" "Oh, my dear chap," replied the Colonel, "no problem at all. Whenever you like. All the best to you both. My congratulations."

Roger left the office on air. It was a very long time before he told Daisy the truth about that evening.

With this obstacle overcome, all was set fair for the great day. After the last parade on August 23rd, he set forth on his motorcycle with Bert on the pillion. In fact, Clem, Roger's brother, was to be best man, but by sticking to the story, Bert could also qualify for 48 hours' leave. Since his home was in Newcastle, a couple of days back in civilisation with a wedding feast thrown in was a welcome treat indeed.

There was to be a problem over the return journey since the petrol ration would have run out by the time they got home, but here, again, luck was on their side. The petrol station at Horley was manned by Canadian soldiers. A couple of words and certain coins resulted in a full tank, which would do all they wanted and more.

August 24th was a wonderful day in every way. The sun shone warm out of a cloudless sky. Daisy, who had had to spend the night in the air-raid shelter because of the constant drone of the German bombers overhead, arrived looking radiant in a lovely dress which she had made herself from white taffeta scrounged mysteriously without the sacrifice of precious clothing coupons, and carrying a bouquet of deep red carnations - a most beautiful bride.

As the service started, the next air raid began, and the sound of distant bombing could be heard, but the vicar was a resourceful man and adjusted the Order of Service to arrive at the words: "... let no man put asunder," which actually confirmed the marriage as early in the ceremony as could be managed - just in case.

They came out from the church under an archway of Scout staves. Daisy was the Wolf Cub leader, and Roger had been Assistant Scoutmaster before joining the army. Daisy carried on both roles since. They walked the few yards to the Crest and Gun, where half the village seemed to be gathered to share in the fun and wish them luck.

Their romance had interested the little community for several years, and the local gossips had predicted either that it would come to no good or that, at best, it would never last. But here was the proof that the scandal-mongers had got it wrong, and the village wanted to be there to share their happiness.

Despite the very meagre supplies allowed by food rationing, the wedding breakfast itself was a magnificent affair with delicacies unseen for months, having appeared as if by magic. There was even a proper wedding cake with a rich fruit interior and real sugar icing instead of the white painted cardboard model which in those days usually had to do duty as a cake. The village certainly made the most of it, and, as they heard later, the lawns and the cricket field across the road were scattered with sleeping revellers. It had been a day to remember.

At last, they managed to get away. An empty carriage in the train from Tunbridge Wells gave them their first moments alone together.

They had chosen a hotel out in the country at Knockholt where, although it was still in Bomb Alley, seemed to promise the best prospect of a few hours of peace before Roger had to return to Aldershot the following afternoon.

They got out of the train at Knockholt Station to walk the half mile up to the Black Eagle, but as they came out of the station, they saw that the whole sky was black with planes.

"The old RAF are out in force today," said Roger to the ticket collector.

"Them's not the RAF," was the lugubrious reply, "them's bloody Huns, and they have been machine-gunning your train ever since Sevenoaks. What have you been up to then?"

They did not bother to enlighten him but started on their walk to the hotel. The next moment they were face down in the ditch as a tremendous dogfight broke out overhead with shrapnel and spent bullet cases raining down.

This was the first of the great daylight raids on London, and the RAF was performing miracles in their attempts to intercept them. The roar of the bombers and the scream of the Spitfires and Hurricanes diving down on them from out of the sun with their guns chattering in an attempt to split up the formations before they reached the capital's outskirts and made progress towards the hotel. This was an adventure they would never forget, and it seemed to them to be a strange way to start their life together.

Suddenly it was all over. The bombers wheeled around and turned for home. Daisy and Roger completed the journey that had taken them two hours instead of the fifteen minutes they had expected.

They strolled through the beech woods of Poll Hill and sat in a field overlooking the valley and did not speak. In total contrast, the evening was sunny and quiet. They and the whole world were at peace, and the war was light-years away.

When dusk fell, however, it returned with a vengeance. All through the night, the hotel they had chosen to ensure peace and quiet was rocked by bombs exploding around it. The pulsating roar of the bombers was incessant as they seemed to be selecting them for special attention.

Daisy and Roger, scorning the proprietor's urgent invitation to accompany him to the air raid shelter, spent their first night of married life under the bed.

Years later, when recounting these experiences to his fellow prisoners, Roger learned that in the chalk downland beneath Knockholt was one of the largest underground ammunition dumps in the country!

A pleasant surprise awaited him on his return to Aldershot the next day. All through their training, a continuous assessment of their potential was made. This had been supported by tactical exercises on the ground, with the sand tray, and a series of written examinations just before he left for his wedding.

Now, on the notice board were posted the results and their final placings and, with his heart in his mouth, he searched the list to find his name.

Being naturally pessimistic, he looked first at the names below the line of those having failed the course and, in consequence, to be returned with ignominy to their units. With a huge sigh of relief, he found that he was not among them.

Bert Veitch, standing beside him looking for his own name, shouted: "Bloody hell, you old sod, look where you are!" He just could not believe his eyes. Out of the entire intake of eighty cadets, he had come second.

Although they had all been asked to state the regiment of their choice on being commissioned, it had also been made clear that this could not be guaranteed and that only those in the top bracket could be certain of their choice.

Roger had opted for the Middlesex Regiment, not only because it consisted of Cockneys, whom he had come to admire during his year at the university, but also because it was the closest of the machine gun regiments to home. And so he was to become a Diehard and only hoped that the nickname would not apply too literally.

Nothing now, short of total disaster, stood between him and his commission scheduled for September 21st. At the first opportunity, he took himself down into the town to be measured for his new uniform.

A fortnight later, he did something so stupid as to threaten his future. Anxious to seize any opportunity of spending time with Daisy, he put in for a day pass for Sunday, September 15th. It suddenly occurred to him that he had never known a roll call to be made before lights out on a Saturday night since they were allowed to be out until midnight and that, in any case, his mates would provide a good cover story for him in the most unlikely event of a check being made.

Accordingly, having collected his day pass on Saturday afternoon, he collected his motorbike and headed for home and his first night with his new wife since the somewhat unusual experience of their wedding day.

But if that had been something of a disaster, it paled into insignificance beside the night of September 14th. The air raid warning sounded at dusk soon after he arrived home. Almost immediately, the familiar pulsating roar of the Dorniers and the machine gun fire of the defending fighters drove them all down into the dank air raid shelter in the field behind the school house.

Watching the night hours ticking away, Roger was about to make the same suggestion when a huge explosion, far greater than the others, seemed to rock the ground. A few minutes later, the village policeman put his head through the shelter door.

"Is there anyone here," he said, "who can give me a hand with traffic control? A parachute land mine has landed on the main road and blown a damned great hole you could put half a dozen lorries in. "There was nothing for it but for Roger to scramble out and spend the rest of the night down by the railway station diverting the Tunbridge Wells-bound traffic.

The following day things were no better. Wave after wave of bombers with their own fighter escort came in from the south. The whole sky was a crisscross pattern of vapour trails as the Spitfires and Hurricanes dived and weaved over and above. Planes would suddenly begin to dive with long trails of black smoke pouring out from them and crash in a great ball of flame. They were not always German by any means.

As the morning wore on, Roger became more and more anxious. This was far worse than anything he had seen before, and it became clear to him that this might well be the prelude to the invasion they had been expecting for so long. If this were the case, his place was at Aldershot and at about 10 o'clock, he got on his bike and headed like the wind for Malplaquet Barracks.

When he arrived, it occurred to him that he must hand in his Sunday day pass, and before doing anything else, he went into the guard room to surrender it. "My day pass," he said virtuously. "I thought there was a bit of a flap on, and I'd better get back to barracks." The Guard Sergeant raised his eyebrows. "Where was you last night, then?" he asked. "Why, back in the barracks, of course, Sergeant."

"I see," came the reply. "Then, in that case, you can tell me what happened at six o'clock!"

Roger was in a blind panic. Here he was a few days before his commission, and he had gone absent without leave at a critical moment. Going AWOL was a crime for which there could be no excuse and, quite certainly, would be the end of him. He felt a cold sweat beginning to trickle down his back.

But the age of miracles was not past, and his guardian angel sent a fairy godmother to his aid in the most unlikely form of Sergeant Fraser.

The Sergeant gave Roger an inscrutable glance and a quick jerk of his head towards the door.

"Jim," he said to his colleague, "something bad has cropped up, and I must talk to you. Just go outside for a minute," he said to Roger, "and come back when I've finished."

Roger was gone in a flash and was thankful to find Bert Veitch, who had seen him come into the barracks and had rushed up to try to stop him from going in to report.

"For God's sake, what happened last night?" he said.

"I'll tell you," replied Bert. "There was stand-to until 6 o'clock this morning because there was an invasion alert. The roll was called, but you were not there and all day passes for today were cancelled. That's what happened."

Roger's heart stopped beating. "Don't panic," Bert went on, "I answered your name for you, but you'll have to get out of the day pass problem yourself." Roger squeezed his arm. Here was a pal, indeed.

Just then, Sergeant Fraser came out of the guard room: "You can go in now," he said, and Roger returned. "Well," said the Sergeant, "what happened?"

Roger's face assumed what he hoped was an expression of complete innocence. "Well, there was a stand-to at six o'clock, and we were not stood down until this morning. I've only just had a wash and shave and forgot about handing in the day pass, as we were told. Sorry about that, Sergeant. Here it is." And he handed the pass to him.

The Duty Sergeant looked at him through half-closed eyes. He was not born yesterday and did not believe a word of the story, but he could do nothing about it. "Get out of here!" he said, "and think yourself bloody lucky."

Roger did both and went off to buy Bert anything he wanted to ask for in the way of alcoholic refreshment.

At last, the great day for their commissioning arrived. There was to be no passing out parade, no ceremony of any kind. Part One orders merely said that newly commissioned officers would dress in their new uniforms at precisely midday and would leave the barracks immediately.

But the show was not yet quite over. Two of the lads who had suffered at Dusty Smith's hands for five long months dressed themselves up in their brand new barathea uniforms at half past nine and stood around outside Dusty's office waiting for him to come out so that he would be obliged to salute them before they left. The others gathered around casually at a safe distance to watch the fun.

At five minutes to ten, Dusty emerged and examined the two cadets from head to toe. "What's this, what's this? What do I see? Two officer cadets improperly dressed and masquerading as officers. On the parade ground, you. At the double!"

The luckless couple performed every gyration known to the drill manual for the next two hours. They marched, marked time, turned to the right, turned to the left, about turned without stopping and always at the double until they were exhausted and their new barathea uniforms were saturated in perspiration.

On the dot of midday, Dusty looked at his watch.

"It is now midday, gentlemen. May I be the first to congratulate you on becoming Commissioned Officers in His Majesty's Army?" He gave them a magnificent salute. Dusty had had his fun.

Roger went back to the hut for the last time, put on his new uniform with the single brass pip on each shoulder and as No.149464, Second Lieutenant Rothwell, he said goodbye to his friends, got on his motorbike and headed for home, a precious week's leave, and his new wife.

Although they had been married for more than three months, they had spent scarcely any time together except for the wonderful few days of his leave before he went to Mill Hill. It would be very nice indeed to be together even in the unwelcoming atmosphere of Mrs Botting's establishment in Bittacy Park Road.

Another reason influencing him was a persistent rumour, which he had kept to himself for the time being, that he was likely to be drafted abroad soon after Christmas. It was difficult to see where he might be sent. He thought it more likely that any movement would be to a posting elsewhere in the country. Nevertheless, this might be a long way away, and it would be impossible for Daisy to be accommodated. Any chance to spend time together was a precious bonus in these troubled times.

It was also true that since the night of November 14th, when the full might of the Luftwaffe had concentrated on the destruction of Coventry, London had been given its first night free from bombing for nearly three months. The raids on the capital had been less intense, and there had even been a couple of nights when the air raid sirens had not sounded at all. He had mentioned possibly accommodating Daisy at his billets to Mrs Botting, his landlady. She had agreed, although with a marked lack of enthusiasm, making it plain that Daisy's stay with her would be 'upon liking' and that she would agree to keep herself to herself.

Accordingly, Daisy returned with him to Mill Hill on the Sunday evening after his weekend leave. She had her first glimpse of the effects of the 'Blitz' from the train window.

There was a raid in progress when they arrived at London Bridge Station. They lost no time in scuttling across the street to the entrance to the Northern Line of the Underground and going down in the lift, which was still working, to the platform.

Here an extraordinary sight confronted them. The whole platform was occupied by recumbent bodies, some on camp beds, some lying on the ground, and some propped up against the curved wall of the station. Some chatted in family groups, while others played cards, read, or looked after small children snuggled up in blankets or carry-cots. Many were already asleep safe in the knowledge that they were so far underground that no bomb, however powerful, could reach them.

Many of the sleepers had brought with them treasured possessions for safekeeping since none knew if their homes would still be in one piece when they returned to them in the morning. A family photograph in an ornate frame, a budgerigar in a cage, and what could be squeezed into a bulging suitcase lay huddled close beside them on the platform.

Although shocked by this pathetic sight, which, more than all the structural devastation on the surface, brought home to them the absolute horror of the Blitz, Daisy and Roger could see no trace of self-pity and, apart from an appeal to no the noisy youngsters to "knock it orf!"

The people of London were humping their way through.

Safe though the Underground usually was, there were occasions when things went terribly wrong. At Belsize Park, on the Morden-Edgware line, several hundreds of feet below street level, a high-explosive bomb had fallen straight down the lift shaft and exploded at the bottom, fracturing water mains and killing many hundreds, both as a result of the explosion and of drowning. At Oxford Circus, large numbers taking temporary shelter in the booking hall only a few feet below the surface had been blown to pieces by a direct hit.

Daisy and Roger stood as far back from the platform's edge as the recumbent bodies would allow, planting their feet between the legs of those asleep and swaying back as the train entered the station. They left the train at Golders Green, the nearest point to the barracks. They made their way by bus and on foot through the blacked-out streets illuminated only by the occasional flash of light from a distant bomb and by the glow from the fires to the south of them.

The house on Bittacy Park Road was dark and unwelcoming. Roger's request that they, or at least Daisy, might be allowed to join the family in the corrugated iron Anderson shelter in the garden was brusquely refused. There was only just room for the family, they were told. However, this consisted of only two people, so the intruders must make their own arrangements. Accordingly, they made their way up to bed listening to the bursting anti-aircraft shells from the mobile gun mounted on a railway truck on the line to Mill Hill East which ran along the bottom of the hill below them, shrapnel rattling on the roof.

When things became too noisy, and there was a danger, not only from bombing but just as much from the rain of shrapnel, they retreated to the dining room. Pulling the table over to the outside wall, they made themselves as comfortable as they could underneath it. They trusted the theory that however much a house was damaged from a near miss, the bottom two or three feet of the wall were always left intact. The table top would, they hoped, protect them from falling masonry.

Although the cupboard under the stairs in the centre of the building was generally reckoned to be the most secure internal shelter, many cases had been of people being crushed or buried alive underneath the bricks and timber, pinning them down and delaying their rescue. By the outside wall, there was less risk of this happening since they would be more accessible to the rescuers.

When they were together at night, this was their regular routine. When, as frequently happened, Roger had to be on duty at the barracks, Daisy had no alternative but to make her way to the public shelter. If she was lucky, she would find a place on one of the bench bunks raised above the floor, along which a small river of muddy water trickled incessantly.

The place was cold, damp, dark and cheerless, and it was clear that the newcomer taking up precious space was far from welcome, and no one spoke to her.

Indeed, her life at Mill Hill was really wretched. She was among strangers and, during the day, had nothing to do except wander around the streets in this rather unattractive part of London. Her few hours of happiness with Roger during the evenings were bought at a considerable price.

One Friday evening, when he was not on duty, they went by bus to Harrow to see her sister. They returned late at night and found themselves at the receiving end of a major raid. The driver stuck it for as long as he could, but he pulled into the side with his bus rocking on its axles from the blasts of air from nearby explosions. The conductor shouted to the passengers upstairs: "Them as wants to go to heaven stay where you are. All the others, come down and get under the bus with me!"

They needed no second invitation.

After half an hour, when things had quietened, they returned to the upper deck and continued their journey. In front of them was an incredible sight. The sky to the south was aglow with a great blaze of light. They were filled with admiration for this cheerful Cockney driver who, seeing what lay ahead of him, drove to his destination at Victoria Station without complaint or hesitation.

They went into neighbouring Edgware the following day, which had received a significant share of the previous night's raid. The pavements were ankle-deep in glass, and there was not a single shop with its window intact. And yet, in spite of it all, business appeared to be as near normal as possible under the circumstances.

They went into a Lyon's teashop to see if there was any chance of a meal. The 'Nippy', as the waitresses were called in those days, was helpful.

"There's no gas or electric," she said, "but I'll put a kettle on the Primus and make you a cup of tea. I think I can find you a piece of cake."

She poured the methylated spirit into the little cup below the main burner of the paraffin stove. When it had burned itself out, she worked vigorously on the pump handle until the blue flame roared under the kettle. They were glad of the tea and the piece of cake, which was still a little soggy, having been too close to the fire hose when the incendiary bomb had been extinguished. However, cake was cake, and they ate it without complaint.

This incident was followed by a period of comparative calm, and one night, there was no air raid warning at all. All through that evening, they found themselves as jumpy as kittens. Strangely enough, they found the silence most unnerving. They had become so conditioned to the noise that they accepted it as a typical pattern of life.

Suddenly, just outside their window, they heard a tremendous swish as if a bomb was falling at close quarters. Daisy dived under the bedclothes and Roger under the bed, and they waited for the explosion, which must, surely, be the end of them.

Nothing happened, and they waited in an eerie silence. Clearly something momentous had occurred - perhaps it was an unexploded bomb which might go off at any moment. Roger got up and went downstairs to investigate. He found that the next-door neighbour had caused the noise, who had emptied a sack of coke onto the concrete backyard.

By this time, life for Daisy had become quite intolerable with Mrs Botting. Things came to a head when she demanded that Daisy should take over a share of the housework as her presence had increased this to an unacceptable level. Ordinarily,

Daisy would have been happy to do so and, indeed, had offered to lend a hand - an offer which had been brusquely refused. Since they were already paying an exorbitant price for her board and keep, they resolved that either they would try to find alternative lodgings or that she must go back home.

Roger mentioned the problem to his Platoon Sergeant.

"No problem. I know just the place, Sir," he said, "a very nice young lady in Bittacy Rise who has a room to spare. She is not on the official billeting list, but I'm sure she would be glad to put you up."

They went immediately that evening and found that the 'nice young lady' was everything the Sergeant had said.

Although the house lacked something of the starchy cleanliness of their previous lodgings, it was homely and comfortable. In contrast to Mrs Botting, she was warm and welcoming. The deal was struck at once, and they paid the starchy Mrs Botting a week's rental and moved in the next day.

They never knew the surname of their new hostess. "Call me Doris," she said, "all my friends do", and so they did.

As far as Daisy was concerned, life with Doris was in complete contrast, and she was glad to turn to and do all she could to help with the house and make life run smoothly. Daisy was no stranger to hard work, and she set to with a will to the great delight of the grateful Doris.

What was outstanding in Doris's establishment was the quality of the food. They had never seen such variety and quantity since peace-time days. Eggs and bacon, butter, jam, cakes, chocolate, gin and whisky - all in great profusion and offered unstintingly. Doris was, indeed, a most generous hostess and excellent company. They had really fallen on their feet.

Another great advantage from their point of view was that Doris went out nearly every evening, not returning until the small hours of the morning, and they had the house to themselves. "Just off down the West End, my dears," she would say. "Have a nice evening and behave yourselves. Help yourselves to whatever is going."

Roger was puzzled by her generosity and as to what Doris did for a living. He assumed she probably worked in a restaurant or club and felt a little uneasy about the origin of all her largesse. It was not long before he found the answer. On the stairs one morning, he found an empty contraceptive packet. Just as he went into the bathroom, he caught a glimpse of his Platoon Sergeant creeping on tiptoe down the stairs on his way back to the barracks.

Suddenly, the truth of the generous supply of goodies, the whisky, the gin, the bacon and butter dawned upon him. Doris was a lady of pleasure and, like so many of her kind, was open-hearted, kind and generous to a fault. As far as they were concerned, Doris's affairs were her own business, and they were happy to continue living off her immoral earnings.

One tricky problem now arose from an unexpected quarter. Roger's mother, not to be outdone by the courage of her new daughter-in-law, announced that she would like to come up to Mill Hill to spend a weekend with them. Nothing they could do or say, no lurid accounts of death and destruction could dissuade her. The only concession they could wring from her was to postpone her visit until "things had quietened down a little".

By evil chance, the first few days of the following week had been unusually peaceful. So they reluctantly agreed that both parents should travel on Friday evening and be met from the bus outside the barracks.

As there was no room for them at Doris's, Daisy set forth to find a bed and breakfast establishment in the neighbourhood. She came back that evening bubbling with laughter.

"Have you found somewhere good?" Roger asked.

"I certainly have," she replied. "The address is Number 13, De'Ath Avenue. The lady's name is Mrs Fear, and the house overlooks the cemetery. Will that be alright?"

Friday evening arrived, and they stood at the barrack gates waiting for the bus. As they did so, the air raid siren sounded. Within a few minutes, the familiar roar of planes could be heard overhead. Amid a tornado of anti-aircraft fire, the first bombs of the evening began to fall. It was clearly going to be a dreadful night, indeed. Perhaps fate was playing a hand in Daisy's house-hunting efforts.

The bus disgorged Roger's parents just as a parachute mine landed behind the barracks, rocking the whole area and sending them all scuttling for shelter.

Somehow they managed to get the terrified parents down the hill to De'Ath Avenue, where Mrs Fear took charge and dragged them both into the shelter with her. There was clearly no room for Daisy or Roger. As it was little short of suicide to venture out, they spent the night huddled in each other's arms under the sink in the kitchen while high-explosive bombs peppered the area lit up by incendiaries.

Towards morning, things quietened down a little, and they judged it safe to venture out back home to Bittacy Rise.

Just as they were crossing the grassed area of a traffic roundabout, however, there came the familiar swish of a bomb falling from very close quarters. Mercifully they were close to a telephone kiosk surrounded by sandbag walls. They dived in and went flat on their faces while the world went mad around them. When they crawled out, they saw that a house not fifty yards away had received a direct hit in the front garden.

Again, it had been a lucky night.

They spent the rest of the night in the comparative safety and comfort of the barracks' lower guard room, drinking mugs of hot cocoa with the Sergeant. Eventually, they made their way safely home up the hill, where householders were still putting out the remains of incendiaries with their long-handled shovels, stirrup pumps and buckets of sand.

Roger's parents went home by the first available train that morning. They had come; they had seen; they had had enough.

But now, a new cloud appeared, and it was one which, although inevitable, they had both dreaded. One morning in early December, Roger was summoned to the medical centre for an examination.

"You feeling alright?" asked the Medical Officer.

"Yes, thank you," said Roger.

"Good," replied the MO. "Is there any reason, as far as you know, that you should not serve in the Tropics?" Although he knew the purpose of the question, he could only say that there wasn't.

"Aren't you going to give me a medical examination?" he asked, still hoping for a reprieve.

"No," said the MO. "No need. You look pretty fit to me. Off you go, and the best of luck."

And that was that.

As far as he could see, the only two possible places to which he could be sent were to the Western Desert, where there was a build-up of troops to protect Cairo and the Suez Canal from the Italian army, which had made a rapid advance from Libya to the Egyptian frontier at Tobruk. The other possibility was to Hong Kong, where the 1st Battalion of the Middlesex, which consisted entirely of regular soldiers, was stationed. It seemed unlikely that a young, inexperienced 'temporary gentleman', as war-time officers were called, would be drafted to that prestigious unit.

There was no point in concealing the truth from Daisy, who accepted the inevitable with her customary quiet courage, and they set about making the most of their last few weeks together. There was much to be done, including a trip to the military tailors in Regent Street for him to be kitted out with khaki drill shorts, shirts, jacket and solar topee, for all of which his kit allowance of £60 proved woefully inadequate.

And now the days slipped inexorably by, and January 2nd, the date fixed for his embarkation, was only two weeks away.

They would have liked to get home for Christmas, but Roger had to be on duty helping to serve the Christmas meal to the men, and they travelled down to Eridge for Boxing Day.

The Underground station at London Bridge had been totally transformed when they arrived. The walls and platforms were decorated with streamers and paper chains, and the Christmas trees were bright with tinsel and a fairy on the top. The brave people of London were not to be done out of their Christmas, and they felt as if they had stepped out into the middle of a party.

They stayed at home until the last moment on the following Sunday, December 29th. Roger said goodbye to his parents, and they caught the last train from Tunbridge Wells.

They had originally thought that Daisy would not come back with him, but Doris had kindly offered to look after her when he had gone and to see her safely home to Eridge. This would allow them just two or three days more together.

Not long after leaving New Cross station, the train came to an abrupt halt, and, raising the blind and peering through the window, they saw a shocking sight. The city was ablaze, and high-explosive bombs were raining down into the holocaust and rocking their train to and fro until they thought it would be blown clean off the rails.

Clearly, the train could not get into the station, and there was nothing for it but to sit tight and hope for the best. They sat holding each other for at least two hours, staring at the inferno and waiting for the end. Their only comfort was that if they were going to be killed, at least they would die together.

At long last, the train inched forward and deposited them at London Bridge station, part of which was still blazing furiously.

Outside the station entrance, where the street was a river of blackened water from the fire hoses, and the stench and heat from the raging fires seemed to wrap itself around them, they dived headlong into the safety of the Underground.

That night, the fire raid on the city was to go down in history as one of the worst of the war. However, civilian casualties were much less than in some previous attacks since comparatively few people lived there and thousands of city workers were home in the suburbs.

The fire raged unchecked for two or three days since, by unlucky chance, the raid had started when the river was at low tide. With the fire hydrants and mains fractured by the bombing, the men of the fire brigade, who took appalling personal risks to do their job, had to drag their hoses across the mud to get at the water for their tankers.

When Roger and Daisy emerged from the Underground at Golders Green, they found that everything was comparatively peaceful. They had left the inferno behind, but their way home was brightly lit by the light from the burning city to the south.

And now their last day together had come, and the young couple said a final sad goodbye. Roger joined the transport for Kings Cross Station along with a dozen young subalterns like himself, all bound for the same destination, wherever that might be. They still did not know where they were bound for. All they had been told was that their field address was RCNMD for Destination K and that they were to join Troopship J at Renfrew docks. "Careless talk costs lives" was the order of the day, and they had to be content with that.

The day, however, was to hold one final surprise. Roger heard a shout from the barrier as the contingent crossed the platform to the waiting troop train. Turning, he caught a glimpse of Daisy and Doris standing on the other side. Doris had clearly done her stuff with her Sergeant and had found, careless talk or no, the station and platform from which the train was leaving, and had brought Daisy for a final goodbye.

A quick word, a last kiss and Roger had to hurry off to join the others, leaving her behind the barrier.

But Doris's powers of persuasion had brought off one final triumph, for scarcely had he settled into the compartment with the others, Daisy was at the carriage window. She was the only other body on the platform, so they had just a few more minutes together before the train moved off.

He leaned out of the window as far as he dared and stayed there until the lone solitary figure on the platform grew smaller and smaller until, finally, she was swallowed up by the darkness and disappeared from his sight.

It was to be almost five long years before they saw each other again.

Chapter 9

Outward Bound

The troop train, its engine disgorging clouds of smoke and steam, jerked its way into the night. Roger slumped down into the corner by the window. No one spoke for a very long time, each one alone with his private thoughts.

They knew that they were to be on the train for some considerable time. Renfrew was a long way away, and the train, like them, seemed in no hurry to get there. They had been told there would be a halt at Grantham for a cup of tea and a longer wait at Newcastle for a meal at the station buffet. They had had nothing to eat since breakfast, and, indeed, anything that he had tried to eat would have choked him, but now Roger was beginning to feel hungry and thirsty, and the thought of a cup of tea became more and more agreeable.

They had left Kings Cross at four o'clock and had no idea how far they had reached. Roger looked around the compartment, dimly lit by only a tiny blue bulb, at his seven companions, some dozing off, others like himself, staring gloomily into the darkness. Some of them had been with him at Aldershot. Cheesewright, who had been so unlucky with his billets. Laurie Wood, tall and reserved, had beaten him by a single mark in their final assessment. 'Pan' Newton, fresh-faced and cherubic in appearance. All knew each other well.

The others, like the big Jimmy James, Ken Cole, 'Willy' Williamson, whose wife was expecting their first baby in three months, Blackaby and Scantlebury had come from an earlier course. All of them had already become friends.

He wondered vaguely what would happen to them all and how many would survive the war if they were involved in combat. He would have been devastated if he had known that, out of this group of young men, he alone would return to England and that all would have been killed in battle, have been drowned on the Lisbon Maru, the prison ship torpedoed by the Americans in October 1942, murdered or have died from malnutrition or disease.

The train began to slow down, and they saw they were drawing into a station. "Grantham," someone said, and they began to pick themselves up, ready to get out for their 'cuppa'. But it was not to be. The train picked up speed again and trundled its way north. It was now well turned six o'clock, and they reckoned it would be another two or three hours at the rate they were going before they had something to eat at Newcastle. From time to time, they were shunted into sidings to wait for half an hour or so and by the time they panted to a halt at Newcastle, it was turned eleven.

The train stopped, and they all poured onto the platform and headed towards the dimly lit buffet. Scarcely had they reached the door, the engine let out a piercing double shriek, and the Rail Transport Officer yelled out through his megaphone: "Everyone back on the train!" So hungry and cursing, they got back in and set off once again.

All through the rest of the night, they continued their intermittent progress, and just as it was beginning to get light, their journey came to an end. They had been travelling without food or drink for nearly sixteen hours and were exhausted, famished and mutinous.

As they scrambled down from the train, they found they were in a dense freezing fog and above them towered a great black shape with a gangway down onto the quayside.

They had arrived at Renfrew docks, and Troop Transport "J" was waiting to receive them. As he clambered up the gangway with his kit, Roger just made out the words 'Empress of Japan' on the side of a lifeboat. He was not to appreciate the irony of this until much later.

Once inside the ship, everything was changed as if by magic. They stood gaping in amazement. It was as if they had been caught up in a transformation scene in a pantomime. Gone were the darkness, the fog, the frost and the wretchedness of a Clydeside wharf. They were in a palatial lounge, brilliantly lit with a luxurious carpet and gilded pillars, warm and welcoming. A Ship's Officer greeted them and invited them to leave their kit where it was and follow him into the dining room for breakfast.

Never was an invitation more gladly received. The men sat themselves down at small tables with spotless table linen and gleaming cutlery and, best of all, a menu the like of which they had not seen since before the war. Every sort of food was there: eggs, bacon, sausages, kedgeree, kidneys, fish, and they stared at it in disbelief. On the table was a great dish of butter and rolls. Without waiting to explore the menu, they pitched in, plastering the bread with butter and wolfing it down.

"Half a minute," said someone, "there's about two weeks' ration of butter here, and we don't know how long it's got to last."

A Chinese steward was standing at the table listening: "You want more butter, Master," he said, "I go and get," and off he went and came back with another great dish. Roger thought of the meagre breakfast Daisy probably made back home in the school house at Eridge. He felt horribly guilty as he was presented with a great plate of bacon, eggs and fried bread, wishing with a great yearning that she could share it with him.

The Empress of Japan was one of the Canadian Pacific liners of 24,000 tons and was still equipped as it had been in peace-time days. They hoped the voyage would continue wherever it was bound for a very long time.

But it had not even started. The Empress lay fog-bound at the quayside day after day, and the first sensations of elation began to wear thin for them all. Inside all was warmth and light, but out on the deck, they were wrapped around with a thick green blanket of fog which soon drove them back to their comfortable lounge and made any possibility of departure out of the question.

One problem was that since the ship was still in Customs bond, the bar had to remain closed, and even a glass of beer was denied to them. As well as this, they weren't to be allowed ashore to sample the hospitality of Glasgow, whatever that might be. They were prisoners in a palace.

On his tour of duty as Orderly Officer, he received bitter complaints from the men whose quarters and menu were far inferior to his own. There were other problems too. Personal supplies of cigarettes and tobacco were rapidly becoming exhausted, and these, too, were in the bonded store and were unobtainable. Added to this was the fact that the ship, which had victualled at Belfast shortly before Christmas, had had a near miss from a bomb, which had thrown part of its refrigeration system out of action. There was a risk that the supplies of turkeys loaded for Christmas would go bad within the next week or so.

The men existed on an unvarying diet of turkey cooked in every way known to the culinary art. On his statutory request of "Any complaints?" at mealtime, he was greeted with a storm of protest.

"It's the bloody grub, Sir. Nothing but sodding turkey day after day. There's no canteen, and we can't get a drink or a smoke, Sir. You're an officer, Sir. Can't you do nothing about it?"

There was very little he or any of his comrades could do, but, in a sudden brainwave, he went to the Commanding Officer and asked permission to go into Glasgow to buy "comforts for the troops".

This permission was grudgingly given, so he went around among his own Middlesex officers and the men placed on their draft and constructed a long shopping list of cigarettes and tobacco to be paid for on his return from his trip.

And so he set off in the fog on a Number 4 tram bound for Sauchiehall Street in Glasgow. To his surprise, he found that his travelling companion was Ah Moon, the table steward who assured him that he knew Glasgow like the back of his hand and could guide him wherever he wanted to go, fog or no fog. Ah Moon, however, had certain words of warning,

"Glasgow no damn good for jig-a-jig," he confided. "Go ashore one shilling, come back nothing."

Roger assured him he was not seeking 'jig-a-jig' but only wanted cigarettes and tobacco. At this, Ah Moon lost interest and abandoned him at the Sauchiehall Street stop, and he groped his way along the fog-bound streets of this unfamiliar city to make his purchases.

Tired but triumphant, Roger made his way, loaded with the orders, back to the Empress only to find that, during his absence, the Customs officials, as a humanitarian gesture, had agreed to open up the bonded store and the cigarettes for which he had paid eleven pence a packet were now freely available from the ship's bars at half that price.

Only one or two of the men agreed to pay for what they had ordered. At the end of the day, he was left with a large quantity of cigarettes which no one would take off his hands. His helpful proposal had cost him nearly twelve pounds, and this, as his weekly pay was four pounds, was a severe blow indeed.

At last, after more than a week, the fog lifted, and the Empress made her way along the Clyde to anchor off Gourock opposite the entrance to Holy Loch. Here was assembled the largest armada of ships he had ever seen. There must have been at least a hundred, ranging from small coasting vessels and merchantmen to great liners, naval cruisers, destroyers and frigates, with the battleship 'Ramilles' in overall command.

The following morning the whole great convoy set sail and, under a crystal-clear blue sky, made its way down the Clyde, with the snow glittering on the Isle of Arran and past Ailsa Craig, the whole stretch of the estuary seemingly a solid mass of shipping.

Two days later, when they were well out into the Atlantic, Clydeside suffered the heaviest bombing of the war. His luck was still holding.

At the entrance to the Clyde estuary, the convoy split into two, the bulk turning south past the coast of Ireland towards Liverpool and the remainder, containing all the largest troopships, twenty-four liners over twenty thousand tons each accompanied by four cruisers, twelve destroyers and the 'Ramilles' turned north and headed for the open Atlantic with an air cover for the first critical two days of fighter aircraft and Sunderland flying boats.

They had not been greatly comforted by the headlines before they left Glasgow, which proclaimed in large black letters: 'The Battle of the Atlantic is on!' They were grateful for the protection of their massive escort.

And now there followed what seemed to be an eternity of sailing with the convoy altering course every ten minutes or so just in case they were being tailed by German submarines whose commanders would have given their eye-teeth for such a prize. But they never knew whether it was its very size and, therefore, its potential for retaliation or whether the hunters were in the wrong area. They were left in peace, and the ships made their way, first north to within fifty miles of the southern tip of Greenland and then westward and southward past Newfoundland before turning east.

They crossed the sharp divide between the grey-green water of the North Atlantic and the clear blue of the Gulf Stream with its warm sunshine, porpoises and flying fish. Throughout the days that followed, they were accompanied by a lone shark which kept station behind them, its triangular fin cutting the water silently and menacingly as if it were waiting for some disaster to deliver one of them up as a tasty morsel.

Roger had always hoped that one day he would travel to see distant parts of the world. The unchanging circle of the open sea surrounding them day after day soon obliterated this ambition. Despite the comfort of his surroundings and the lavish diet, which was in such contrast to the frugal meals to which they had become accustomed, life became almost unbearably monotonous.

Days were spent searching the horizon for some sign of life. Their evenings gossiping or drinking in the lounge where a double gin could be purchased for threepence and speculating on the number of miles covered during the past twenty-four hours, hoping to come up with the correct answer in the daily sweepstake.

The battleship and two cruisers had left them a day or so earlier and, as they learned later, had headed eastwards into the Mediterranean. Because of the blockade by the Italian navy, it was no longer considered safe to risk troop transports, those bound for North Africa being obliged to circumnavigate the whole continent.

At last, on January 25th, after being out of sight of land for nearly a fortnight, they sailed on to a buoy apparently in the middle of the open ocean. In a few more hours, the coast of Africa appeared. In line ahead, the convoy passed through the narrow entrance through the palm-tree-lined sandspit and into the vast stretch of water, forming the harbour of Freetown, capital of Sierra Leone. The sight of land and the end of the most dangerous part of the journey came as a great relief. Just as the ships were filing in, a single plane approached them from the sea and flew down the entire length of the convoy. As it passed overhead, they saw the red, white and blue of the French air force on its wings. Everyone stood up on the decks and waved and cheered, but Roger, remembering a similar plane at Aldershot and the consequences of its visit, shouted: "Look out! Get your heads down!"

The day after their arrival was January 25th - Burns Night, and in a temperature of 95 degrees, they were served with haggis and 'Bubbly Jock', the last of the turkeys which, by now, had become very well hung indeed. The men were serenaded by the Pipe Major of the Royal Scots who were travelling with them and celebrated as only Scotsmen can on such an occasion.

Although they were glad to get away from the fetid heat of the harbour, everyone was a little anxious on leaving Sierra Leone. The previous convoy had run into serious trouble en route to Cape Town. Two ships had been sunk, one so severely damaged that it had limped into the harbour a good week after the others. The appearance of the French raider over the convoy and the message that it would undoubtedly carry back with it to Dakar roused fears that the German submarines would try a repeat performance.

All was well, however. They crossed the equator on a cool and cloudy afternoon. They took their obligatory ducking and shaving from Father Neptune in the ship's minute swimming pool with commendable stoicism.

They arrived at Cape Town on February 8th and, to their great delight, were allowed ashore. They saw a long line of cars by the roadside as they entered the dock gates. A warm invitation to a meal in their home and a trip around the countryside came from each vehicle. Cape Town was delighted to see them and opened its heart and its doors to them with great enthusiasm and embarrassing generosity. They were informed that they had been automatically elected members of every club in the town and were not allowed by the members to pay for a drink in any of them. The memories of that beautiful city remained a little blurred for many of them. Luckily, after a very protracted session at the Junior Civil Service Club in Plein Street, Roger's resolution to make a solo ascent of Table Mountain departed from him when glancing down behind him, he came to his senses halfway up. Before he had got into any serious difficulty, he made his ascent by a more orthodox route by cable car.

One day he found himself the guest of the Minister of Defence. He was escorted to the seaside resorts of Muizenburg and Fishoek on False Bay to the south of the town. He sat in the sun on the sand with a splendid picnic, a huge bunch of grapes and an immense feeling of well-being. The war was a long way away, and if only Daisy could have been there to share it with him, he would have been in paradise.

At first, he could not fathom the reason for such a welcome offered to them all, regardless of rank, until it was explained that it was generally assumed that all the troops were on their way 'up north' to defend Africa. They quickly learned to admit to this, whether it was true or not and, by now, they had learned from the ship's crew that the Empress was bound for Singapore.

He had written something to Daisy every day. Even though he knew that his letters would be censored, the hour or so he spent with her every evening seemed to bring her close, and this time was very precious. Cape Town allowed him to post his letters and a parcel home.

At last, after ten days of this opulent living, they sailed around the Cape and into the Indian Ocean. They sailed through calm seas of vivid blue with shoals of flying fish and schools of porpoises playing 'last across' in front of the ship and crossed the equator for the second time. The threat of attack by U-boats had now lessened, and most of their escort had left them, although the convoy of troopships had not diminished in size.

Then, one morning the Empress veered off to the west while the remainder of the convoy, together with all that was left of the escort, continued to the north. It was clear that they were all heading for the Red Sea and the Suez Canal to reinforce the 'Desert Rats' in Egypt and Libya, where a push to drive the Italians back into Tripoli was being planned. They learned later that the bulk of their fellow travellers had, in fact, been sent to Greece to halt the German advance there and that many of them had been killed or taken prisoner in Crete later in the year.

They found themselves in Mombasa Harbour within a day of leaving the convoy. After two days of refuelling, they set out eastwards, unescorted across the Indian Ocean bound for Bombay.

One day, not long after they had left Mombasa, a seaplane appeared from the south and circled the ship. As it flew low overhead, they saw, to their surprise and consternation, that it had the black crosses of Germany on its wings.

The ship immediately got the wind under its tail and seemed to be trying to turn itself into a speed boat. The plane had come from an armed German raider about whose presence they had heard rumours. With no escort, it was clear that this was no time to linger in the sunshine of the Indian Ocean.

All of a sudden, life became uncomfortable in the extreme. Glasses and plates rattled on the tables, the whole ship shuddered with the vibration of its engines at full speed, and the frequency of boat drills increased dramatically.

On these, Roger had found himself in the back row side by side with Cheesewright, which, given that gentleman's reputation for inviting disaster, depressed him considerably. They estimated their chances of being able to get anywhere near a raft or lifeboat to be so low that, finding themselves by the entrance to the saloon, they resolved that, should the worst happen, they would go in and treat themselves to free drinks as the ship went down.

However, all was well, and after another three or four days, they found themselves in Bombay Harbour with a whole afternoon to go ashore. This was a real treat after being cooped up for so long. They wandered along the street by the magnificent railway station to the Gateway to India, looking at the stalls of the letter writers, corn removers and the staged pavement fight between a cobra and a mongoose. Its tail bushed out like a flue-brush crouched back and flew at the throat of the cobra, which flicked its head to one side and then darted down at the little creature, missing it only by a fraction of an inch. It was all a bit of a sham since it was most likely that the mongoose had no teeth and the cobra no fangs, but they had been well-trained and put up a most convincing show.

They left Bombay the following day following the coal-fired liner Aquitania belching black smoke from its four funnels across the Bay of Bengal down the Straits of Malacca. At Singapore, everyone disembarked at Seletar naval base and, except for the small Middlesex contingent, became reinforcements for the Singapore garrison at Changi. Here, a little more than a year later, they suffered terrible hardships at the hands of their Japanese captors. Many were sent north to the notorious Burma Railway and the River Kwai, where hundreds perished from starvation, disease and torture.

Transport from Singapore to Hong Kong was apparently difficult to arrange. They could only be transported three or four at a time in small coasting vessels, so they must wait until a boat could be found. Roger, Dicky Hill, Pan Newton and Cheesewright were the last to leave and were accommodated, first in the Adelphi Hotel near the cathedral and later at a tented transit camp at Bidadari in the centre of the island, where they met the draft of officers and men whom they were replacing.

His time at Bidadari was, by far, the most enjoyable part of the whole trip. There was not much to do, no parades to attend, and they spent their time exploring Singapore town or the countryside. They visited rubber plantations, swam and climbed to the top of Bukit Timah, the only hill of any size on the island, and saw mangrove swamps and the Causeway joining Singapore to Johore Bahruss, which the victorious Japanese army was to pour across onto the island in less than twelve months.

In the evening, when the day's oppressive heat had been cooled by the inevitable afternoon rain, they sat outside their tents, lounging in comfortable bamboo chairs with a long glass of something cold. They would look up at the brilliant blue-white stars in the inky black sky, telling each other what a filthy climate this was and how much they longed for a good old-fashioned London pea-souper and enjoying every minute of it.

As he sat there in the quiet, soft tropical night, Roger's mind wandered back over the extraordinary event that had brought him to this place. He recalled that not much more than twelve months ago, he had stood on Tonbridge station kissing

Daisy goodbye on his way to Stoughton Barracks and the acid tongue of Sergeant Fox, all that happened in between and, finally, the last sad day of parting and the long voyage halfway across the world which now separated them from each other by many thousands of miles. His heart ached for her.

Now a new chapter was about to unfold. After a fortnight in the comfort of the transit camp, they were ordered back into the town to embark on the 'Anshun' for the six-day journey to Hong Kong.

Both the 'Anshun' and its skipper came straight out of a Joseph Conrad novel. Roger was in company with a Dusty Miller for the second time in his army career.

But there was a complete contrast between the two. The ramrod, dignified, highly disciplined Sergeant Major of No. 170 Octu could not possibly have been more different from this shambling, shirt-sleeved skipper with his greasy cap pushed back from his forehead and a cigar stub protruding from his mouth.

He was a hard-bitten, hard-swearing, hard-drinking man, although Roger never saw him anything other than cold sober. He could not afford to be otherwise, for the 'Anshun' was one of those coasters whose decks were crammed with Chinese passengers. Passengers who lived, cooked, ate and slept in the open were separated from the first-class passengers, of whom only five could be accommodated, by sturdy iron railings which formed a cage around the cabins and guarded by two very large Sikhs armed with rifles. Piracy was still rife in the South China Sea, and no one could afford to take risks.

Dusty Miller had all the right qualities for his job. To complete his Joseph Conrad image, he was an inveterate and skilful poker player.

Cheesewright, Pan Newton and Dicky Hill, who all fancied themselves as card players, accepted his invitation to join him in a game which started almost as soon as they left Singapore and continued every evening until they reached Hong Kong.

Cheesewright and Pan were sadly out of pocket when they reached Hong Kong. The debonair Dicky Hill had been obliged to sign an IOU to Dusty Miller for £126 – a sum he did not possess in the whole world.

On April 2nd, precisely three months after they had climbed aboard the Empress of Japan, the 'Anshun' nosed her way through the Lye Mun channel and dropped anchor near the Star Ferry. Roger, looking out at the quayside of Kowloon, saw a Chinese coolie trotting along with a bamboo pole across his shoulder, a piano hanging from one end and a vast balancing weight from the other.

He had arrived in Hong Kong.

Chapter 10

Hong Kong

As they stood on the deck of the Anshun, waiting for the tender to take them to the mainland, they looked around, fascinated at the teeming life of the stretch of water which separated the island of Hong Kong from the mainland of the New Territories. The sprawling city of Kowloon fringing the northern side of the harbour.

The water was dotted with the squat wooden bulks and great square sails of the sea-going junks trading up the coast to Swatow and Shanghai and across to Formosa lying at anchor. Smaller three-masted vessels were the sugar junks plied between the islands and up the Si Kiang - the Pearl River - to Macau and Canton.

To the south, the square inlet of Causeway Bay was a mass of sampans - smaller boats rowed and steered by long oars - so closely packed that walking from one to the other would have presented no difficulty.

One of these pulled up alongside as they leaned over the ship's rail. The wife of the owner, dressed in a worn black jacket and trousers, her wrinkled face bronzed nearly black by constant exposure to the sun, offered up a basket of fish for sale. She wore a huge-brimmed conical-shaped hat of plaited rice straw, the brim of which was turned down in a sort of circular fringe. According to Miller, who was standing by them, the hat proclaimed her to belong to the Hakka tribe.

Looking down into the sampan, they saw that the whole foredeck was occupied by half a dozen scrawny hens and a couple of pigs. Under the canvas hood, which shaded the centre of the boat, were three or four youngsters playing with a mangy lurcher dog of dubious parentage. It was a miniature floating farmyard.

At the front of the boat, the owner was crouched over a small charcoal fire and was obviously cooking something in an earthenware pot.

Let into the side of the sampan was a large tank covered in front by wire netting with a wooden lid. Inside were swimming a dozen or more large fish, making the device an aquarium and live food store, constantly supplied by fresh seawater. This was clearly a self-contained and self-supporting family unit. Miller explained that its members rarely went ashore, instead buying their rice and other essentials from trading sampans which moved up and down the harbour.

The whole of the narrow shore of the island to the south was closely built-up with imposing buildings in the centre, dominated by the hundred-foot skyscraper tower of the Hong Kong and Shanghai Banking Corporation (later to be HSBC), at that time by far the tallest building on the island. Tailing off beyond Causeway Bay into the bustling slum area of Wanchai with its blocks of tenement flats and warren of narrow lanes lined with food stalls and the shops of craftsmen and traders.

Rising sharply behind the built-up area was a chain of hills rising to over 1,000 feet with a scattering of trees sprinkled with dozens of white buildings. These were prestigious homes of the wealthy. The whole scene was dominated by Victoria Peak, with its roadway circling the summit. Climbing steeply up towards it like a caterpillar, the little tramway which, given the length of the tortuously winding roadways which snaked their way up the face of the peak, was the quickest route to and from the town.

On the other side of the harbour to the north was the flat peninsula of Kowloon, a solid mass of buildings nosing its way towards the island, reducing the gap between it and the city of Victoria to little over a quarter of a mile. Across this stretch of water, the ferries, their decks crowded with passengers on both the upper and lower decks, passed to and fro unceasingly.

At some distance behind the built-up area of Kowloon stretched a high ridge of hills running from east to west. The highest point looked precisely like a crouching lion accompanied by her two cubs and, much higher in the background, rose the conical peak of Tai Mo Shan, the Big Hat Mountain, so-called as Miller explained, because, during the summer monsoon, it wore a cap of cloud which was a warning of rainy weather to come.

At that moment, there was a bumping against the side of the ship and, looking down, they saw it was the launch which was to take them ashore and land them at the Star Ferry Pier by the terminus of the railway line opposite the Peninsula Hotel. This is where they had been told to report and await the transport to take them to the Middlesex barracks at Shamshuipo, some four miles north.

Here they learned that the truck would not arrive for a couple of hours and, as it was now past midday and there was no telling when they would get a meal, they decided to see what they could find in the hotel - a most imposing building which seemed to hold the promise of astronomical bills.

Not a little overawed by its splendour, Dicky Hill, Pan Newton, Cheesewright and Roger made their way into the restaurant amid a sea of white linen and silverware, with immaculate waiters waiting to pounce on the nervous newcomers.

Roger was all for escaping while the going was good, for all the finery of their surroundings confirmed their suspicions as to the size of the forthcoming bill. Still, the debonair Dicky Hill, undeterred by the enormous IOU he had just left behind with Dusty Miller, insisted on taking charge of the menu.

"Just leave things to me, chaps," he announced and, calling over an immaculate waiter, glanced carelessly down the menu. "We'll all have the same," he announced.

"We don't want to confuse these fellows. 'You speakee English?'" he enquired of the waiter.

"Of course, Sir," came the reply in a perfect English accent, "what would you like to order, gentlemen?"

Dicky, who had studied pidgin English on the journey from Singapore and had hoped to air it at the earliest opportunity, was a little taken aback but maintained his dignity: "We'll all have Porterhouse steaks," he announced grandly.

The waiter bowed slightly, his face an inscrutable mask, and departed with just the faintest raising of the eyebrows. The others glanced at each other, most impressed. Clearly, Dicky was a man of the world and knew his stuff when it came to dealing with waiters, no matter what their nationality.

They waited with growing impatience for the arrival of the food.

After nearly an hour, by which time they were becoming increasingly famished and anxious lest their transport should arrive before the meal was finished, the waiter appeared with a large trolley on which were piled four of the largest plated dishes they had ever seen. The waiter took off the lids, and they stared in disbelief at their contents. On the silver platters were the four most enormous slabs of meat, each more than sufficient for four portions and each representing at least a fortnight's meat ration for a whole family back in England.

Just as they were settling down to tackle this formidable mountain, an orderly arrived.

"Your transport is here," the orderly announced. "I'm sorry I am a bit late, gentlemen, and I must ask you to come straight away."

"What about the bill?" asked Roger. "How the hell are we going to settle it?"

The waiter stepped forward. "That is perfectly alright, Sir," he said. "If you just sign the chit, I will see it gets to the barracks, and it will be added to your mess bills at Shamshuipo. Good afternoon and thank you for your custom, gentlemen."

Dicky's grand gesture cost them each more than a week's pay and did little to increase his popularity with them. However, as they were soon to find, this was to be the least of their financial worries.

The truck turned left into the long straight avenue of Nathan Road. They soon left behind them the prestigious buildings around the waterfront. They were quickly threading their way along the crowded street between rickshaws and taxis beneath high blocks of tenement flats with long laundry lines hanging on poles from the upper storeys. Tiny shops and food stalls along the pavement edges decorated with banners and signs brilliantly painted with Chinese characters sending out a bewildering variety of pungent, spicy and fishy smells.

After about twenty minutes, they pulled up at the guard room at the entrance to Shamshuipo barracks.

In front of them, a wide roadway led through the whole complex to buildings at the far end and extending to the waterfront. They learned later that these were occupied by the 2nd/14th Punjabi Regiment, who shared the barracks with them. On the left of this approach road, stretching its entire length, was a vast parade ground flanked on its far side by a tall white concrete block of flats several stories high. Each block with a wide verandah which, they were told, was Jubilee Buildings, which were to be their future home.

A side road branched up to the right about halfway along the roadway. It was lined on either side first by the various company offices and, behind them, a complex of concrete huts which housed the cookhouse, mess rooms and quarters for the men. The roadway ended at the garrison church and hall, forming the barracks' northern extremity. Their truck took them halfway up this side road and deposited them at the Battalion office, where they lined up to be greeted by Colonel 'Monkey' Stewart, the Commanding Officer of the 1st Battalion.

He was a little man who walked with a pronounced limp and whose wizened face provided a clue as to his nickname. He looked along the line of his new officers, his lips pursed and with his eyebrows raised.

"Stand properly to attention, gentlemen," he said in a slightly grating and disapproving voice. "This is the 1st Battalion, and it has very proud traditions. You will maintain these to the highest degree at all times. You are fortunate to have been selected to join the regular battalion and serve with professional soldiers. I trust that we shall feel equally fortunate to have you with us. In the first place," he went on, "you are all incorrectly dressed. Heaven knows where you got those uniforms from, but they are all wrong, and you must have them replaced at once. The tailor will call on you tonight."

They stared at him aghast. They had all bought their tropical kit from the same suppliers in Regent Street. They had been assured that every item was correct. It seemed that the style and cut of uniform for the 1st Battalion differed from all the others.

"And while you are being measured for your new uniform, you must also order your mess kit - we can't have you in the mess on dining-in nights unless you are properly dressed. Good luck to you all, and I trust that you will all share our pride in the Regiment and will uphold its traditions. You may dismiss, and you will be shown to your quarters."

And then he added, "Welcome to Hong Kong" almost as an afterthought.

The Colonel gave the men a smart salute and returned to his office, leaving them bewildered and apprehensive about the future. They had no idea what was meant by mess kit or how much extra expense this would involve.

They were soon to find out. The mess kit consisted of tight navy-blue trousers of fine serge with a black stripe down the seams. With supreme difficulty, the trousers had to be drawn on over soft black leather Wellington boots which reached halfway up the calves. This was topped by a white starched dress shirt with a detachable collar with turned-down points that stood straight around the throat and had to be so stiffly starched that it threatened to choke one. When one perspired, the collar collapsed into a limp, soggy band around the neck. This was held in place by a single-ended black bow tie, which was the very devil to tie correctly. It was absolutely forbidden to replace it with a ready-made imitation.

The jacket, of which one needed two, was very tight and short, reaching only to the waist, and was fastened by silver buttons bearing the regimental crest. A plum-coloured silk cummerbund about six inches in width was fastened around the waist and covered the top of the trousers. This had to be secured according to a strictly designated pattern. The whole outfit was topped by a navy-blue forage cap bearing a silver regimental badge.

As the Colonel had said, wearing this dress was *de rigueur* on Thursday evening dining-in nights. It could only be avoided with the greatest of difficulty. The minimum cost of this outfit was something over £80, equal to several months' salary. This, together with the new khaki drill uniform and topee, amounted to more than £100. This, added by instalments to their monthly mess bill, was a severe blow to them all.

Roger sat gloomily on the balcony of his new home in Jubilee Buildings. He bitterly contemplated the sand-covered parade ground below, casting his mind back over the events of the last nine months since his commission. He remembered the perils of the Blitz, which he had shared with Daisy, who was now nearly ten thousand miles away and was still facing sleepless nights fire-watching and listening to the drone of enemy bombers overhead. Meanwhile, he was living a life of comparative luxury, dressing up in fancy clothes in a city where food rationing was unheard of and where the night sky was brilliant, not with the fires from burning buildings, but from neon lights from a million street lamps and from busy shops and restaurants.

He had not volunteered for military service to lead this artificial life. A life light years away from the war, in a situation where it seemed probable that he would be forced to do so for the remainder of hostilities. He wondered miserably what the situation would be if, as at that time seemed quite possible, the war was to be lost.

After all, in April 1941, the only protection against invasion was the narrow strip of water between Britain and France. Apart from the contribution made by troops from the Commonwealth, it was without allies. The full might of the German Army was poised, ready to deal the final blow. Here he was, dressing up in monkey jackets with silver buttons and leading the life of a peace-time regular army officer. He resolved that, as soon as the opportunity occurred, he would risk the inevitable wrath of Monkey Stewart and ask for a transfer to a fighting unit, however futile such a request might prove. He must, however, leave a decent interval before doing so and make up his mind to make the best of a bad job in the meantime.

He imagined why Monkey Stewart might react unfavourably to Roger's request. Monkey was a professional soldier in command of a most prestigious regiment of which he was fiercely proud and whose traditions he was dedicated to uphold. And, no doubt, he, too, would have wished to be in the thick of the action. Up to the present, all his officers had been regulars. Many of these had been posted back to England to make a more positive contribution to the war effort. As Roger knew, having met them at the transit camp in Bidadari on their way home, they had been replaced by young, inexperienced subalterns, "temporary gentlemen" who knew nothing and probably cared less about the traditions of his beloved regiment and whom he must, God help him, try to mould into officers worthy of their good fortune.

Another problem they had to cope with was that for three months, they had led a carefree and largely undisciplined existence on board the troopship apart from boat drills and the undemanding occasional duty as Orderly Officer. Now they were to be plunged into the resumption of a strict military regime under the critical eye of Monkey Stewart, supported by the Adjutant, Company Commanders and, perhaps the fiercest of all, the Regimental Sergeant Major, whose withering glance could reduce one to a height of a couple of inches even though accompanied by words of icy politeness and who ate junior subalterns for breakfast.

The most immediate problem, however, was one of finance. Almost the worst crime one could commit as an officer, especially in a regular regiment, was getting into debt. Roger was not allowed to use bus transport but must either walk or take an expensive taxi into town, so he was to be virtually a prisoner in Shamshuipo until he had cleared the debt to the tailor for his uniform.

He would have been even more distressed if he knew that his imprisonment would be for real within a few months.

Chapter 11

Diehards

After this unpromising start to their life in Shamshuipo, things began to settle down. They gradually got into their new routine.

As far as military duties were concerned, he had little difficulty settling into the strict routines of regimental life. His experiences at Guildford and Aldershot had been good training. He thought with gratitude of the discipline inflicted by Sergeant Fox and Sergeant Fraser. However rough this had seemed at the time, and, having been pushed to the limit himself, he knew what to expect of his men, how much they would take and how to get the best response from them. He felt grateful not for the first time that he had been obliged to work his way up from the ranks and had not been given the instant commission he wanted.

Above all, he learned from his service as a ranker to respect and appreciate the qualities of the men in his Cockney platoon. They had an impish sense of humour and enjoyed a leg pull and a laugh. Although many were real rogues who could scrounge almost anything you might care to name, they were invariably cheerful and resilient physically and mentally. What they would not tolerate was any attempt to put on "side" or to be the recipient of sarcasm or "bull-shit", as they described it.

Provided they were treated properly, they were intensely loyal. They expected a fair deal from their officers and, if they got it, were happy to give it in return. To be referred to as 'My Orficer' was an accolade of approval, but it had to be earned.

Much of the work was routine drill parades and inspection of huts and kit in which Roger learned to rely heavily on the support of his Platoon Sergeant, who was always at hand to rescue him from the inevitable blunders into which his own lack of experience frequently plunged him.

The request "Carry on, Sergeant" was a lifeline to which he had frequent recourse as when, on the parade ground under the watchful eye of 'Monkey' Stewart on one occasion, he had his own platoon marching in line abreast inexorably towards the water's edge, having wheeled them to the right instead of the left, and could not think of the appropriate command to rescue them from a watery grave.

Much more enjoyable were the route marches out into the New Territories. He could see the paddy fields with their patient, black-clad women, knee-deep in muddy water, their backs bent over as they pushed the rice seedlings down into the slime. The farmers ploughing up the tiny pocket-handkerchief fields with their water buffalo. Each patch of ground was enclosed by earthen banks on which grew a wild variety of vegetables: tomatoes, lettuce, sweet potatoes, beans, swamp cabbage and a dozen others unfamiliar to him. All of them watered, as his Sergeant explained, from the little pond in the corner into which was tipped manure, mainly from pigs and humans, and which, from the lush growth of the vegetables on the banks, seemed a most effective, if not very hygienic, fertiliser as he was to find to his cost later.

As it was now towards the end of April, and the temperature and humidity were increasing in readiness for the onset of the monsoon, these route marches became increasingly exhausting. The return to barracks was more and more welcome. On the last long mile, all one could think of was the cold shower and relief for the aching feet waiting for them in Jubilee Buildings on their return.

The week-long exercise on Hong Kong Island was even more enjoyable than the route marches. The training occurred at his Company's Headquarters at Ty Tam Gap, east of the island, in a well-equipped series of cave-like rooms strategically dug into the rocky escarpment overlooking the main road from Wanchai to the Stanley peninsula. Here, the much more relaxed regime reminded him irresistibly of numerous peace-time scout camps. It was a real treat to sit outside in the cool evening listening to the whirring of the cicadas and the rustle of the wind in the trees.

The strategic role assigned to the Diehards in defence of Hong Kong was to man a series of machine-gun posts scattered at intervals around the island's south coast. These posts were intended to fend off attacks from the sea, which, it was assumed, would be the only possible way of assaulting the colony.

The likelihood of a land-based attack from the north of the mainland, where the forces of Chiang Kai Shek had been at war with the Japanese for three years or more, would provide a protective shield. For the same reason, the heavy coastal batteries at the southern tip of the Stanley peninsula were sited to deal with approaching hostile convoys well before they came within range of the Middlesex machine guns. The approach from the Chinese border at the Shum Chun River was lightly guarded by a chain of pill-boxes along the intervening hill range known, perhaps not inappropriately, as the Gin Drinkers Line. This was held by the 2nd Battalion of the Royal Scots, the only other British regiment, and the 2/14th Battalion of the Punjabis.

His platoon had positions in pill-boxes, not unlike those he had helped to make along the River Thames, built along the shoreline on the western edge of Ty Tam Bay and around the end of the peninsula towards Big Wave Bay. The bay's broad sweep of white sand was later to be the place of execution on December 18th 1943, by the Japanese, of Hector Gray, a flight lieutenant of the Royal Air Force and two of his companions.

Part of Roger's duties was a daily inspection of these positions. One, in particular, involved a long narrow pathway from the road past a tiny village, no more than a huddle of shacks with a dozen or more pigs and a scattering of babies and chicken, to the edge of Ty Tam Bay from where a primitive landing stage provided for a rowing boat ferry across the inlet to Stanley Village.

The villagers had been terrified by an enormous python, alleged to be some sixteen feet long, which had killed and swallowed a baby and a pig to the great consternation of the inhabitants.

The incident had occurred several weeks previously, and it was thought quite likely that, having digested its meal, the python might well return for a repeat performance. Roger had been warned to be on the lookout for the snake on his way down to the pill-box.

He had received the news without much enthusiasm, having not received any instruction in anti-python procedures. He hoped devoutly that he would not be put to the test, particularly as the path led down through waist-high grass, which swished against his legs as he brushed his way through it.

However, duty was duty, even though one was not all that courageous. On Roger's second visit to the gun site, as he passed the village, he was stopped in his tracks by a swishing and a movement in the grass around a bend in the path just ahead of him. He was about to meet the python on its way to lunch.

With his hand shaking, he pulled his revolver from its holster and reflected gloomily that he had never, so far, fired the damned thing in anger. He wondered what would happen to his wrist if he had to pull the trigger. Perhaps if he stood still and did nothing, the thing might decide to go away and leave him in peace. On the other hand, it was obviously incumbent on him to rid the village of its menace. He thought of the kudos which would be his when he dragged the corpse back into the village.

Screwing up every last dreg of his resolve, he turned the corner of the path to see a little girl and a dozen baby chicks playing happily together in the long grass. Very red of face, he continued his journey down to the gun position and kept very quiet indeed about the whole discreditable incident.

However, two days later, he reaped a rich revenge. On his way in his truck along the road above the village, the python was crossing the highway in front of him. There were a couple of bumps as the wheels went over the snake, and that was the end of the matter. But the villagers had not exaggerated. When they measured it, it was seventeen feet six inches long.

Back at the camp, a particular pleasure was to climb the hills immediately behind it. From there, Roger could see the splendid view from Lion Rock northwards over the New Territories into China proper and south across Kowloon and the harbour to Hong Kong and the surrounding islands.

Best of all, he watched the China Clipper fly in from San Francisco, as it did once a fortnight. Circling around, he saw it touch down in a welter of spray in Kowloon Bay to offload at the level strip of Kai Tak airport. The airport was only large enough in those days to take small planes, and it was the home of the small detachment of the RAF base - the only air defence of the colony.

The arrival of the great flying boat was a most welcome sight as it invariably carried letters from Daisy. The plane returned his letters to her in as little as a fortnight as opposed to the four or five weeks taken by sea.

The Chinese tailor had called the day after their arrival. Within twenty-four hours, the uniforms and mess kit had arrived and were a perfect fit, as was invariably the case. The tailors were incredibly skilful at copying garments. There was a story, which Roger had no doubt was true, that an officer, having made a small triangular tear in his jacket pocket, which he had cobbled roughly together, ordered the tailor to make an exact copy. The new jacket arrived the following morning with the tear, immaculately repaired, reproduced faithfully.

The only problem was to pay for it all, and this would take several months, during which living was going to be very difficult. Roger just could not afford to buy a drink in the mess, even at the ridiculously low prices.

The last straw came with the arrival of his first mess bill, which showed more than thirty dollars charged for drinks.

When he protested, it was explained that even though he had not bought any for himself, he was expected to pay a share of those drunk by official visitors on guest nights.

There was only one thing for it. Somehow or another, Roger had got to get a transfer away from the regiment. With the courage born of desperation, he asked for an interview with Monkey Stewart.

As best he could, he outlined his problem and explained that living in barracks without getting into debt was impossible.

Monkey listened attentively and, when Roger had finished, asked, "And exactly what do you propose to do about it?"

"Well, Sir," mumbled Roger, "the only solution I can find is to ask for a transfer to a unit in the field where I shall not have to be involved in these expenses. After all, Sir, and without wishing to give offence, I did not volunteer for service in the army to live in the peace-time routines of a regular battalion."

It was probably the most difficult, foolish and courageous thing he had ever done. Monkey stared at him in disbelief. Here was a junior subaltern, still wet behind the ears, who had had the incredible good fortune to be posted to what, in his view, was the finest regiment in the British Army, asking to leave it within a couple of months of joining it.

His face turned a strange livid white and then purple-red as his mouth opened and closed without a sound emerging. He looked to Roger as if he was about to have an apoplectic fit, and he was terrified by the sight. At last, after what seemed an eternity, Monkey gasped out, "Am I mad, or are you mad, or is the whole bloody world mad, tell me that!" "I am very sorry, Sir," stuttered the now petrified Roger.

"Sorry! Sorry, I should think you bloody well are sorry!" grated the Colonel. "Get out of my office and get back to your duties and let me hear no more of this bloody nonsense!"

Roger fled. He had committed the blunder of a lifetime and would be a marked man from then on. But, in his youth and inexperience, he had misjudged this remarkable man, as he was to find out before many days had gone by.

The day after his memorable interview with Monkey, he was on duty as Orderly Officer. This entailed a long list of inspections of every aspect of barrack life. Regulations decreed that he must be accompanied by no less a personality than the Regimental Sergeant Major, of whom every right-minded subaltern stood in awe.

They trudged around the barracks, Roger faithfully ticking off each item as it was completed. After his stormy interview with Monkey Stewart, it seemed essential to carry out this duty with meticulous accuracy so as to begin the long and seemingly impossible process of getting himself back into the Colonel's good books.

The last item on the list was the inspection of the swill bins outside the cookhouse. Roger had seen these carried away each day by the Chinese contractors who bought them for their contents to be sold, no doubt at a handsome profit to farmers in the New Territories.

Towards the end of the inspection, the Sergeant Major said: "Well, I think that's about the lot, Sir," as they steered towards the kitchen. "Everything seems to be in order, I think. Thank you, Sir. Good night."

"Half a minute, Sergeant Major," said Roger, looking down his list. "We haven't inspected the swill bins yet."

"Oh, those," returned the Sergeant Major. "We never bother about the swill bins, Sir."

"Why not?" asked Roger. "They are on the list and wouldn't be there if we didn't have to inspect them." "No. No, Sir," insisted the Sergeant Major. "With respect, Sir, they are one thing we never look at."

There was something in the Sergeant Major's voice which interested Roger. It might have been exasperation with this young whipper-snapper of an officer or, just possibly, something else.

Without really knowing why he did it, he said: "Well, Sergeant Major, I'm going to break an invariable custom. We'll go and inspect the swill bins. Show me where they are!"

With the Sergeant Major, red of face, following reluctantly behind him, they went round to the collection of bins at the back entrance to the cookhouse. Roger took off the lid of one of them. Inside was a most unappetising mess of cold porridge, cabbage leaves and potato peelings.

"There you are, Sir," said the Sergeant Major. "That's all there is to see. I hope you are satisfied, Sir."

Again without really knowing why he did it, Roger thrust his malacca cane deep down into the swill and rummaged it around. Then he felt it come up against something large and solid. Fishing down, he pulled out a beautiful uncooked leg of lamb.

Suddenly the truth dawned upon him. This was one of the perks of the cookhouse staff, who hid real food under a covering of swill. This was then to be washed off by the contractors who sold the contents at handsome prices to the restaurant owners in the town whilst the cook and his staff and, possibly others, reaped a handsome rake-off.

"Come on, Sergeant Major!" he said. "We'll turn out every bloody bin and see how far this thing has gone."

And so all the bins were tipped out onto the ground, and each revealed a whole Aladdin's cave of contraband food destined for the restaurants of Kowloon and Hong Kong.

The Sergeant Major looked at the damning evidence without any real surprise.

"Are you going to report this, Sir," he said, "or would you like me to deal with this matter privately?" "Of course I'm going to report it, man," returned the triumphant Roger. "What the hell do you think?"

"Perhaps you should leave it with me, Sir," the RSM insisted. "You must understand that these things do go on in China and 'squeeze' is a part of everyday life and," with an inscrutable glance, "I wouldn't like you to become unpopular so soon after your arrival here. It might make things rather difficult for you, in a manner of speaking."

Although he understood only too well what the Sergeant Major was trying to say, Roger stood his ground and prepared his written report accordingly.

Later, on the grape-vine, Roger heard that various NCOs in the catering and Quartermaster's departments had lost their stripes in the unofficial enquiry which followed. Still, by this time, he had become a little wiser and, understanding more of the advice of the RSM. He heard no more of the matter.

The following day he received a summons to Monkey Stewart's office and, with some trepidation, once more appeared before his Commanding Officer.

But this was to be a very different interview from the previous one.

The Colonel was quiet and composed: "Ah, yes, Rothwell," he said, "I have seen your report. You did a good job, but you must not expect to have made many friends. Just leave things with me, and I will deal with them. Now," he went on, "I understand that the Command Education Officer, who is a friend of mine, is looking for an assistant who has had some experience in educational matters to take charge of a scheme to provide some courses of general interest to occupy the men. There isn't a great deal for them to do just now, and some are getting restless hearing the news from home. Also, Major Wood, the Command Education Officer, is scheduled to go to Singapore for a couple of weeks in the autumn. He would like his deputy to hold the fort while he is away."

"Of course," he went on, "you would not be able to live in barracks, and I think the best thing would be for you to be billeted in the Hong Kong Club for the time being until you can find more suitable accommodation. You would be entitled to all the various allowances - subsistence, lodging, fuel, light and so on, so you needn't worry about finance any more. Well, what do you think about the proposal? You don't have to agree to a secondment, but I am sure that you will be wise to do so."

Roger was speechless. Here was the perfect solution to all his problems. He would be almost his own master living independently and doing the sort of job for which his training in civilian life had prepared him. Best of all, his financial problems would be at an end because his allowances would amount to more than his pay. He would be comparatively well off, provided the charges at the Hong Kong Club were not excessive.

He felt a great wave of gratitude for this wizened-faced little man and stuttered out that he would be delighted to do all he could to make a success of the job. He started to thank him for making it all possible, but the Colonel cut him short.

"There's no need for thanks," he said. "It's my job to try and put square pegs into square holes, and I wouldn't have suggested it unless I thought you were capable of doing it. The best of luck to you. Report to Major Wood at Command Headquarters tomorrow morning. And," he added with something like a grin, "don't work too hard at setting the world to rights!"

Roger went back across the parade ground to Jubilee Buildings in a daze. He just could not believe his good fortune. In an instant, his whole outlook had changed, and, of course, he had Monkey to thank for it. Clearly, this fierce little man had a heart of gold and cared for the welfare of his officers just as he cared for that of his men. However, Roger could never determine how much of his decision was due to the need to get him out of reach of any reprisals following the incident of the swill bins. Whatever the reason, his luck had held.

The following day he caught the Star Ferry across the harbour to Command Headquarters, where he was interviewed by his new CO, and by the end of the week, he was installed in the Hong Kong Club. He had become Assistant Education Officer to the China Command.

The next time he found himself in Shamshuipo Barracks, it would be under very different circumstances.

Chapter 12

Command Headquarters

The Hong Kong Club was a sombre and imposing Victorian building which boasted that it had the longest bar in the world, a claim hotly disputed by its counterparts in Shanghai and Singapore. It had a dark and cavernous dining room with a vast choice of menu to match. Roger counted no fewer than forty items for breakfast alone, including cold kidneys, grilled mushrooms, kedgeree and game pie, bacon, eggs and sausages, cereals, fruit and even porridge. It was a place where one could live in stolid comfort provided that, as in Roger's case, one was not looking for a life of gaiety and fun.

His room on the third floor of the building opened onto a wide verandah with a stone balustrade and tall arches overlooking the cricket club ground, a vast expanse of carefully tended grass surrounded by spiked iron railings.

To the left of the cricket ground lay the complex of buildings which housed HMS Tamar, the naval dockyard and, looking ahead up the slope of the hill, he could see the square white outline of Command Headquarters and, to the right, the square tower of St John's Cathedral and, above it, the trees and gardens surrounding Government House.

The morning after arriving at the club, he climbed the hill past the Peak Tram station and through the trees to report to his new boss at Command Headquarters.

Major Wood received him courteously and set out the scope of the job he was to undertake. He was a round-faced man with a cleft chin and a close-cropped moustache covering a long upper lip. Walter de Burley Wood, known, for some reason which no one could ever discover, as 'Jack' to his friends, was called, less reverently, Whisky de Beer by all the rest. Although Roger, as he came to know him better, became aware of the logic behind this nickname, he never saw him offensively the worse for drink. On the contrary, the more he took on board, the more courteous he became until one was reminded of a royal courtier of olden days bowing ever so slightly as he handed his guests a large tumbler of gin and tonic which consisted markedly of more of the former than of the latter.

Above all, he was a very kindly and cultured man, a scholar, a lover of literature and, as he had been a barrister of Lincoln's Inn before joining the army. He knew instinctively that this was someone to whom he could relate and that they were going to get on well together. He would have been astonished had he been told at that time that the day would come when each was to owe his life to the other. Once again, by a lucky accident, he had fallen on his feet. He knew at once that in his office behind the wide verandah with its magnificent view across the harbour to the hills behind Kowloon and away towards mainland China he was going to be as happy as was possible away from his girl who never left his thoughts and to whom he wrote every evening without fail.

His principal job, as Monkey Stewart had explained, was to organise courses and activities for the British troops from the Middlesex and Royal Scots Battalions and the ancillary services – Signallers, Engineers, Ordnance and Service Corps who had been showing signs of anxiety and restlessness at the bad news from home.

His first task was to determine what type of activity would appeal to them. This involved consultation with their units and an assessment of the likely cost of the project, the books and equipment that would be needed and where he was likely to find suitable instructors.

His researches revealed a bizarre variety of suggestions ranging from English literature, languages including French, Urdu and Cantonese, mathematics, elementary psychology, to boot and shoe making and repair, motor car maintenance, radio construction and repair, navigation and dinghy sailing.

All of this was to be achieved within an overall budget of HK$25,000 – the equivalent of about £1,500 – which meant that financial corners had to be cut wherever possible, which called for considerable ingenuity.

He discovered, for example, that, provided one was not fussy about the quality of paper, uncut edges and numerous misprints, editions of textbooks pirated in Shanghai could be bought for a quarter of their usual price from a downtown bookseller. For a second time, this brought him into contact with 'squeeze', responsible for his discoveries in the swill bins at Shamshuipo and his consequent transfer to his present job.

To assist him in this venture, he had been allocated a clerk, Corporal Ken Sawyer – known, inevitably, to all and sundry as 'Tom', who, surprisingly enough, belonged to the Royal Army Veterinary Corps employed initially to look after the mules of the Indian Army contingent.

Whenever a consignment of books arrived at the bookshop, Tom was despatched to collect them and, as time went by, Roger was intrigued to find that, from week to week, a fresh copy of the unexpurgated edition of 'Lady Chatterly's Lover' appeared on the Corporal's personal shelf in his office. The book was officially unavailable in

England because of the explicit accounts of the sexual activities of the lady and the gamekeeper. When the collection amounted to seventeen copies, Roger could contain his curiosity no longer and asked for an explanation of their origin.

Tom explained that each time he collected a consignment of textbooks, the shop proprietor insisted on his accepting a 'commission' and, to save trouble in selecting a different title each time, he stuck to Lady Chatterley with a faithfulness equalled only by that of her amorous gamekeeper.

The Royal Corps of Signals Sergeant who was to conduct the radio maintenance course presented him with a long and expensive-looking list of components from a supplier in Ice House Street. The Sergeant's estimate of the likely cost was in the region of HK$1,500, but this, he advised, would be open to negotiation since it would be expected by Chang Tak, the proprietor of the shop, that a period of haggling over the price would inevitably take place before the deal was settled.

Accordingly, armed with his list, Roger presented himself at Chang's establishment, a modern-looking shop in the steeply sloping street. Chang Tak ran his eye over the list and, producing a large abacus - a contraption much like a child's bead frame without which no Chinese trader appeared able to operate - and whisking the little wooden balls to and fro along the wires for some time, said, "That will come to 1,900 dollars, Master. Where shall I send the parts?"

Roger, who had done some amateur dramatics in his previous existence, feigned an expression of deep shock.

"That is quite ridiculous," "he replied. "I have been told by experts that the proper price is HK$900, but because I don't want to argue about it, I will give you HK$1,000." Chang's face set into an inscrutable mask, which Roger already recognised as a sign that a haggle lay ahead. However, he recognised the faint upturn of the corner of the lips that negotiations were still at an early stage and that the salesman was going to enjoy himself.

"That sort of deal would make me bankrupt," he said, "but because it is for the British Army, you can have it for HK$1,750, although I shall have no profit at all."

"Very well," replied Roger, "I can see we are wasting each other's time, and I shall have to find another supplier who will let me have the goods at a proper price." He made as if to leave the shop.

Chang pursued him to the door. "Look, Master," he pleaded, "as my last offer, my very last offer, you may have your list for HK$1,500, and that is all I can do."

Things were going well, and Roger's hopes rose: "I tell you what," he said, "I will give you HK$1,150 and not a cent more, take it or leave it." Once more, he moved towards the door.

Chang raised his arm to bar his way. "Master," he said, "let us not quarrel about this small matter. I will make a great sacrifice and bring the price to HK$1,350 and get into big trouble with my employers."

"Make it HK$1,250," Roger said, "and we can do business, and I can come back to your shop for more things another time."

Instantly, Chang's mask dissolved into a broad smile, and he held out his hand. "Very well, Master," he said, "and I hope to see you again soon."

As he was leaving the shop, Chang followed him to the door. "What make is your radio set?" he inquired.

"Good Lord," returned Roger," what makes you think that I can afford a radio on my pay?"

Chang persisted: "Here is a very good set," he said, "It is a GEC Overseas Six. You can receive London direct with it."

"That's as may be," returned Roger, "but I have told you, I can't afford to buy a radio, and that's all there is to it. Good morning to you." And out he went, happy with the success of his first real haggling session.

He was late back from work that evening, and as he came to his room, he heard the unmistakable tones of a BBC announcer: *"And here is the news from London. Last night, the RAF carried out another successful raid over Dortmund inflicting heavy damage. All our planes returned to their bases without loss."*

A GEC Overseas Six stood on the shelf next to the window, complete with an outside aerial working as loudly and clearly as if it had been at home. There was no doubt in his mind where it had come from, and a little cold trickle ran down his spine. Here was a blatant example of 'squeeze', and now he was the one involved.

Shops in Hong Kong stayed open to all hours, and he went at once to the phone. "Mr Chang," he said, "this is Lieutenant Rothwell. Will you come at once and take back your property."

Chang Tak's silky tones came back down the line: "What property, Master? I do not know of any property."

"You know bloody well what property," returned the indignant Roger. "It is the Overseas Six that you have put in my room without my permission, and you can damned well come at once and take it back. You're not getting me involved in your schemes, so I shall expect you here within an hour."

"You talk in riddles, Mister Rothwell," replied Chang. "You are making big mistake. Perhaps someone else - a friend maybe has made you a little present. I am very busy now and cannot take something, not mine. I think you are fortunate you have good friend. Goodnight, Mr Rothwell."

And that was the end of the matter. In vain did Roger go round to the shop first thing next morning. Chang Tak was adamant, and the inscrutable mask adopted by the Chinese when they were no longer listening descended on his face. Roger reluctantly had to give up. Chang had determined that a lucrative trade with the army lay ahead. Roger's goodwill in this was a sensible investment. Roger kept the set and his own counsel. Although the radio was a godsend and brought him closer to home, he took care never to do any further business with the wily Chang.

The radio episode occurred a little while after he had left the Hong Kong Club and was installed in the Courtland Hotel on Kennedy Road, a little way up the hill and on the same level as Command Headquarters. The move was a matter of self-protection brought about one Thursday evening by an unexpected encounter with his Commanding Officer, Monkey Stewart and the Second in Command, Major Hedgecoe.

Thursday evenings were special at the barracks at Shamshuipo. All officers were required to appear for dinner in full mess dress - Wellingtons, cummerbund, monkey jacket and all whether they were in barracks or not. His newfound freedom was no exception to the invariable rule, and he came into the dining room in his usual khaki drill kit.

Scarcely had he sat down at his solitary table than Monkey, his face a dull shade of purple, stalked over and hissed: "Don't you know this is Thursday?"

"Yes, Sir," replied Roger. "What is the matter?"

"I'll tell you the bloody matter," returned the furious Monkey, "you are improperly dressed, that's what is the matter. Get out of here, and don't come back until you are wearing the correct uniform!"

Roger knew better than to argue and went.

He did not come back that evening. The following day, he discussed his problem with Frank Austin - the Chief Cipher Officer who was a member of the Army Education Corps, who had been seconded to his new post but who still took a lively interest in the affairs of the Corps and with whom Roger had established a good friendship.

"No problem," said Frank, "come and live in my place in Kennedy Road. I'll fix it up for you this evening. You can't go on like that."

Frank was as good as his word, and the next day, Roger had left the club and was comfortably installed in a little room at Courtland with a glorious view across the harbour and a weekly bill considerably less than at the club.

Before this had happened, however, two things had occurred which made a lasting impression on his mind. One night early in June, he woke up shivering with cold.

He picked up whatever covering was available – all his clothes, even the bedside rug, and snuggled down beneath them, but it was useless. The shivering had turned into a violent shuddering, which was quite impossible to control. Worse still, it seemed as though his head was going to burst. It was as though someone was inside with a sledgehammer and was trying to break through his skull.

He stuck it as long as he could, got up, dressed and got back into bed, clothes and all, but it made no difference. The unbearable cold and violent cramps that seemed to lock all his joints told him something dire was happening.

He lay under the coverings all night, sometimes icy cold, then suddenly changed to burning heat. All the time, this uncontrollable shuddering rocked the bed, and the hammering inside his head was unbearable.

How he did it, he could never clearly remember, but somehow he was in a rickshaw and had told the coolie to take him to the medical room halfway up the hill to Command Headquarters.

The MO put his hand on his forehead, thrust a thermometer under his tongue, looked at it, and grinned. "104 Fahrenheit," he said. "It's Bowen Road Hospital for you, my lad. You've got a nice little dose of malaria, I reckon. We'll take a blood test, but we must get you into bed and a dose of quinine inside you before things get any worse."

And that was that. For the next ten days, Roger found himself inside the military hospital. Within eighteen months, he was to return under very different circumstances and with a much more complicated catalogue of complaints than a simple attack of malignant tertian malaria.

The attack lasted for some ten days, the rigours returning every other day and ending in a violent perspiration which soaked clothing and bedding but which gave a blessed relief from the violent shuddering and the blinding headache.

During this time, on June 21st, the welcome news of the German invasion of Russia arrived. This was the first real hope of a turning point in the war since, at that time, before the rapid enemy advances to the gates of Leningrad and Stalingrad, it seemed impossible that the Germans could succeed in overcoming the vast Russian resources and maintaining lines of supply over the immense distances involved.

The diversion of the German effort away from the West, where Britain still stood alone, and the likelihood that Hitler had abandoned his invasion plans for the time being at least, together with the certainty that it would result in a reduction in the nightly air raids over London, brought great comfort to them all and seemed to bring the longed-for return home a step closer.

Not long after his discharge from Bowen Road and whilst he was still feeling weak from his illness, he noticed one evening that the sky at sunset was a vivid green such he had never seen before, and in the streets, he saw that the shopkeepers were busy carrying all their wares indoors and were closing heavy wooden shutters and tying down whatever could not be brought inside.

"Big wind come," explained Ah Soon, his room cleaner. "Typhoon come Hong Kong side damn soon. All peoples stay indoors. You not go out, Master, when wind come."

That night, in the small hours, Roger was woken by a tremendous howling and shrieking from great gusts of wind beating against the shutters of his room while the whole building seemed to shake under its force.

Imprisoned by the shutters, he could see nothing, so he dressed and went down to see what was happening outside. Forcing his way into the street, he saw tall sago palm trees bending over double and sweeping the ground with their fronds. A big shop sign came hurtling through the air and smashed itself to pieces against the iron railings of the cricket ground. He ducked back inside for safety and pondered on the wisdom of trying to struggle up the hill to work in the morning.

At about eight o'clock, the great gusts seemed to die away with intervals of comparative calm in between. Roger decided to make the effort to get up to headquarters.

As he was still feeling somewhat shaky on his legs, he decided to find a rickshaw coolie who, for ten cents, would take him up the hill. This was not as easy as he had thought, as the streets around the club were without their usual throng of the little carts and their ragged blue-clothed owners. At last, he found one huddled in a sheltering corner who insisted on a fare of a dollar before he could be persuaded to accept the job.

As they were still haggling over the price, the wind dropped as if by magic to a complete calm. The sky, which had been heavy with inky black clouds and torrential rain, suddenly cleared with the sun shining through as if promising a fine hot day. What was curious about this strange phenomenon was that the air seemed filled with a crowd of birds and brilliant butterflies - more than he had ever seen - flying in a cloud of colour in the brilliant sunshine. The great storm was over, and he climbed into the rickshaw. As he did so, the sun disappeared behind a dense black sheet of cloud. With a great shriek, the wind, which had previously been blowing in gusts from the south, came back in an uninterrupted torrent of air, even stronger than before, from the opposite direction. He had had the comparatively rare but very doubtful privilege of witnessing the 'eye' of the typhoon.

With a yell, the coolie dropped the shafts of the rickshaw and fled for shelter. Roger, trapped inside the thing, clung on for dear life as he felt it being bodily lifted high in the air and hurtled clear over the spiked railings of the cricket ground and depositing him among a heap of splintered wreckage in the middle of the sacred turf.

He clung on helplessly for a minute or so while the gale shrieked around him, then, extricating himself from the debris of the rickshaw, crawled back on hands and knees to the shelter of the club and thoughtfully went back to bed to add a page to his letter to Daisy to tell her of his adventures.

Two days later, he had the encounter with Monkey and Major Hedgecoe and, taking the Peak Tram from the bottom station by the cathedral, went up to Kennedy Road with his possessions to install himself in his new home in the Courtland Hotel and the next stage of his life in Hong Kong.

Chapter 13

Courtland

Although by no means luxurious and, probably by modern standards, rating no higher than two stars at most, the Courtland Hotel was spotless and comfortable. It was presided over by Mrs Moneypenny and her husband (in that order). The guests were either junior officers like himself or clerical employees in one or other government departments.

His room was small but quite adequate for his needs. Its window looked out over the harbour, its view extending away over the New Territories to the blue hills of the Chinese mainland.

In common with most other similar establishments, the toilet facilities were primitive by European standards. They consisted of a metal commode, known appropriately as a 'thunderbox', which was emptied twice daily, its contents being sold to a local contractor for onward sale to vegetable farmers in the New Territories to be tipped into their fertiliser storage ponds. The price for night soil of European origin being considerably greater than for the native variety because of its greater nutritional properties is a point to be considered when eating salads and uncooked root vegetables. Eating raw vegetables or salad invariably resulted in an attack of Hong Kong 'Dog', the symptoms closely related to Gippy Tummy, Singapore Dog and Delhi Belly. These laid the sufferer low for a couple of very uncomfortable days and placed a heavy burden on the capacity of the thunderbox.

The only available lounge was the large dining room with picture windows looking across Kennedy Road to the high retaining wall of the garden belonging to the house on the next higher level, fringed with tall coconut palms. Roger quickly found life in this new establishment much more agreeable than in the Hong Kong Club, and he very quickly found himself accepted into the social circle and made many new friends.

Principal among these was Frank, the Cipher Officer who had also come from a teaching background, and Wally from the Royal Signals, who introduced him to the mysteries of Mah Jong. Many off-duty evenings were spent manipulating the little ivory tiles with their Chinese characters depicting winds, bamboo and dragons of various colours so that he found himself happier and more at home than ever since he had joined the army eighteen months previously.

Above all, apart from the wearing of uniform and the necessity of giving and receiving salutes, he felt himself to civilian life free from the petty and meaningless mumbo jumbo of restrictions, restraints and regimental protocol. His financial situation had also improved dramatically. This was further enhanced by the lower charges at Courtland compared to the club, so he was comparatively well off, with his total income at just over £40 per month.

As a result, he was able substantially to increase his allowance to Daisy, who, typically, as he was to find on his return home at the end of the war, had spent not a single penny of it and had existed on her meagre pay in the Land Army so that a comfortable amount would be available for their new home.

He was now able to get out into the town and to buy presents to send home – a gold and jade good luck charm bracelet for their first wedding anniversary, a silver embroidered satin kimono for her birthday and food parcels containing tea, chocolate, tins of butter and other items either unobtainable or strictly rationed back at home.

He also discovered a cabinet maker working in a little ramshackle booth on Shanghai Street behind the Peninsula Hotel in Kowloon. For a few dollars he would make teak chests lined with camphor wood and, without using either pattern or template, carve them in deep bas-relief with dragons and scenes from Chinese mythology. Roger started to build up a set of these ranging in size from a tea caddy to a blanket box, dreaming of the day when they would become part of his home.

Indeed, life seemed so settled that he began to think seriously of the possibility of Daisy coming out to Hong Kong to join him and to live in comfort and safety for the remainder of the war. That these plans never materialised never ceased to be a matter of great thankfulness throughout the whole of his life.

However, his closer contact with the town revealed a new side of life in this most prosperous of cities, for behind the bright lights, glitter and general opulence of the place lay an undreamed-of world of poverty and squalor. Beggars washed out their rags of clothing in the stream of water which cleaned out the gutters, a dead baby lay abandoned on the side of the street and emaciated children clinging to his legs and begging for "cumshaw" – a few worthless coins and chanting "no momma, no papa, no whisky soda". He quickly learned that the exotic and romantic odours of the East consisted mainly of foul drains and unwashed humanity.

On one occasion, when walking down Ice House Street with a friend, Doctor Scriven, he saw a woman dressed, as always, in a shabby black tunic and trousers staggering down the steep hill towards them.

"Just a minute," said Scriven, "she's just going to have a baby!" and, grabbing hold of her, he dragged her into a doorway from which she emerged five minutes later with the tiny crying bundle in her arms and strode off down the street.

"Will she be alright?" demanded the shocked Roger, who had watched the little drama with horror.

"Yes, of course," returned Scriven, "just as easy as shelling peas!" They carried on down the street as if this had been a daily occurrence - which it probably was.

He soon learned that it was unwise to intervene in any life-threatening catastrophe since many of the uneducated and superstitious Chinese believed that their fate was preordained and that whoever interfered with destiny made themselves responsible for the remainder of their lives existence in this life.

On another occasion, on his way through Wanchai he saw an apparently dead child lying in the gutter and stopped the truck to investigate.

"For God's sake, don't touch it, Sir," shouted his driver," or you will have to pay for its burial. Leave it there until the meat wagon picks it up."

And so, reluctantly, he drove on, leaving the pathetic little bundle lying in the garbage at the side of the road while the passers-by stepped out of their way to avoid the body.

By no means all of the population lived in squalor, however. Their wealth could often be assessed by the splendour of the family funerals. The richer the family, the longer and more splendid the funeral procession, which was escorted by several brass bands, each playing different tunes. The richer the family, the greater the number of bands; Roger once counted seven in a single procession. The resulting cacophony still further enhanced by the explosions from hundreds of fire-crackers.

The deceased was carried in a coffin made, often as not, from the curved slabs of tree trunks, sometimes with the bark still on, and brought in a richly decorated car bearing a huge photograph of the dead person.

If, as most frequently happened, the family lived in an apartment high above street level, a bamboo staircase would be built down from the window, and the coffin was carried down this rickety contraption to deceive the devils that would be fooled by this device and would be waiting by the door to leap into it as it came out. The devils were also assumed to be extremely greedy, so vast quantities of imitation banknotes purporting to be for millions of dollars would be scattered onto the roadway as the procession went to the cemetery. The devils, already disorientated by the racket from the brass bands and the fire-crackers, would stop and pick them up, giving the deceased a good head's start on the journey.

On arrival at the tomb, which would be closed by a vast circular boulder, much as in biblical days, the coffin would be thrust inside without a moment's delay. The boulder rolled back into place before the exhausted and frightened devils could get inside. After which, the white-clad mourners would return quietly home, satisfied that the dead relative would rest in peace for eternity.

This belief in a personal devil, which followed close at their heels, made driving through Wanchai an exciting business as, not infrequently, a pedestrian would dash across immediately in front of the truck so that the devil would be killed; its victim left in peace for eternity. The hospitals often received the broken limbs of those who had left it too late. Still, the risk was philosophically accepted, as was all life and death. What worried them was not death itself but the manner in which it came.

Poverty was accepted as the norm, and the poor seemed able to exist on a small bowl of rice and an occasional scrap of fish or vegetables.

As with all the residents of Courtland, Roger's needs were attended to by a "boy" responsible for cleaning the room, waiting on him at table, seeing to the laundry and carrying out any shopping or other chores.

Ah Sing, Roger's "boy", whom he shared with Barney Crowley across the corridor, was a gaunt little man who kept two wives and several children in the space underneath the building, which, because of the steep slope of the land, was built up on stilts at the back. For his services, he received the princely sum of five dollars a week from Roger and Barney with a "cumshaw" of two dollars at the end of the month if he had given no cause for complaint, and this sweetener ensured devoted service.

Now, a total monthly income of a little short of £5 meant that, although he could keep himself and his family in comparative comfort, anything that could be made on the side was not unwelcome.

Roger had bought himself a very pleasant pale-blue and white imitation Ming-type vase which stood on the shelf by Daisy's photograph. Ah Sing was commissioned to keep this filled with fresh flowers on the understanding that he would be paid as necessary but at least once a month. He enthusiastically accepted this task, and Roger was delighted with the constant and ever-changing variety of hibiscus and other exotic flowers that never failed to fill the vase.

He was also a little concerned over the probable size of the bill with which he would be faced when the day of reckoning arrived. He communicated his anxiety to Ah Sing, who merely gave a slight shrug of the shoulders and assumed his mask of impassivity, which meant that Roger would get no information until the time was adjudged to be appropriate.

At last, however, he could contain himself no longer and refused to let Ah Sing leave the room until he had been told how much he owed. Ah Sing looked thoughtful and finally volunteered tentatively: "Two dollar, Master."

This was ridiculous - all these beautiful flowers for a whole month for two shillings and sixpence. "Now look here, Ah Sing, this must be wrong. Do you mean twenty dollars?"

"No master," returned the impassive little man. "Two dollar". Then with the ghost of a smile, he added: "House next door have got very nice flower."

Roger saw no reason to interfere with this happy arrangement. Clearly, Ah Sing had come to a sensible business arrangement with the gardener, who undoubtedly took his due share of the 'squeeze'. Ah Sing was earning his "cumshaw".

His new job brought him a great deal of satisfaction and interesting new experiences. His education scheme developed well and soon was running itself without too much effort on his part. However, his visits to classes held in the evenings often meant a long day's work, which often left him exhausted in the high humidity of a tropical summer.

In addition, he had to oversee the education classes for the Indian regiments, mainly in English language - for which certificates could be awarded, which gave a much sought-after increase in pay. These were conducted by the two Army Education Corps Sergeants, Cullimore and Fabel, who were qualified teachers and needed little or no supervision. Still, it was often necessary to speak to the students. So he found it helpful to learn a little Urdu - the lingua franca of all Indian troops, and this occupied what spare time he had.

Lastly, and most interestingly of all, Frank Austin asked if he could give him some assistance in the Cipher Office - a tiny room built inside an outer room and subject to intensive security precautions.

Official approval having been given and the Official Secrets Act having been duly signed, Roger happily accepted his additional responsibilities. Still, he was a little dashed to find that his turns of duty were invariably at night since cables sent in the afternoon from England would start to arrive at about 10 p.m. Those sent in the morning from Canada would begin to come in at two or three o'clock in the morning with the result that his tour of duty meant two or three sleepless nights each week.

The codes were of different kinds - some in groups of letters, others in figures - all contained in reference books like dictionaries kept in a large safe with a complicated coded locking system which had to be opened and closed each time a different code was used. This code was never written down, and if, as occasionally happened in the small hours of the morning, the sleepy operator was unable to remember it, he had to lock the safe, lock the door of the inner office, lock the door of the outer office, lock the main headquarters door and walk the half mile or so back to Courtland to wake a sleepy and somewhat irritated Frank to have the code whispered into the ear and then repeat the whole wearisome procedure in reverse.

Top security messages came through on the Type X machine, a complex affair like a giant typewriter which was controlled by five drums, each with a sort of metal tyre around them which had to be twisted to the setting designated for that particular day and which then rotated with each letter so that the code changed with each letter and was virtually impossible to crack.

The code for the day was shown as the first group of letters on the telegram, and this controlled the whole message. The message which had arrived by teleprinter was fed into the machine, which spat out the cipher groups at one side and the decoded message at the other. Frequently, however, the decoded message appeared as gobbledegook, and the unfortunate decoder had to spend anxious minutes - sometimes hours - trying to get into the mind of the sender to find out what he had done wrong.

Certain messages were of such high security that they were received with a special prefix. These had to be sealed with wax in a special envelope which was then placed in a locked box, of which only the General's A.D.C. had the key and, after locking the offices, these had to be taken by hand no matter what time of night to Flagstaff House several hundreds of yards along the road to the A.D.C, who had to be roused from his sleep and the sealed box handed personally to him.

Most of this type of message came from Canada at about 3 or 4 a.m., and the special prefix was used regardless of the contents. Roger had great satisfaction in taking details of how many bedsteads would be required for the two battalions scheduled to arrive from Canada in November and in listening to the sleepy curses of the A.D.C. when he had unlocked the box and unsealed the envelope, but rules were rules, and cipher officers were not expected to do anything other than to obey orders.

Despite all these elaborate security precautions, however, Roger was horrified when, at the hairdressers in the town, he was asked by the proprietor if he thought that he might stand a chance of getting the contract for cutting their hair when the Canadian soldiers arrived in Hong Kong!

All normal messages arriving during the night were put into an out tray, which was collected by a Chinese orderly the following day and distributed to the various headquarters offices, and, unlikely though it seemed, he wondered if this could be the source of the security leak.

In view of the extremely tight security surrounding the movement of the Canadian troops, Roger communicated his anxieties to Colonel Newnham, the senior officer in charge at Command Headquarters, but was told crisply to mind his own business.

After the surrender to the Japanese on Christmas Day, it was discovered that the orderly who collected the message tapes was a senior member of the Japanese secret service.

Chapter 14

Storm Clouds

August and September, typically for Hong Kong, were hot and humid, with temperatures rarely below 80F and with maximum humidity. During the daytime, the slightest exertion created an unquenchable perspiration. When writing, one had to have several layers of blotting paper under the forearm to soak up the sweat and prevent the document from disintegrating.

Roger soon realised the truth of Noel Coward's jingle: "Mad dogs and Englishmen go out in the midday sun", but, unfortunately, his work made observance of the advice inherent in the rhyme quite impossible. He would get back to Courtland in the evening limp, exhausted and thankful for a tepid shower - sudden immersion in cold water being to invite all sorts of uncomfortable maladies - a long glass of ice-cold Tiger beer and a change of clothes which, as often as not, would be the third of the day.

These minor sufferings and inconveniencies notwithstanding, life took on a very agreeable pattern. The job seemed to be going well; Major Wood approved of his work and was complimentary of the results of the project, and he had found pleasant companionship with Frank and Wally. His ill-gotten radio kept him more closely in touch with home. The regular arrival of the China Clipper bringing regular letters from Daisy and taking back the accumulation of his nightly messages to her all contributed to a feeling that life could be worse.

The comparative cool of the evenings gave the welcome opportunity of a trip from the Kennedy Road station of the Peak Tram only a few yards along the road - and an exhilarating ride on the little rack and pinion railway to the top station from where Lugard Road made a quarter of a mile circuit of Victoria Peak - "Topside More Far" to give it its pidgin English name.

From here, one had the whole panorama of the island fading into the blue distance over Stanley and the fishing village of Aberdeen to the south. While to the north, a magical fairyland of twinkling lights from the entire stretch of coastland of the island fringing the black water of the harbour and, continuing beyond it from the great promontory of Kowloon, thrusting its way towards it. It was a sight that no one who had seen it would ever forget. Hong Kong was aptly named the "Pearl of the

Orient", and it was difficult to realise that beneath all this beauty lay poverty and squalor unequalled in almost any other big city in the world.

On other evenings he liked to stroll along Kennedy Road, which, soon after Courtland, stretched along the side of the hill through a fringe of sago and coconut palms, jacaranda and Flame of the Forest trees.

From here, overlooking the tenement flats of Wanchai, rose an orchestra of clicking sounds as from a vast army of grasshoppers. They were made by the slapping down of a million Mah Jong tiles from the gambling houses below. These were accompanied by the reedy discords of oriental music from restaurants and brothels. It was all most evocative of the Far East, and its strangeness was exhilarating but made one feel very much alone and a long way from home.

At weekends he would go with Frank and Wally across the island by bus or taxi to Repulse Bay, where they had invested, for a few dollars each, in a mat shed - a ramshackle rectangular construction of woven fibre mats on the sandy foreshore which gave shelter from the heat and made a convenient changing room for dressing after their swim, an activity often brought to a sudden and painful end by an encounter with swarms of minute jellyfish which despite their diminutive size packed a vicious and temporarily agonising sting.

After such a session, they would make their way up through the Flame of the Forest trees, which fringed the sand to the Repulse Bay Hotel near Stanley Village for a welcome cold beer. Little did they think that within a few months, this would be the scene of a desperate shoot-out from room to room along the corridors with the invading Japanese after the style of a Mid-Western film.

Occasionally, on a Sunday, Roger would be invited for a traditional Sunday lunch with his two Sergeants, Bert Cullimore and Tony Fabel, who shared a little bungalow by the side of the path leading down from Kennedy Road to Command Headquarters.

Here they were catered for by their amah-of-all-work, Ah Chat, an enormous balloon of a woman round as she was as high with a constantly grinning face and with a genius for cooking. At these meals, the fare was invariably roast beef with Yorkshire pudding and all the trimmings, followed by a huge treacle pudding, all of which had to be consumed to the last crumb for fear of offending Ah Chat. In a temperature approaching the nineties, this was a real ordeal. Sometimes there would be an invitation from Major Wood who, with his good-looking and charming wife Evelyn, many years his junior, had an apartment across the harbour in Kowloon. Together with her natural gifts and his gallantry born of Gordon's gin, they made a wonderful host and hostess.

Following the example of most of those who lived away from barracks, Roger ordered himself a pale grey sharkskin suit and a pair of civilian-type shoes, the whole outfit costing no more than ten pounds in all for these social occasions, and felt that, for his leisure time at least, he was virtually back in civilian life.

Having reconnoitred various establishments, including that of Hang On, whose sign proclaimed him to be a "Gentleman's clothes maker. Ladies have fits upstairs", he resolved to place the arrangements for the suit and shoes in the capable hands of Ah Sing, who took charge of the entire operation using the telephone in Roger's room.

The tailor and shoemaker arrived simultaneously. Roger was invited to stand on a sheet of paper while one drew around his feet and the other performed some bewildering gyrations with a tape measure. All of this while Ah Sing watched the proceedings with keen interest. Roger gloomily contemplated the sartorial disaster that seemed likely to result from this pantomime and went to bed wishing he had never consulted his 'boy' on the matter.

When he got up the next morning, Ah Sing brought him with his tea and slices of pomelo, which formed his waking cuppa, the new shoes and suit which had been made overnight and both of which fitted him to perfection. His confidence in this extraordinary little man had not been misplaced.

Not everything was as straightforward as this, however. It was wise to keep a watchful eye on even the simplest purchase, while it was sheer folly to leave any item of value not securely locked away. His buying of a tube of toothpaste, for example, which he put into his pocket unexamined, revealed an empty void inside the immaculate box, the contents having been skilfully removed by the unwrapping of the seal at the base before he had bought it.

The summer wore on into September in intense heat and brilliant sunshine interspersed with heavy outbursts of monsoon rain and another typhoon which, although severe, failed to reach the high standard of the first. Other clouds unconnected with the atmosphere were beginning to appear. Although adhering strictly to the rules of complete silence imposed by the Official Secrets Act, Frank and Roger never discussed them. Nevertheless, the contents of many of the coded messages to and from the War Office showed increasing concern over the activities of the Japanese further north in mainland China.

The Japanese invasion of China in 1937, carried out with characteristic brutality, had given them command of Shanghai, the Yangtse Valley, and much of the territory northwards and south into Kwang Tung province. Secret service reports spoke of manoeuvres and a military build-up in the area beyond the Shum Chun River, which marked the frontier between the New Territories and mainland China.

As official anxieties deepened, women not engaged in essential occupations such as nursing and important clerical duties were urged to leave the island, most heading for the security and unrationed comfort of Australia, where they stayed for the remainder of the war. Others undertook the long and rather risky journey back to England where, although the threat of invasion and the attentions of the Luftwaffe had now receded, life was by no means without risk and, to the ladies used to the luxury life of Hong Kong, stringent food rationing was a most unattractive prospect.

Evacuation was, however, not obligatory. Many chose to stay and accept what seemed to most at the time was the very remote likelihood of hostilities breaking out in this remote corner of the world so far removed from the theatres of war.

Major Wood, who was due a month's leave and sensed a developing crisis, decided that Evelyn, his wife, should return to the United Kingdom where their daughter, Ronnie, was living with her grandparents and spend as much time as possible with her before their separation. The major went with her as far as Singapore, leaving Roger in charge of the office with a promise of a recommendation for promotion when he returned if all had gone well during his absence.

Early in October, the first positive signs of trouble ahead came to the surface. For some time, the Japanese government had openly shown political support for the German advances and successes in Europe. This was further strengthened by the glee with which they greeted the occupation of Greece and the failure of the British advance against the Italians in North Africa, which had brought them from their advance base in Tobruk to within reach of Tripoli. Thanks to massive reinforcement by Field Marshal Rommel, they had been pushed back to El Alamein, leaving the enemy poised to strike at Egypt and the Suez Canal.

Japan, possibly sensing that the collapse of British resistance in Europe was imminent, stepped up its anti-British propaganda campaign and began moving troops into southern China.

One alarming evidence of this threatening attitude occurred towards the end of October when every commissioned officer in the command received a letter, posted in Shanghai and accurately addressed personally by name, rank, regiment and appointment, containing abusive propaganda and urging them to take no action when the day arrived for Japan to liberate the enslaved colonies under British control.

Most treated the letter with hilarity, safe in the belief that Singapore, with its powerful naval forces, would be more than a match for anything the Japanese could produce. It was inconceivable that in view of the distances involved and the densely forested terrain of Malaya and Burma, any attack by land forces could have the slighteset chance of success.

Headquarters staff and those who had access to the confidential information coming in through the cipher office were less sanguine. The fact that the Japanese intelligence had been able to obtain such accurate information about its personnel suggested an extremely efficient Secret Service, and, not for the first time, Roger and Frank expressed uneasiness about how decoded information was distributed to the various departments by the Chinese orderly.

Clearly, also, the security of the colony, separated from Japanese troops only by the Shum Chun River in Kwang Tung Province a bare fifteen miles to the north of Kowloon and with the protection afforded by Singapore more than 1,500 miles away, was becoming a matter of increasing concern in the War Office. Amid all this activity, Major Wood returned from Singapore on what was to be almost the last boat to make the journey and took charge once again. Roger, now becoming increasingly concerned at the unpromising situation, suggested that perhaps it was time for him to return to his regiment. Although disappointed, he was not surprised that his request was turned down out of hand because of all the increased activity in the cipher office.

The provision for Command Headquarters in the event of hostilities was to transfer to a complex series of underground bunkers known to all and sundry as the 'Battle Box'.

The Battle Box had been constructed by covering the deep gully between Command Headquarters and the Victoria Barracks with a bomb-proof concrete roof with its outer wall facing northwards across the harbour. It consisted of a fourteen feet thick barrier of reinforced concrete which, it was thought, not even the heaviest bombardment could shatter. This was a theory soon to be put to the test and, fortunately for the occupants, proved to be accurate. Although, since the toilet provision had thoughtfully been placed along the back of the wall, those using it during the battle were to experience some extremely uncomfortable sessions as the six-inch shells thundered against the other side and deposited them on the floor.

The whole set-up appeared uncomfortably like a trap to those ordained to occupy this subterranean accommodation. For the first time in his life, Roger came to understand the significance of claustrophobia. He resolved that should the worst ever come to the worst, he would get himself up to the surface and take his chance there.

The cipher office was a tiny cell, badly ventilated and poorly lit, adjoining the GOC's quarters so that messages could be passed through with the minimum of delay. Most of the available space was taken up by the Type X machines, with the book codes piled up on side tables since the need for the security precautions of the former office had now disappeared.

By Saturday, December 6th, it was clear to those at the sharp end of intelligence reports that the threatened storm was about to break.

Life in the colony as a whole went on as usual. A large party at the Jockey Club following a rugger match against the army and a reception by the senior Canadian officers attended by the commissioner of police while the Canadian troops enjoyed their first free evening were busy exploring its many delights.

Over it all, however, hung an uneasy feeling of impending trouble. By midnight, parties broke up well ahead of schedule as rumours circulated that Japanese forces were on the move.

The following morning a report was received in the cipher office of substantial Japanese troop movements only a few miles to the north of the Chinese border. The information became so serious that the ADC sent a senior staff officer to the cathedral where General Maltby was attending morning service at which the Middlesex Regiment was on church parade. The GOC left and immediately summoned an emergency meeting of the Defence Council at Government House with the result that all troops were placed on standby and ordered to man their battle stations.

Roger, who was not on duty that night, went back to Courtland to catch a few hours' sleep, unaware that this was the last night he would ever spend there.

The unaccustomed ringing of the telephone in his room woke him up at about 7.30 a.m.

It was Frank, and from the tone of his voice, he was extremely agitated.

"Get down to headquarters as fast as you can," he said, "something tremendous has happened."

Roger's heart stopped beating for an instant; Frank was never one to get excited.

"What's up, for goodness sake?" he demanded.

"I shouldn't really tell you over the phone," replied Frank, "but about quarter to five this morning, the special intelligence unit reported a broadcast from Tokyo saying that war with Britain and America was about to break out. As the likelihood of their being so stupid as to attack the United States and bring them into the war was unlikely, we thought it was probably just another piece of their propaganda. Still, we have just had a signal in to say that Japanese planes have attacked the American fleet at Pearl Harbour, and all hell is a-popping."

Roger was completely thunderstruck for a moment, but when he came to his senses, the full implication of the situation came home. If the Japanese had attacked the American navy, this must achieve what everyone had been hoping for years: that America would have no choice now but to come into the war in support of the

Allies. This must mean the eventual defeat of Germany and, unless they caved in unconditionally, of Japan as well. Surely now, the end of the war was in sight, and a great surge of hope welled up within him.

However, a chilling thought struck him as he threw on his clothes. If the Japanese had been so rash as to attack America without a formal declaration of war, would they not also do the same for Britain? Was not Hong Kong the nearest and most vulnerable target for their attack, and how long would it be before they began?

He was not to wait long for the answer. As he was making his way along Kennedy Road, he heard the noise of aircraft overhead. Looking up, he saw three planes circling over the harbour and the poached egg emblem of Japan under the wings.

Suddenly a shower of paper drifting down over the town came from one of the planes. One fell near him, and he picked it up eagerly.

It was a leaflet addressed: "To the British Soldiers." In one corner was a German soldier holding a Nazi flag and standing on a Union Jack covering the British Isles. In the other, standing on a tiny island, a very small and ugly British soldier scowling up at two enormous and handsome jack-booted Japanese pointing up towards their new ally and, in between, the message: "*We want you to know one thing. The very day when Japan makes its furious attacks on Hong Kong and Malay, it is also the day that Germany makes its long-planned landing in the British Isles. The end of Britain has come!*"

As he was considering this dramatic piece of information, another leaflet fluttered down in front of him. Under a large headline: "Very, very courageous British soldiers" was a map of Britain and Europe covered with swastikas while the Italian flag occupied the Mediterranean and Africa and Japanese flags covered China and South East Asia. A very implacable Japanese soldier thrust his bayonet into a tiny British flag in Hong Kong. Underneath were the words: "*You are very courageous, we know. But in this war, there won't be anything that you can do. Even with your courage, you will get no place. It is really useless and meaningless to resist. Have the courage to face the real fact and come. Come for a peace without fighting. Come like a real man. We will listen. It will be a 'man to man's talk', and we will guarantee your life.*"

He was hurrying along the path towards the Battle Box, half appalled and half amused digesting this dramatic turn of events and trying to come to terms with the grave significance of it all. From a distance, he heard the unmistakable whistle of falling bombs and, looking back down the harbour, saw brilliant flashes of flame coming up from Stonecutters Island to the west of the harbour, followed a few seconds later by enormous explosions as the missiles found their target on the heavy gun positions strategically placed there for the defence of the harbour.

He broke into a trot, and just as he approached the little bungalow where he had consumed the gargantuan Sunday lunches with the Education Corps Sergeants, he heard the scream of dive bombers sweeping down towards him from behind, clearly bent on the destruction of Command Headquarters two or three hundred yards away. Instinctively he flung himself through the door and threw himself face downwards on the floor. As he did so, the entire building seemed to jump into the air and settle down amid a rain of plaster and shattered glass. A cluster of high-explosive bombs had straddled the little house on three sides, evidently missing their intended target.

He lay for a few moments among the rubble, shocked and numbed. When he tried to pick himself up, he found he was pinioned by something large and soft. A solid wooden barrier pressing down on him from above stopped him from extricating himself. Then to his astonishment, he heard the unlikely sound of someone laughing.

Tony Fabel was trying to lift up the heavy sideboard under which he had been thrown by the blast whilst clasped in his arms was the massive yielding bulk of Ah Chat, the Amah.

When they had extricated themselves, and the gap between the bottom of the sideboard and the floor had been measured and compared with the girth of Ah Chat, they discovered that by some extraordinary trick of the blast, he and the fat Ah Chat had together occupied a space no more than nine inches high. At that moment, they heard the wail of the air raid siren sounding a little late in the day.

The 'all clear' never sounded. The war with Japan had begun.

Chapter 15

The Battle for Hong Kong

Down in the Battle Box, everything was in turmoil, with telephones ringing in every room. In the cipher office, Frank was busy with the Type X machine sending out the first of the situation reports known as "Sitreps", and Roger was set to work with book codes to despatch a small mountain of telegrams.

So far, although intelligence reports from across the border suggested otherwise, there had been no visible sign of movement on the other side of the Shum Chun River. The assumption was still that the main attack would come from the sea. If this were to happen, everyone was uncomfortably aware that the available naval force of two destroyers and six motor torpedo boats, some of them manned by members of the Hong Kong Volunteer Defence Corps, would be able to achieve little against a large-scale seaborne naval attack. The only hope of repelling an invasion from the sea would be the heavy artillery based at the southern tip of Stanley Peninsula and the shore-based machine gun posts of the Middlesex Regiment sited near likely landing points.

No one could tell whether any major enemy invasion fleet was assembling in the offing since, as well as silencing the guns on Stonecutters Island, the first wave of aerial bombardment had destroyed the few planes based at Kai Tak. All that could be done was to watch and wait.

They did not know then that the two destroyers who had set sail immediately after the air attack were never to return, having been ordered to make their way to Singapore to join the main fleet. This was to avoid being the victims of a superior naval force or the recipients of the attention of the Kamikaze suicide bombers whose mission in life would be to crash their planes loaded with bombs onto the decks of their targets.

For the same reason, all merchant shipping capable of putting to sea did so and headed south with the destroyers for the Philippines or Malaya. It would be almost four long years before any of them returned.

Only when the destroyers did not come back within a couple of days did the truth dawn upon them that there was no possibility of rescue from Singapore apart from a remote chance of support from the two battleships known to be operating in the South China Sea. The little garrison stranded on its island was to be left to do the best it could with the meagre resources available: six regular infantry battalions consisting, at most, of 6,000 men, of which the 2,000 Canadians who had arrived only a couple of weeks before the outbreak of hostilities and, notwithstanding their determination and courage which they later demonstrated most convincingly, were basically inexperienced and untrained and with no knowledge of the terrain over which they would be operating.

It seemed clear, also, that this last-minute reinforcement of the garrison had been a defiant piece of bluff designed to dissuade the Japanese from initiating a land-based attack and that these young Canadians were to be sacrificed along with the rest of the luckless troops if the ruse failed.

The only remaining support came from the part-time Hong Kong Volunteer Defence Corps consisting of civilian employees in the dockyard, government offices, banks and other business concerns. They were enthusiastic but with little real military training or experience, their main asset being that they would be familiar with the terrain over which they would be fighting.

Indeed, the only garrison members with direct experience of enemy action were the few, like himself, who had recently arrived from England and had experienced the Blitz.

It now seemed clear to him that his place was back with his regiment, and he immediately made a fresh application to do so but with no success. His role, he was told, was to stick with his job until events made this no longer possible. At this point, he would join a mobile unit consisting of such odds and sods of administrative personnel as might be available for the defence of headquarters or to take part in any emergency activities that the situation might demand. That was as far as he could get.

His immediate concern was to get some sort of message of reassurance home to Daisy, who, he guessed, must be beside herself with anxiety over this totally unexpected turn of events. So, as soon as he could get away for an hour, he went down to the cable and wireless office on the waterfront behind the Hong Kong Club and was lucky enough to still be able to send her a telegram saying that all was well and that she was not to worry – an entirely fatuous exhortation.

This was the last she was to hear of him for more than two years except for a message from the War Office telling her that he had been posted as 'Missing in Action', which was somewhat less than comforting and did little to reassure her.

Having destroyed the gun positions on Stonecutters Island as well as the puny defence offered by the Royal Air Force at Kai Tak and keeping out of range of the obsolete First World War 3-inch guns manned by the H.K.V.D.C. at Saiwan at the eastern end of the island overlooking the approach to the harbour through the narrow Lye Mun passage, the Japanese aircraft had total command of the skies and were able to attack their chosen targets with impunity.

Immediately after the Defence Council meeting on December 6th, all troops had been dispatched to their battle stations and, within a few hours, were ready for action.

The Royal Scots, Punjabis and Rajputs had taken up their positions along the Gin-Drinkers' Line south of the narrow Shing Mun River, about four miles in length across the narrow neck of land. They formed a horseshoe-shaped line with the well-fortified Shing Mun Redoubt, a modern and well-equipped command post in the centre under the command of Colonel Simon White. The Royal Scots held the vital western sector protecting the Lai Chi Kok Road into Kowloon, while the Indian Regiments were responsible for the eastern part of the line and the coast road from Fan Ling and Tai Po.

The Middlesex had occupied their machine-gun posts along the southern fringe of the island while the two Canadian regiments, the Winnipeg Grenadiers and the Royal Rifles of Canada, occupied the central range of hills on the island from Victoria Peak to Mount Collinson in the west.

All bridges in the New Territories between the Shum Chun and Shing Mun Rivers were blown.

Having ceded the greater part of the New Territories, virtually indefensible given the meagre manpower available, Hong Kong was as ready as it was possible for it to be to withstand the onslaught of the Japanese army. Troops were mindful that without reserves and any depth of defence or hope of reinforcement, the Gin Drinkers' Line stood between the invaders and the northern shore of the harbour should the attack come from the north.

With the air defences totally eliminated, the protection of the navy removed, and the artillery which covered the harbour entrances destroyed, the outlook was bleak indeed. There was little the defenders could do but sit it out, hump their way through, and hope the threatened attack would not materialise.

They did not have long to wait to find out. Early in the afternoon of Tuesday, December 9th, the observation posts in front of the Gin Drinkers' Line saw large-scale movements of Japanese troops on the other side of the river and by 11pm, advance units of the Imperial Regiment 228 were clearing the barbed-wire defences in front of the Shing Mun Redoubt in preparation for the main assault.

There was little the defenders could do but watch and wait. With the enemy troops who had managed to infiltrate unseen behind them under cover of darkness, the Redoubt was overwhelmed almost without a shot being fired.

With the loss of their central control point and vital communications centre, the Royal Scots defending the western part of the line and the main approach road to Kowloon held out for eight hours. They withdrew in disarray at dawn to form a new defence line running from the waterfront at Shamshuipo and stretching around the northern fringes of the town towards Kai Tak.

Having destroyed the western part of the defence line and with unhindered access across the Shing Mun River, the Japanese, using another of their crack regiments, many of them disguised as Chinese coolies and crossing the estuary of the river in sampans, turned their attention to the Punjabis and Rajputs holding the east of the line.

The Indian regiments fought gallantly but were no match either numerically or tactically for their vastly superior enemy. They were also forced to draw back to the new defence line except for a few isolated platoons trapped in the hills. By the evening of December 10th, the Japanese controlled the whole New Territories except for Kowloon. Because of its closely built-up residential area, the city was clearly indefensible for any length of time. The woefully inadequate defence line could hold out only long enough to cover the withdrawal of the survivors across the harbour by Star Ferry and any other form of water-borne transport which could be commandeered.

By this time, the telephone cables linking Hong Kong with the rest of the world had been cut, leaving wireless telegraphy as its only contact with the outside world. The report broadcast from London on December 12th that "the gallant garrison of fortress Hong Kong" had redeployed within its island was received with less than enthusiasm by its beleaguered members, who now could do nothing but wait for the inevitable catastrophe.

They were hopelessly outnumbered, a mere six thousand fighting troops, already seriously depleted during the fighting on the mainland, with no heavy artillery or armour, no protection from either the air or sea, now facing an invasion force estimated to be in the region of forty-five thousand highly trained and mobile men. All of whom had had three years' experience of battle in China and who, in the true spirit of 'Bushido', were determined never to surrender or to abandon their advance as long as one of them was still on his feet.

The only hope was a rumour that help was on the way from a massive Chinese force under the command of Chiang Kai Shek, which was said to be advancing to their rescue from the north. Although they were eager to repeat the story, no one in his heart believed it.

Chiang's army never arrived, nor was there any possibility it could.

Isolated groups of survivors who had succeeded in extricating themselves from the trap continued to make their way by night across the harbour to the comparative

Hong Kong from Victoria Peak

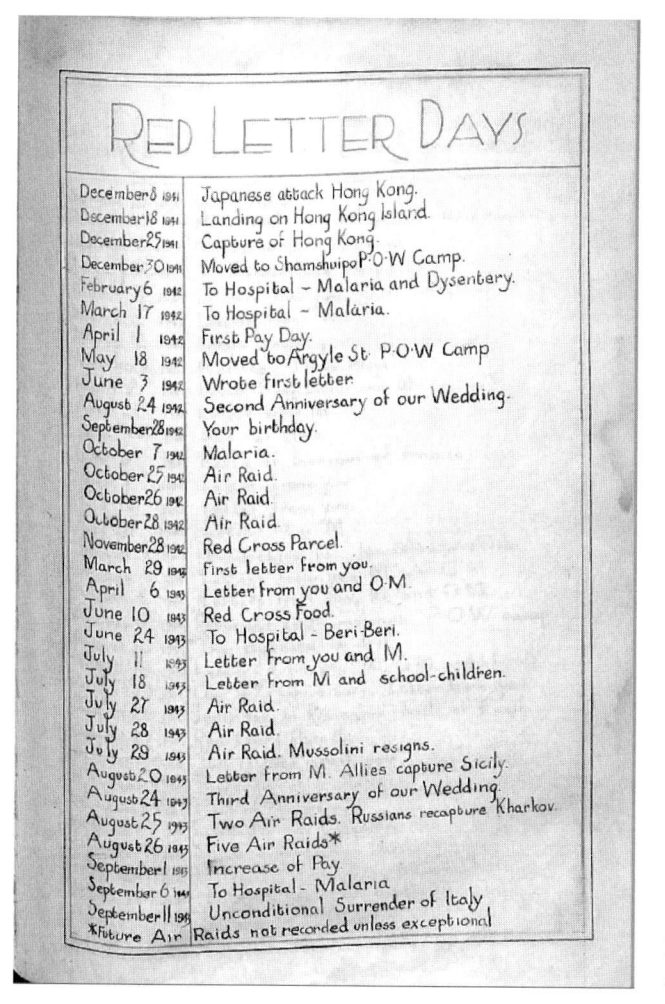

Red Letter Days

December 8 1941	Japanese attack Hong Kong.
December 18 1941	Landing on Hong Kong Island.
December 25 1941	Capture of Hong Kong.
December 30 1941	Moved to Shamshuipo P.O.W Camp.
February 6 1942	To Hospital - Malaria and Dysentery.
March 17 1942	To Hospital - Malaria.
April 1 1942	First Pay Day.
May 18 1942	Moved to Argyle St. P.O.W Camp
June 3 1942	Wrote first letter
August 24 1942	Second Anniversary of our Wedding.
September 28 1942	Your birthday.
October 7 1942	Malaria.
October 25 1942	Air Raid.
October 26 1942	Air Raid.
October 28 1942	Air Raid.
November 28 1942	Red Cross Parcel.
March 29 1943	First letter from you.
April 6 1943	Letter from you and O.M.
June 10 1943	Red Cross Food.
June 24 1943	To Hospital - Beri-Beri.
July 11 1943	Letter from you and M.
July 18 1943	Letter from M and school-children.
July 27 1943	Air Raid.
July 28 1943	Air Raid.
July 29 1943	Air Raid. Mussolini resigns.
August 20 1943	Letter from M. Allies capture Sicily.
August 24 1943	Third Anniversary of our Wedding.
August 25 1943	Two Air Raids. Russians recapture Kharkov.
August 26 1943	Five Air Raids*
September 1 1943	Increase of Pay
September 6 1943	To Hospital - Malaria
September 11 1943	Unconditional Surrender of Italy

*Future Air Raids not recorded unless exceptional

Roger kept a detailed log of events whilst in prison

Letters from Daisy started to make their way through

Red Letter Days

September 28	1943	Your birthday.
October 12	1943	Major Wood returns from Bowen Road Hospital
November 6	1943	All dogs in Camp destroyed.
January 30	1944	To Bowen Road Hospital.
March 3	1944	Letters from you, O.M and Clem.
March 5	1944	Letters from M.
March 12	1944	Letter from you.
March 24	1944	Produced "Three Plays"
April 2	1944	Letter from Clem and M.
April 21	1944	Letter from M.
June 5	1944	Fall of Rome
June 8	1944	Heard of Invasion of France
July 4	1944	Letter from you
July 18	1944	Letter from you.
July 31	1944	Letter from M.
August 3	1944	Production of "Ten Minute Alibi"
August 4	1944	Letters from you, M, and O.M
August 8	1944	Letters from you, M, and O.M
August 9	1944	Returned to Shamshuipo P.O.W camp
August 10	1944	The Barnett incident.
August 15	1944	Letters from you, M, O.M, and Clem.
August 24	1944	Our 4th Anniversary. Letter from you
August 26	1944	Surrender of Roumania. Fall of Paris.
August 27	1944	Red Cross Parcels.
August 30	1944	Two letters from you
September 5	1944	Surrender of Finland
September 7	1944	Fall of Antwerp
September 8	1944	Surrender of Bulgaria
September 14	1944	Allied troops enter Germany
September 18	1944	18 letters from you, M and Clem.
September 20	1944	1,000th day of captivity
October 15	1944	To Hospital - Malaria
October 16	1944	Big Air Raid - over 40 planes

Red Letter Days

November 13	1944	To Hospital - Malaria.
January 16	1945	Raid by more than 300 planes.
February 1	1945	Russian troops enter Germany
February 6	1945	American troops enter Manila
March 3	1945	Red Cross Parcels
April 24	1945	Russian troops enter Berlin
May 9	1945	Unconditional Surrender of Germany (7y 45)
August 9	1945	Russia declares war on Japan
August 11	1945	Rumour of Japanese surrender. Malaria.
August 16	1945	Confirmation of Japanese surrender.
August 30	1945	British Fleet arrives in Hong Kong.

The end is in sight

Roger in Safari Kit - straight out of "It Ain't Haf Hot, Mum"

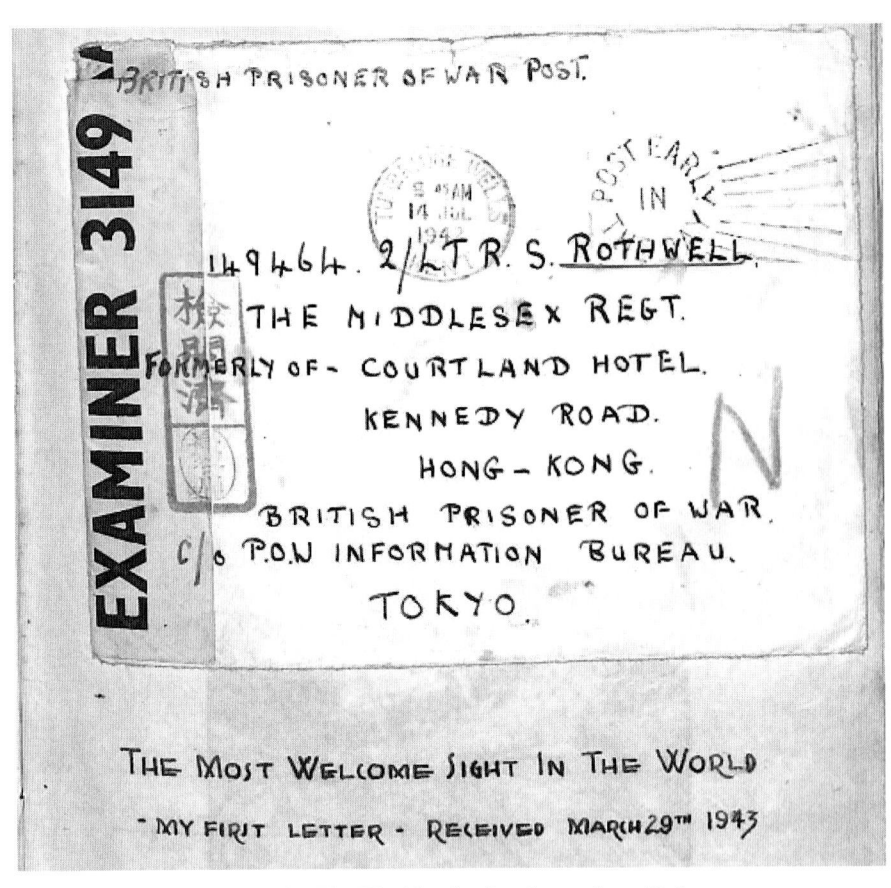

The Most Welcome Sight in The World - the first letter from Daisy

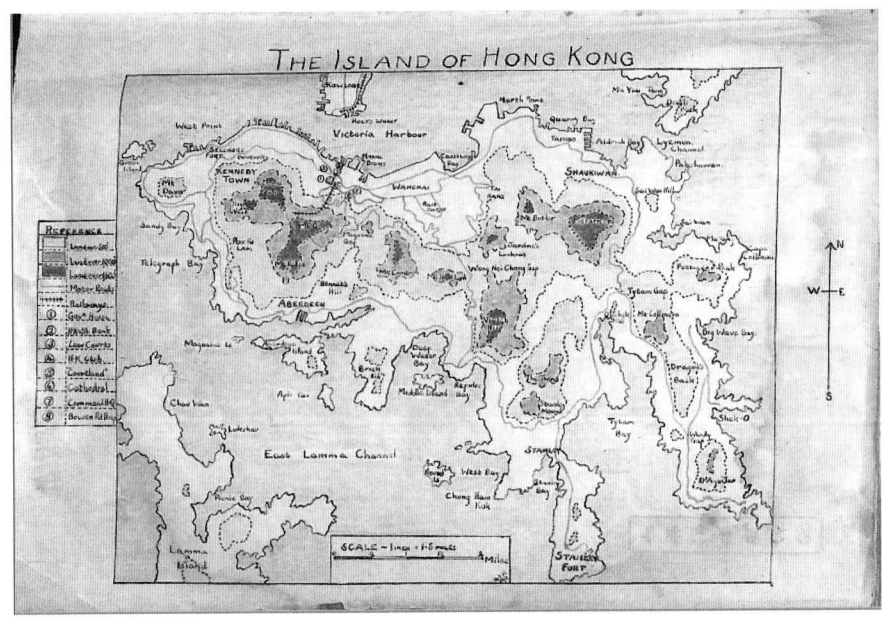

To while away the long hours, the men drew detailed maps of Hong Kong

Praying for contact from Daisy

PRAYERS OF A P.O.W - No 2.

THE PRAYER

You know, Lord, how when letters came
Addressed to R.S.R by name,
How much I treasured every word –
Please, Lord, don't think that I'm absurd –
But things seemed brighter altogether
And grey skies changed to sunny weather,
And there was real joy in life
When I had letters from my wife.
But eight long months have passed away
Since that extremely happy day.
So don't you think I'm nearly due
To have another one or two?
It's not, Lord, that she doesn't write,
You know she does each Sunday night;
But something happens on the way
Which causes all this long delay.
Lord, I would be Your grateful debtor
If I could have another letter.
It's very comforting to know
That she was well two years ago;
But here's the news I really seek –
Is she safe and sound this week?

20·2·44

Darling,
This is your book; the only present I can bring you from a Prisoner of War Camp.

I hope it will give you pleasure, and help to bridge over these empty years during which only our hearts have been together.

And anyway, my darling I know you will value it, if only because the making of it has filled some lonely hours for me, and brought you even closer.

Argyle St. P.O.W Camp
Hong Kong
16·iii·43

Thinking of the future and of Daisy

Heerard Hotel
Lancaster Gate
London, W. 2
Dec. 8, 1960

Dear Mr. Rothwell,

I thank you very much for your kind letter.

I recognize your way of writing you put in my autograph more than fifteen years ago.

So suddenly I am happening to be in your country which I have been dreaming about these many years. I find people here very good to me, especially since appearing in the programme they greet me kindly. I am becoming a great Londoner! My church gave me a three month leave of absence, I may stay here a month at least.

I intent to visit Canada and U.S. and finally Hong Kong on my way back to Japan.

And so, in the meantime I shall be able to have the pleasure of seeing you and Mrs. Rothwell and also your son and daughter.

Thank you again for your kind letter.

With every good wish to you all.

Yours very sincerely

John K. Watanabe

A letter from John Watanabe - the man who saved Roger's life

Watanabe San

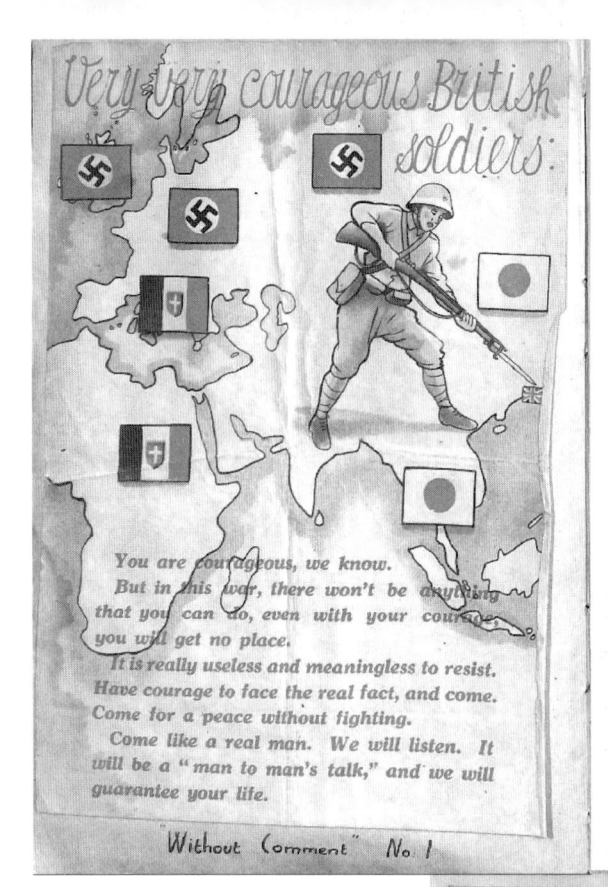

Appealing to the soldiers to come quietly

Useless to Resist

Surrender or face annihilation

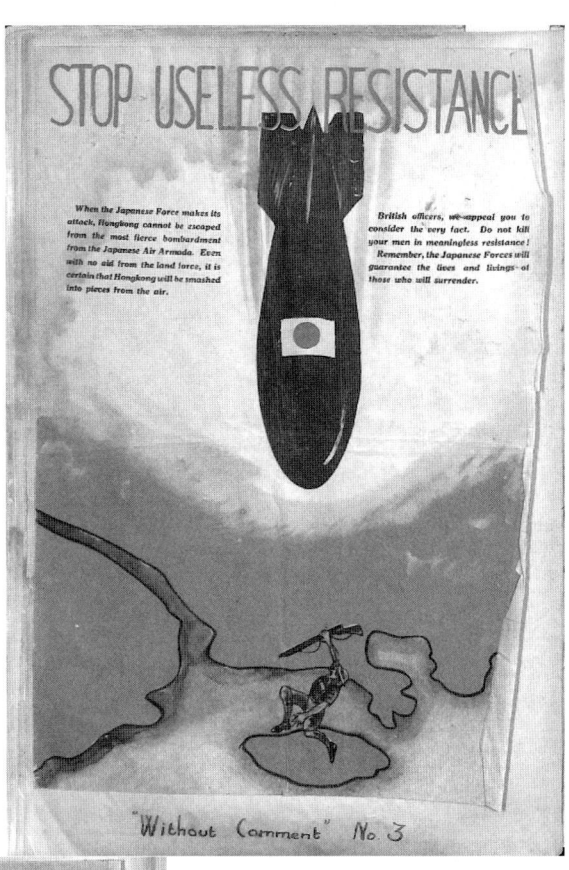

Appealing directly to the Officer rank to surrender

Japanese propaganda leaflet to break our spirits

Britain as a powerless circus act

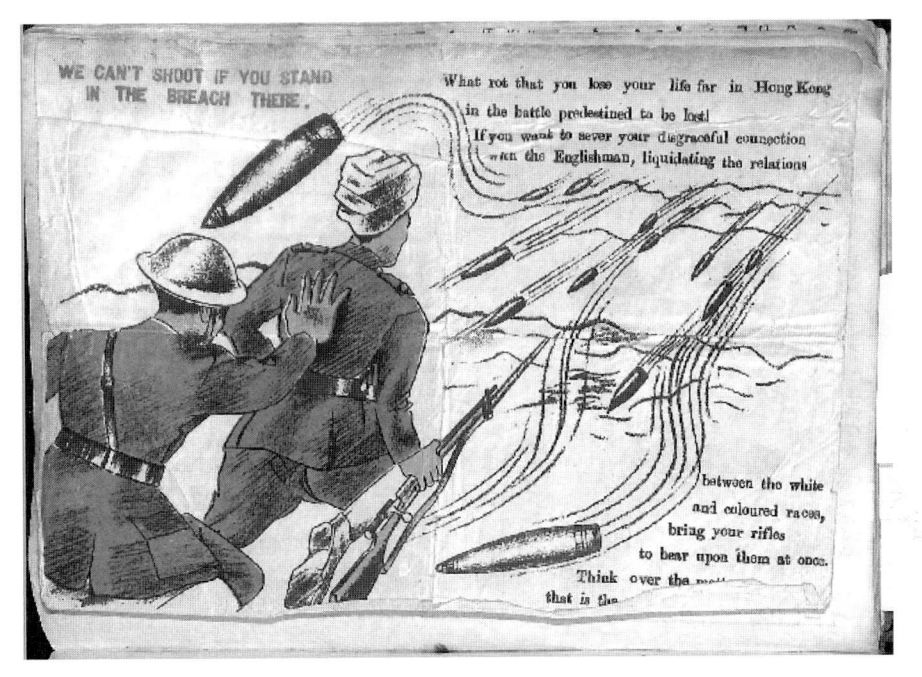

Discouraging dissent in the ranks

Pencil sketch of the PoW camp by fellow captive K. Sawyer

"Argyle University" timetable of study – Roger teaches French to the men

37 subjects were available to "students"

Coupons for Loot

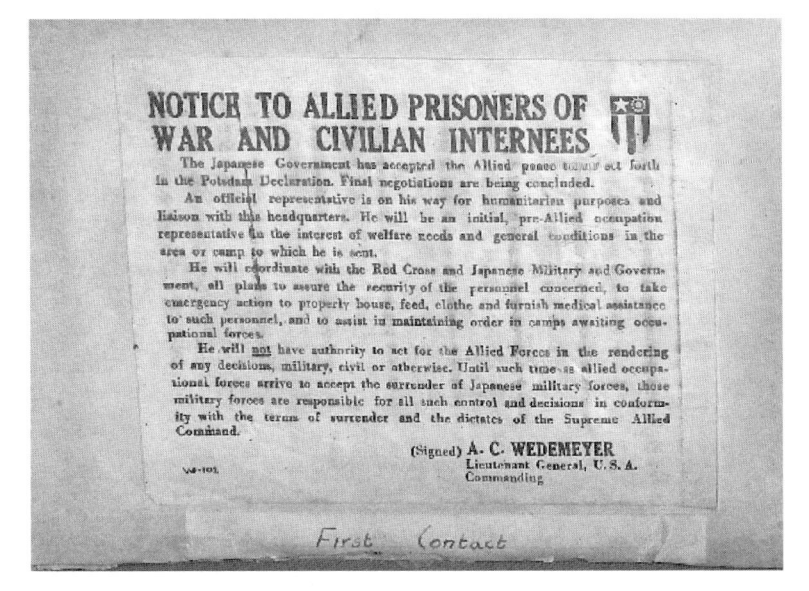

A notice signalling that the end of the nightmare was close-by

The text reads "This certificate is used for current transactions and can be exchanged for Japanese currency at the Bank of Japan and its branches, agencies, and savings offices."

軍用手票 "Military Payment Certificate" - currency used by soldiers in occupied Hong Kong

The Union Jack flies again in Hong Kong

More bold propaganda - this time in Chinese

捷訊，傳單．

日本軍之武勇！

星加坡已完全陷落了！！！

星加坡隕落的事實已證明英軍之柔弱，及大東亞之香港馬尼拉早已陷落了，星加坡─英美侵略東亞之根據地─也終於陷落了。

我們現在日軍已將英美之惡勢力一概驅除了！

我們應感謝大日本皇軍把我們東亞人的土地完全收復這樣，英美已不能再侵略及壓迫我們大東亞的民族了，我們在日本的統治下可以自由生活，安居樂業了．

全亞的民族起來吧，不願做英美奴隸的人們．

復興我們的東亞努力建設大東亞吧！

起來吧，東亞與大日本親善提攜

Without Comment No 8
(translation opposite)

Translation of the chinese text - boasting of a Great East Asia, free from Western forces

VICTORY TIDING'S CIRCULAR

Singapore has already completely fallen!!!
The fact of Singapore's fall already proves clearly the weakness of the English forces, and the military prowess of the great Nipponese army.

Hong Kong and Manila fell very early! Singapore - the Anglo-American base for agression in East Asia - has also completely fallen! Today the Nipponese forces have completely put to rout the infernal power of the Anglo-Americans! We ought to give grateful thanks to the great Nipponese Imperial Army for the complete return of our East Asian peoples' birthplace; thus the Anglo-Americans will not again be able to seize and oppress our great East Asian commonwealth! We, under the leadership of Japan, will be able to live in freedom and to follow our occupations peacefully! Come on then! Don't be willing to be the slaves of the Anglo-Americans. Come on then! East Asian peoples. We will join in good fellowship with Great Japan, restore our East Asia, and with our might firmly establish it as Greater East Asia!

Appealing to Indian soldiers with the promise of good treatment if they surrender

Attempts to turn the Indian soldiers against their colonial oppressors

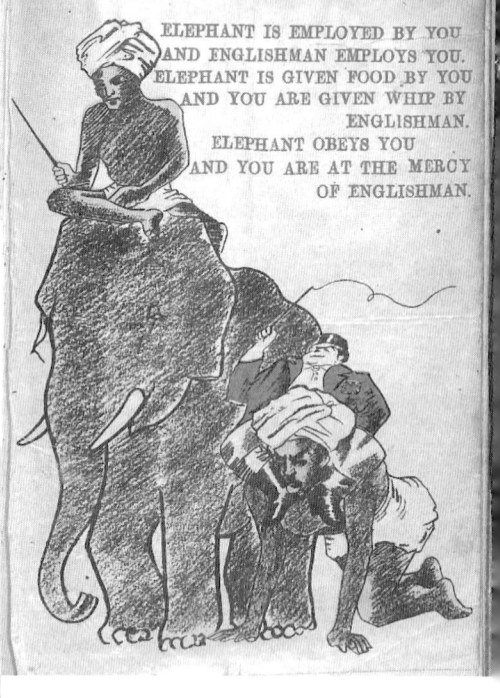

In stark contrast to other propaganda, although the message is the same, "resist and you will be shot"

safety of the island. One of these groups, the remnants of a platoon from the Punjabis, managed to get a signal across that they were holed up in Kowloon and were going to try to reach the Star Ferry pier at dawn. As a ferry was berthed at the Hong Kong side pier, a small group from Roger's 'Odds and Sods' was despatched to take it across and cover the withdrawal.

There was an uncanny silence as they chugged across the harbour in the darkness of early morning, everyone waiting for the burst of fire, which they were sure would greet them when they came within range. However, nothing happened, and the ferry tied up while they crept out, hearts in their mouths, towards the railway station opposite the Peninsula Hotel to assess the situation.

Suddenly they heard the roar of an engine, and a truck containing David Mather, the platoon commander, and a group of his men, raced round the corner from Nathan Road, hotly pursued by another loaded with jabbering Japanese loosing off with machine guns in a hail of bullets in all directions, none of which, luckily, found their mark.

There was no time to stand and fight. Everyone raced back to the ferry, which cast off and headed for the island, exchanging fire with the enemy on the shore until the ferry disappeared from their sight in the gloom and tied up safely at the pier in the Hong Kong side of the harbour.

By the next day, the Japanese, now in complete control of the mainland, had brought up their heavy artillery and mortars and commenced a bombardment of the island, which lasted all day and into the night. The town, stretching upwards towards the high ground behind it and clearly within view of the enemy's observation posts, was a perfect target for their gunners.

The unhappy defenders were amazed at the accuracy of the fire. Still, they would have been less surprised if they had known, as they were to discover later, that the attack on Hong Kong had been a routine exercise in Japanese staff colleges for several years. Every battery commander had a book of statistics for each pre-ordained position giving the range and elevation of each target. All that had to be done was to consult the appropriate table, set the gun and pull the trigger.

The north-facing wall of the Battle Box was a favourite target. Shells pounded it relentlessly but, fortunately for those making use of the toilet facilities on the inside of the wall, didn't penetrate its fourteen feet of reinforced concrete.

That afternoon, Roger made his way back to Courtland, now in the direct line of fire, to salvage some clean clothing. As he was climbing the steps which led up from the pathway to headquarters, there was a violent explosion immediately in front of him as a mortar shell hit the retaining wall of the garden opposite. Immediately he felt a violent blow at the side of his head, which threw him backwards down the steps leaving him stunned and dazed in a heap at the bottom.

His first thought as he picked himself up was, "My God, I've been hit!" and, putting up his hand to probe the wound, which he was sure must be there, he was astonished to find no blood or any trace of injury. Then he realised that his steel helmet was lying some yards away behind him. When he picked it up, he found that the webbing strap on the right side of his head had been cut neatly through as if by a knife. A jagged piece of shrapnel which was on the ground, still too hot to pick up, had sliced through the strap.

Once again, his luck had held.

The day following this first spasm bombardment, a launch bearing a white flag was seen coming across the harbour. A totally unreasonable surge of hope flashed through them. Surely the Japanese were not coming across to call it a day.

They were not, of course. The launch contained a delegation demanding a conference with the General and Governor and to urge them to agree to the surrender of the colony and to save unnecessary bloodshed and loss of life, which, they said, would inevitably follow if the defenders were foolish as to continue a useless struggle which would, in any case, result in total defeat.

History does not record the General's reply, but from the sudden departure of the launch and the immediate resumption of the bombardment, his answer was, undoubtedly, a very dusty one. They settled down to a steady rain of shells and mortar bombs, which succeeded in knocking out the only remaining gun positions at Saiwan, covering the eastern end of the harbour and doing enormous damage in the town itself.

The next day saw a sudden lull in the attack, and everyone drew a breath of relief.

But it was to be short-lived, and, in the afternoon, it began again more intense than before. Taking advantage of the unusual quiet spell, Roger got along to Courtland for a couple of hours rest on his comfortable bed and a bite to eat when the shells started once more to pound the area around Command Headquarters. Even in the middle of the blitz in London, he had experienced nothing like the ferocity of this latest attack. Roger crouched down in Frank's old room in the basement rather than risk the exposure of his second-floor bedroom. Hungry as he was, he did not feel like eating.

This was just as well, for a mighty blast rocked the whole building, shattering the dining room window and filling the whole place with debris and the stench of cordite. Recovering from the shock of the explosion, he went upstairs to see from his window where the shell had landed.

He soon found out. It had come in through the outer wall of his room. It had exploded on the other side against the wall of Barney Crowley's room, reducing both to a shambles of broken bricks and mortar. Miraculously, however, the cupboard on which his radio and the blue flower vase and, best of all, the photograph of Daisy which she had sent a few weeks earlier were undamaged except for the glass shattered by the blast.

He took the photograph, removed the broken glass, dusted it off, and carefully put it inside his jacket. He knew he must never part from it again. It would protect him and bring him luck. He felt as though he would need it.

The intensive bombardment proved to be the prelude to the arrival of another delegation offering final terms for the surrender of the colony, after which the General must accept responsibility for defeat and the inevitable slaughter which must accompany it. Still, this last attempt proved no more successful than the first. The Japanese returned empty-handed and angry with General Maltby's defiant refusal to negotiate ringing in their ears.

Throughout this period, leaflets urging surrender continued to rain down from the attacking planes together with the bombs.

One, addressed to *"The Highest British Officer"* and showing a dishevelled collection of British soldiers picking their way through the rubble of the town and receiving a Nazi-type salute from an immaculate Japanese officer, bore the legend: *"In this war, you have no chance of victory. If you want to save your men and yourself it is best to stop resistance at once. We will guarantee your lives and your livings."*

Others addressed to the Indian troops were designed to incite them to mutiny. *"Attention!"* read one. *"Come. Indian soldiers. We treat you specially good"*, while another showed a be-turbanned, half-naked Indian on his hands and knees carrying a John Bull figure on his shoulders armed with stock-whip and belabouring a seemingly unresponsive elephant and its mahout. The caption for this flight of fancy read: *"Elephant is employed by you, and Englishman employs you. Elephant is given food by you, and you are given whip by Englishman. Elephant obeys you, and you are at the mercy of Englishman."*

These rather unsubtle psychological approaches would have been amusing except that they showed the mentality of the enemy who would, probably within a short time, be their captors and, quite possibly, their executioners.

The next few days passed with little sign of further action apart from the unceasing bombardment of the island from across the half-mile stretch of the harbour. During this time, they received the terrible news that the two battleships, Prince of Wales and Repulse, on patrol in the South China Sea, had been sunk by kamikaze planes crashing onto their decks with a full load of bombs. This seemed to be the final blow and extinguished any last possibility of relief from any quarter. They were on their own without a single ray of hope. They could only resolve to give as good an account of themselves as possible before their inevitable fate overtook them.

Perhaps the most galling realisation of all was that all the defenders' heavy artillery, based at the southern tip of the Stanley Peninsula, was pointing seawards. The hilly terrain to the north made it impossible for any fire to be brought on to the invader on the mainland since the elevation needed to clear the summit would land their shells well behind the Japanese positions.

As far as Roger was concerned, the only ray of comfort was that the plans for Daisy to come out to join him in the peace and security of Hong Kong had come to nothing.

Early next morning, the elderly members of the H.K.V.D.C.'s Dockyard Defence Corps, who had formed themselves into a small group known affectionately by one and all as the "Hughseliers", found their building in the middle of a host of khaki-clad Japanese who had come ashore by a fleet of sampans under cover of the smoke and who had silently surrounded the area undetected by the defenders.

Under the command of Mr Cock, the Chief Executive of the Dock and known affectionately by everyone as 'Cock of the Dock', the old men, many of them with experience from the First World War, put up a determined and gallant resistance but to no avail. The dock itself, essential to the invaders as a harbour for the offloading of men and material, was in the hands of the enemy.

The bravery of the old men and the stubbornness of their resistance may have earned the respect of their enemies. Thus they escaped the massacre which was the fate of nearly all those who fell into their hands during the battle.

But if the night landings on North Point had taken everyone by surprise, daylight revealed a much greater disaster.

Moving swiftly and silently through open country and avoiding roads and defended areas, the invaders had cut across scrubland and through Quarry Gap between Mount Parker and Mount Butler, bypassing the Middlesex Company Headquarters at Tytam Gap and had reached the southern coast at the head of Tytam Bay in Roger's old platoon area.

This manoeuvre had succeeded in cutting the island in two, isolating the whole eastern end and, by establishing a line from north to south, had effectively made a nonsense of the entire defence plan. The plan had relied on a coastal perimeter defence and a line of defensive positions stretching along the high ground from east to west, which could now be rolled up sideways almost unhindered.

The whole island's eastern end was now at the mercy of the invaders. Those unfortunate enough to find themselves cut off behind the enemy lines were the first to experience the fanaticism and brutality of the representatives of the Land of the Rising Sun.

Typical was the occupation of the field dressing station at Sai Wan at the island's eastern extremity. Here the invaders seized and raped the nurses whilst forcing the unarmed medical orderlies to dig a long, narrow trench by the side of which both men and women were forced to kneel with their heads bowed. Behind them, they heard the sound of swords being drawn from their scabbards.

After a word of command from the officer, the swords swept downwards, and the headless bodies toppled forward into the trench.

Among them was a medical orderly, Corporal Leitch, who heard the whistle of the descending sword and felt an instant of numbing pain before he, too, fell unconscious into the mass grave and was buried under the bodies of his companions.

Some time afterwards, it may have been hours or even days, Leitch had no way of telling – he regained consciousness – and clawed his way through the heap of corpses which covered him.

Dazed and as if in a dream, he crawled out and, on hands and knees, went blindly forward, unaware of the direction in which he was heading. All he could remember after this was an agony and an eternity of crawling and stumbling until, by some miracle, he found himself in friendly hands and being carried to a field hospital and, from there, to the military hospital at Bowen Road.

By some miracle, he had crawled unseen through the Japanese positions.

The sword which had been intended to behead him had struck against the top vertebra of his spine and had glanced upwards and, instead of severing the neck, had sliced the flesh at the base of his skull from the left ear to the right leaving a deep gash some ten inches long.

The heat of the bodies on top of him had caused the blood to coagulate, thus saving his life and substantiating his claim to be the only man alive to have been beheaded and have lived to tell the tale. Thenceforth, he called himself and was known by everyone as 'Swords-I-Hate-'Em' Leitch.

Down in the Battle Box, there was no panic, and everyone moved about his work quietly but with a numbing sense that the end could not be far away and each wondering what fate awaited them.

Suddenly a shot rang out from the command room used as headquarters by General Maltby and his senior staff officers. Frank and Roger stared at each other in horror. Had their commanding officer shot himself rather than surrender to the enemy? It was a moment that no one there would ever forget.

After an instant of silence and to their great relief, they heard the voice of the General who, from the tone and forcefulness of his remarks, was still very much alive and not a little angry. The shot had come from a careless orderly who had forgotten that he still had a round in the breach of his rifle and had caught the trigger against the corner of a desk.

Not inappropriately, the bullet had penetrated a copy of King's Regulations.

That afternoon with the Japanese making steady progress towards the hastily organised and woefully inadequate defence line, which had now been turned through an angle of ninety degrees, an order came through from the command room that the ciphers should be destroyed to prevent them falling into the enemy's hands and putting the security of the entire system at risk.

The melancholy task of breaking up the Type X machine fell to Roger. He sat with a hammer, chisel and screwdriver, smashing up into tiny fragments and completely dismantling each of the five drums to make sure that no single electrical connection remained intact. As he did so, he recalled how, only a few weeks before, when wrestling with a particularly intractable malfunction in the middle of the night, he had exclaimed: "When this bloody war is over, the first thing I am going to do is to smash this damned thing to smithereens."

As far as he was concerned, his war was all but over, and his wish was fulfilled, but not in the way he had hoped.

The only consolation was that his work underground in the Battle Box was now at an end, and he could, at least, get himself above ground and take his chance in the open air with his 'Odds and Sods'.

Chapter 16

Capitulation

The skilfully planned and brilliantly executed manoeuvre of the enemy had achieved its primary objective: ultimately frustrating the planned and carefully rehearsed strategy of defence and throwing the established lines of communication into chaos for a few vital hours, throwing the central command structure into confusion. Local commanders were left to respond to the defence of their area on a purely ad hoc basis using their initiative and operating independently, relying mainly on motorcycle dispatch riders for communications.

The nature of the terrain, consisting mainly of hilly, scrub-covered ground with no east/west roads apart from the main road along the waterfront in the north and that fringing the south coast, was all that the advancing Japanese could have wished.

Their strategy was to move swiftly and silently under cover of vegetation in small groups in a series of reconnaissance and fighting patrols rather than along a continuous front. Their ability to appear unexpectedly in widely separated locations succeeded in causing maximum confusion to the defenders, whose main objective was to occupy and hold the high points from which they might hope to detect the enemy's movements.

The fact that they could contain the advance for as long as they did despite their heavy casualties is a great tribute to their courage and determination.

The enemy's tactics also increased the difficulties faced by the defenders, whose training was based on the philosophy that there comes a point in an action when losses have become so heavy that any further attempt to advance can no longer be justified. In this case, the unit must consider itself pinned down until the opportunity arises to withdraw to avoid further casualties or until reinforcements reach them.

Not so the Japanese, in whom the belief had been instilled that there was no such situation as being pinned down and that surrender or retreat in the face of the enemy was unthinkable. To die in battle was to procure a passport to immortality.

It was no uncommon thing, therefore, when as occasionally happened during the battle, they found themselves at close quarters with a numerically superior force for those in the rear of the action to toss grenades into the melee killing friend and foe alike or to fight to the last man.

As a survivor from one such incident observed, this was no way to fight a war.

"It's not bloody well fair," he commented, "you can see that the little bastards don't play cricket!"

And so, by slow degrees, using the guerilla tactics at which they were so skilful, the enemy pressed forward until they were able to cut the vital north/south link between the town and the Stanley Peninsula through Wong Nei Cheong Gap.

Here, at Overbays House, a large building overlooking Repulse Bay, they cornered a group of forty or more of the defenders, which included Roger's friend 'Wally' Wallington, with whom he and Frank Austin had spent many carefree evenings playing Mah Jong only a week or so previously.

Having accepted the surrender of their captives and having seized their weapons, the Japanese herded them into a room on the first floor and closed the door, leaving their victims to ponder on their likely fate. Suddenly, the door was flung open, and half a dozen hand grenades were tossed into the room, where they exploded, reducing the tightly packed occupants to a pulp of blood and torn flesh.

A few minutes later, those who survived were finished off with the bayonet.

A tiny handful of those who had been close to the window when the grenades were thrown in had managed to break out and leap down into the garden below, where more were mown down by rifle and automatic fire, only one or two escaping through the bushes and surviving to tell the tale.

Wally was not among them.

On a hillside above Stanley Village, when the burial parties went out to bury the dead after the battle, they found the body of Willy Williamson, who had shared Roger's carriage when the train had left King's Cross Station not a year previously and who had received the news of the arrival of his baby with such delight. His horribly mutilated body had been tied to a length of rope fastened to a tree where he had obviously been used for bayonet practice.

Up on the catchment of the Tytam Reservoir, Lieutenant Scantlebury and the thin-faced, dark-haired Falconer who had also shared the carriage with him on the way out from England, advancing cautiously along a gully built to take stormwater into the reservoir, blundered into a group of the enemy and were mown down by a hail of automatic fire.

By December 21st, the enemy had reached the narrow neck of land leading to the Stanley Peninsula. At the southern tip of which was sited the heavy artillery, still pointing uselessly seaward, having been unable to contribute to the battle, which now provided a haven for civilians and the survivors of the gun positions at Saiwan. They had managed to get through the enemy-held areas and whose fortifications provided the opportunity for an organised desperate last stand.

The approach to the two-mile-long peninsula was occupied by the little settlement of Stanley Village. Here, one of the fiercest battles of the whole action took place.

Here, the cheerful Blackaby, who had been in Roger's carriage at King's Cross and invited the fury of Monkey Stewart after the route march, heard noises coming from a shed in the village near the seashore. Climbing onto the roof, he dropped a grenade down the chimney to flush out the intruders.

He had not seen a group of Japanese crouching down on the other side, who shot him down just as the grenade exploded. His companion, Ken Cole, another carriage occupant on that cold January day, escaped onto the beach where, from behind a large boulder, a group of the enemy leapt out, thrust their bayonets into him and left him for dead. Ken had a great gash on his left arm, which he had raised in front of his face as the blows were struck, opening up his arm from shoulder to wrist.

Undoubtedly this saved his life, and after the surrender, he was picked up nearly dead from loss of blood. He was taken back to hospital, where he survived to tell the tale with a weal matched only in size by that on Corporal Leitch's neck.

Many were not so lucky, and a group of the 'Odds and Sods' took shelter in the Repulse Bay Hotel, where Roger, Frank and Wally had enjoyed their glasses of iced beer after their swim at Repulse Bay, only to find that the building was already occupied by the enemy. A fierce gun battle occurred along the corridors like a second-rate Western movie, with attackers and defenders shooting from the doorways and dashing back into the bedrooms.

The survivors from this melee escaped through the windows and made their way back to safety across the hills.

On the other side of the island, the Japanese were making slow progress into the town through the narrow alleys of Wanchai to the fringe of the Happy Valley racecourse, where they took up their position on the far side of the arena in the grandstand building.

Captain Martin Weedon from the Middlesex Regiment acquired a Bofors anti-aircraft gun, ran it along the street and, using it as a field gun, blew the stand to matchwood, despatching its occupants to the care of whatever gods were assigned to look after them in the next life. For his daring exploit under intense fire, Martin was awarded a well-deserved Military Cross at the end of the war.

Street fighting is a slow and desperately dangerous proceeding. It was not helped by the large numbers of Fifth Columnists and Chinese agents recruited by the

Japanese, who sniped from the windows of the tenement flats at passers-by and made progress along the street. Some of the 'Odds and Sods', attempting to escort a group of Indian coolies employed as sweepers and cleaners by their regiments, marched at the head of their squad in the manner of true British sahibs, turning to find themselves alone. The Indian sweepers had not shared the military codes of their enemy and had disappeared into the back alleys of Wanchai.

Quite apart from the overwhelming odds stacked against them, the defenders were faced with another major problem.

The colony's water supply was obtained from several reservoirs, the most important of which, the Shing Mun, had fallen into Japanese hands on the first day of the battle. The others close to the Taikoo Docks, together with the vital Tytam Reservoir, had been captured immediately after the landing, leaving only two near Aberdeen Village by Bennet's Hill, and at Pok Fu Lam in the west, to the south of Victoria Peak in the defenders' hands.

The consequence was that a severe water shortage developed in the densely populated area of Victoria and drinking water became almost impossible to obtain, and increasing thirst became a real problem.

The local press continued to publish its reports on the situation, putting on the best gloss it could, mainly to reassure the civilian population and prevent a panic that would have further increased the defenders' problems.

The Hong Kong Sunday Herald on December 21st, by which time the battle for Stanley Village was in progress, still continued to speak optimistically of reports of relief on the way. It reported, *"an army of 100,000 Chinese troops advancing along six different routes towards the Shum Chun River"*. It went on: *"According to an official communique, a message has been received from General Yu Hon Mow that his forces are now within a very short distance of Hong Kong, and the relief of the garrison may be expected shortly."*

Such reports cheered everyone up even though no one believed them. By December 23rd, the tone had changed. In the Hong Kong Telegraph of that day, which proved to be its final edition, no mention was made of General Yu and his mythical army. The reports read: *"Fighting continues along the lines held yesterday"* and *"Briefly, the situation remains unchanged"*, but the desperate nature of the situation was revealed in a sinister footnote, which read: *"Small parties of our administrative, military personnel not normally equipped or trained for active combat but now fighting in advance posts have shown great determination and courage; in many cases beating off enemy units attempting to overrun their positions and, in other cases, fighting to the last. The value to operations of such fine resistance by such isolated parties cannot be over-estimated*." While recognising the contribution made by such 'Odds and Sods' groups as his was flattering, Roger knew that the end could not now be far away.

By Christmas Eve, the situation had become desperate, with pockets of Japanese appearing on the wooded slopes of the hills above Command Headquarters. A group of the 'Odds and Sods' was despatched to attempt to flush out one of these.

The plan of attack was a simple one. The patrol was to wear gym shoes to deaden the noise of their approach. With hand grenades hanging from their belts, they were to surround the position at dusk and, at a given signal, hurl their grenades into the enemy position, lying flat on their faces to avoid injury from the resulting shrapnel, and then to go in with bayonets to finish off any survivors.

The plan went well. Fortified with a ration of rum, the group crept forward in total silence, advanced through the undergrowth, and, guided by the subdued chatter of the enemy, surrounded the position. The whistle blew, the grenades were hurled, and the little group kissed the ground. Instead of the expected series of explosions, there was a deathly silence broken only, a few seconds later, by howls of rage from the Japanese who had been struck on various parts of their anatomy by lumps of metal and who appeared extremely discontented, loosing off their weapons in all directions.

The Quartermaster Sergeant who had issued the grenades had neglected to arm them with their fuses. The gallant squad, who had counted on winning this particular part of the war and a pile of medals, ran for their lives in a most inglorious retreat. Later that evening, when Roger and his little squad, having recovered from their ill-fated adventure, were back in their positions on the slopes around Headquarters, an intensive bombardment from across the harbour began to rake the area.

The attack took the form of an area shoot in which a row of shells worked its way along the top of the area and then moved down to the bottom, from where it returned to the top in a methodical and, fortunately, entirely predictable manner.

Roger, who was using a balcony of Command Headquarters as an observation post, and having had one or two narrow squeaks from shells landing on upper and lower floors, one of which caused a fire in the room below him, judged that the time was right for him to go to the rest of the squad, which was under the command of Corporal Ken Sawyer (his former clerk who had collected the seventeen copies of Lady Chatterley Lover) to see what casualties had occurred.

The men had dug a narrow slit trench and had got down into it for shelter from the nearest line of shell bursts. They had strict instructions that they were not to fire unless they had a clear target to aim at since to give away their position needlessly would be to invite disaster.

As he was going up the hill towards the position, there was a sudden burst of Bren gun fire from the trench. He was about to dash up to enquire the reason and to remonstrate with the gunner when a mortar shell landed inside the trench with a deafening explosion, reducing it to a gaping crater.

When he reached it, he found a pulp of blood and broken bodies and, by some miracle, Ken Sawyer standing in the middle of it all, dazed and speechless but without a scratch on him. It had been his lucky night.

Christmas Day dawned with a clear blue sky and the promise of a beautiful day to come. Roger thought of the Christmas of a year ago, which he had spent with Daisy, and could only imagine the agony of mind with which she would be greeting the new day in a few hours' time. She would have had, no doubt, a lurid, if optimistic, account of the battle from the radio and the press. He could feel, as he was to do again later at a moment of supreme danger, that she was very close to him in her prayers. The thought brought him a surge of nostalgia and comfort.

If, as seemed probable, this was to be his last day, he felt sure that she would be with him and that she would know beyond all doubt what had happened to him.

As the morning wore on and the sound of gunfire came ever nearer, such of the 'Odds and Sods' as could be gathered together agreed that they would go out and make a last stand, killing as many as they could of the enemy before they went under themselves.

At about half past three in the afternoon, they found themselves in a bend of the road leading down from Victoria Barracks into Wanchai. Everything had gone uncannily so quiet. Then, to their astonishment, a column of Japanese, five abreast, came marching up the road towards them.

They could scarcely believe their luck. Here, at last, was an actual target at which they could shoot – an enemy which they could actually see, and they opened fire with what weapons they had. The Japanese appeared at first not to be deterred by this obviously unexpected attack but, after a pause, took cover and began to retaliate.

At this moment, a motorcycle roared up behind him, and the Sergeant riding it tumbled off the machine.

"For God's sake, Sir, stop firing. These are the occupation forces coming to take over the town under the terms of the surrender!"

"Put this man under arrest," ordered Roger, who had been warned about the activities of Fifth Columnists.

"Don't be a damned fool," shouted the Sergeant, "I've got a written order from headquarters." And he produced a scrap of paper signed by Colonel Newnham saying that the garrison had surrendered at 3.17 p.m. and that all troops were to lay down their arms.

"If I were you, Sir," said the Sergeant, "I'd make myself scarce. I don't think you will be very popular with our Japanese friends".

They needed no second bidding and got themselves back to Headquarters as fast as their legs could carry them. This incident was to be repeated numerous times by similar groups over the next few hours. It was not until seven o'clock in the evening, four hours after the surrender, that the last shots were fired. Hong Kong was at peace under the control of its new masters.

On his return to Headquarters following the surrender, he fully expected to find the place swarming with the victorious Japanese. He was surprised to find everything quiet and pretty much as normal, the only difference being that there was no more noise of shelling. It appeared that one of the terms of the surrender had been that the Japanese would maintain their positions and that the defeated garrison, having laid down their arms, should be mustered in designated areas and await instructions from their captors.

Roger added his revolver to the growing pile of discarded weapons without any great sense of nostalgia. The damned thing was a .45 Colt with a kick like a mule which had nearly broken his wrist on the only occasion that he had fired it in anger, leaving him quite sure that the bullet had gone nowhere near its target. Fortunately, the sniper at whom it had been aimed had been equally inaccurate, and they had decided, consequently, to call the exchange off. They had gone their separate ways without further ado.

With nothing more to be done, he sat down in the late evening sunshine to ponder on the situation. Despite the general calm, the prospect was not a pretty one. One thing was clear. His days as a fighting soldier were over if they could ever have properly been said to have begun since, apart from the occasional skirmishes with the 'Odds and Sods', he had never had a real crack at the enemy. Still, he had always managed to be on the receiving end with no chance of hitting back.

His had been an inglorious war to which he had made pathetically little contribution. Indeed, he had done nothing heroic and was uncomfortably aware that his king and country could have gotten on equally well without him. Most of the time, under fire, he had been extremely frightened but had been comforted by being told by a seasoned warrior that the man who claimed not to have been frightened under such circumstances was either "a bloody fool or a bloody liar".

And now he was about to become a prisoner of a nation whose concept of the sanctity of human life had already been clearly demonstrated to be very different from his own. The future was uncertain in the extreme, and he regarded it with acute apprehension.

Back in the school house at Eridge, Daisy was sitting down to a family Christmas lunch with her father and mother and Roger's parents.

As the meal was being served, the news bulletin on the Home and Forces programme gave the first news of the surrender of Hong Kong, together with a lurid account of some of the atrocities suffered by the defeated garrison.

Daisy pushed her plate away, and they sat in silence, broken only by Roger's father achieving the most tactless remark of his whole lifetime by saying: "I wonder what my old boy is having for his dinner today."

It was the last straw. Daisy, who had borne the anxieties of the last few weeks with great courage, burst into tears and ran from the room.

At Command Headquarters, Major Jack Wood was optimistic.

"Don't worry, laddie," he said when they were discussing what was to become of them, "the Japanese will be anxious to prove how civilised they are and will be especially correct in their handling of officers. I don't doubt we shall be separated from the men, sent to Tokyo, and accommodated in a hotel for the rest of the war."

Roger received this news with incredulity and wondered how such an intelligent man could be so naive. Still, in the years when they were sharing the same misery, starvation and deprivation in the squalor of Shamshuipo and Argyll Street prison camps, he was tactful enough never to remind him of his optimistic pronouncement. Jack Wood was a cultured and civilised gentleman and expected the remainder of humanity to observe the same standards.

The following two days passed without developments of any sort; no Japanese appeared, and they sat around waiting for something to happen. By now, food was beginning to run short and with no water, they were both hungry and very thirsty.

There was, however, some food and water to be had at Aberdeen on the other side of the island. Roger was despatched with a truck to see what could be salvaged from there.

The trip was not without its hazards.

Although the enemy had made no further advance since the surrender, it was probable that isolated groups might be stationed along the road which went past the university and wound its way down the island's west coast to the little fishing village.

He had been warned that if he was stopped, he would offer no resistance, allow the Japanese to search both him and the truck, and help themselves to anything that took their fancy. This was needless advice since, with no weapon to defend himself, it was difficult to see how he could do anything other than submit without protest.

He left everything of value behind at headquarters. Because he had heard that one unfortunate chap wearing a ring when he was stopped had lost both the ring and the finger, he covered his own immovable wedding ring with sticking plaster. He bound up his hand as if it was injured.

The wisdom of this move was proved when, on the way to Aberdeen, the truck was stopped and, none too gently, he was subjected to a thorough search and, when nothing of value had been found, he was pushed back into the truck with nothing worse than a jab in the kidneys. He continued on his way with a gasp of relief. At least he saved his ring and, quite possibly, his finger.

At Aberdeen, he found flour, tinned meat and bread under the care of a small group of Punjabis squatting in the open around a fire covered by a sheet of iron on which they were cooking chapattis. The meal consisted of flat pancakes of flour and some dubious-looking meat which he shared gratefully with them, sitting cross-legged on the ground and doing his best to communicate with them in his basic and limited Urdu.

Loading the truck with supplies and some cans of water, he made his way back to headquarters without further incident and was received with more enthusiasm than he felt he deserved.

The following day they were warned that the Japanese were soon to occupy headquarters and that they were to be moved out to a Prisoner of War camp which had been prepared for them.

In view of this, they were advised that the next couple of hours were likely to be the last for them to be able to move about freely and that if any of them had access to any property that they wanted to take with them into prison now was the time to get it. So Roger made a beeline for Courtland to see what he could lay his hands on.

To his surprise, he found the faithful Ah Sing still living alone in his squat under the building and for the first time in his life, the little chap displayed real emotion.

"It very good, Master," he said, "now I come with you."

"You damned well won't," retorted Roger. "You keep as far away from white man as you can, and you never say you worked for Englishman."

Ah Sing made no reply but busied himself, packing what could be found of Roger's underwear and spare clothes into a suitcase while Roger hunted through the rubble of his room, selecting treasures to go with him into prison. It seemed to him that the most important possession would be books, so he packed his copy of Shakespeare, the New Testament, a copy of 'Wind in the Willows' which he had won as a school prize together with The House at Pooh Corner and E.V. Lucas's 'Sussex' together with a bundle of Daisy's letters. Into the case also went pencils, a fountain pen and two ink bottles.

The case was now full and very heavy. Putting it up onto his shoulder, he fished in his pocket, pulled out all the cash, which amounted to about fifty or sixty dollars, and pressed it into Ah Sing's hand.

"You have been very good, Ah Sing," he said. "You take money. You go away, and you not tell Japanese that you work for me. Savvy?"

The inscrutable mask descended once more over Ah Sing's face. "I come with you, Master. I carry case," he said doggedly and, taking the suitcase onto his own shoulder, marched off in the direction of headquarters.

"Come back!" shouted Roger. "Don't be a bloody fool. They will shoot you if they see you with me." He plodded on with Roger, shouting and cursing, trotting along behind him.

When they arrived, Command Headquarters seemed to be crawling with Japanese. Two of them ran up, snatched the case from Ah Sing, threw it at Roger and with a prod of a rifle butt in his back, pushed him forward onto his face.

As he picked himself up, he heard a shot and, looking round, he saw Ah Sing face downward on the ground, a dark stain spreading across the back of his blue cotton jacket.

He had paid the price of loyalty, and Roger was a prisoner in the hands of the Japanese.

Chapter 17

Humiliation

Roger was deeply distressed by the murder of Ah Sing, not only because he had developed a real liking for this impassive little man for whose death he had unwillingly been responsible, but because it was further proof, if this were needed after the brutal slaughter and torture of his friend Willy Williamson and the atrocity at the Sai Wan medical station, of the mentality of their captors, which boded ill for their treatment as prisoners in their hands.

The gruesome accounts from the burial parties despatched to locate and bury the dead in the days following the surrender spoke of the evidence of savage butchery and mutilation of the bloated and decaying corpses, which was their horrific task to identify and deal with. These still further fuelled anxiety for the future. The former Command Headquarters was one of three marshalling areas chosen by the Japanese for their prisoners, the other two being at North Point by the Taikoo Docks, where the landings on the island had taken place and where the buildings of the sugar factory offered temporary accommodation, and at Stanley Barracks on the southern tip of the peninsula which was later to become the civilian internment camp.

On the morning of December 30th, almost twelve months to the day from his farewell kiss to Daisy at King's Cross Station, the thousands of survivors were lined up five abreast in a long column stretching several hundreds of yards along the roadway around the perimeter.

Roger found himself standing by his friend Cheesewright from his regiment, who had been at Aldershot with him and survived the bombing of his five billets at Mill Hill. 'Cheeters' was a good chap to be alongside in a bad situation despite his apparent propensity to invite disaster. His taciturn face was always ready to break into a cheerful grin. He had an irrepressible sense of the ridiculous, even under the most trying circumstances. At that moment, he could not have chosen a better companion. He was badly in need of someone who could make him laugh.

Sitting between them in the rank was Captain Tommy Thompson of the Pay Corps nursing a circular brown paper parcel. He was cuddling it as affectionately as if it had been a baby.

"What have you got there?" demanded Cheesewright.

Thompson clutched the parcel to his bosom. "It's a Dundee cake," he said, "it came out from England by the last mail. My wife sent it out to me for Christmas."

Cheesewright's face assumed an expression of acute anxiety: "Well," he said, "I wouldn't let them see that if I were you."

"Why not?" enquired the luckless Thompson.

"Why not?" repeated Cheesewright, his voice fraught with concern. "Why not? My dear chap, I've never seen anything look more like some sort of bomb than that. If I were you, I'd get rid of it as soon as you can. If they see you with it, they won't stop to ask questions. They'll shoot you or behead you on the spot! You'll have to hide it somehow. You poor chap, I wouldn't be in your shoes for all the tea in China."

"How can I hide it?" asked the unhappy Thompson, his face turning a pale shade of green. "It's too big to put anywhere without it being seen, and I don't want to throw it away."

Cheesewright's face lit up as if struck with a brilliant idea: "I'll tell you what, old chap, Knocker and I will take the risk of helping you out, won't we, Knocker?"

"Of course," Roger replied without having any idea what it was all about, "what do you want me to do?"

"Why, we'll help him eat it, of course, and then he can throw away the tin before the little bastards see it." "Would you really?" said the gullible Thompson, greatly relieved. "I say, that's very decent of you."

And so, solemnly, the cake was cut into three generous portions, shared, and the tin thrown away. It was a bit of a dirty trick to play on the poor gullible chap, but Roger was extremely hungry at the time, not having had any real food for three days. It was the last piece of civilised nourishment he was to have for nearly four years. Never has a chunk of cake tasted so good before or since, nor has he ceased to feel a twinge of guilt and a surge of gratitude to the devious Cheesewright.

While they were squatting down finishing the last of Tommy Thompson's cake, he glanced down and saw, lying at his feet, a little cream-coloured rectangular ivory block about an inch square.

It was a Mah Jong tile, and, picking it up, he saw that it was a Green Dragon, the most prestigious piece in the whole set and worth more than all the others.

He put it in his pocket and held the talisman tightly in his clenched fist. Here was a clear token of good luck, and he felt a surge of confidence flood through him and knew that, as long as he had the little tile in his possession, he would survive whatever ordeal lay ahead.

(He was not wrong; the tile never left him throughout his years in prison.)

And now, at last, they were ordered to their feet, grasping a wild variety of bags, sacks, parcels and suitcases holding such possessions as they had managed to grab. The dishevelled, dirty and ragged column moved down the hill up which he had so often trudged on his way to work, encouraged to keep in line and keep together by guttural shouts and prods from the rifle butts of their captors.

"Just like a cage of bloody monkeys," said Cheesewright

The long column moved down past the cathedral and the Hong Kong Club to the waterfront near the Hong Kong and Shanghai Bank, on the top of which a large white flag of surrender was flying. Here they were halted in the little public park presided over by a statue of Queen Victoria, who gazed down upon the ragbag of her defeated subjects with an expression of disapproval which seemed clearly to say: "We are not in any way amused." It was a sentiment they all shared.

For an hour or so, they sat around in small groups ringed around by the rifles and bayonets of their guards, some smoking what was to be the last of their cigarettes, some catching up with lost sleep, a few dispiritedly playing cards, no one talking much and all alone with their private thoughts and fears.

At last, they were shouted to their feet and pushed into their ragged column of five abreast. Jack Wood was still optimistic: "Now you'll see, laddie, we are going to be taken aboard troopships to be to transported to Japan."

But he was wrong. At the Star Ferry Pier, they were hustled onto the ferry, packed like sardines and taken across to the Kowloon pier, where David Mather and his Indian troops had escaped, thanks to the 'Odds and Sods' a fortnight earlier.

Here they were lined up once more in front of the Peninsula Hotel, where they had been confronted with the gargantuan meal on the day of their arrival. Roger, the effects of Captain Thompson's cake having worn off, thought nostalgically of that monumental steak and, even more longingly, of the companions with whom he had shared the meal and some of whose decomposed bodies were now lying in shallow graves in various parts of the island.

More shouting and pushing from their guards, and they staggered to their feet and moved off around the corner of the hotel into Nathan Road - the four-mile-long straight stretch leading to Shamshuipo, which, it was now becoming clear, was to be their destination and to which the prisoners, some already exhausted, some clearly ill, nearly all loaded with kitbags, parcels and cases, were to be forced to walk on an afternoon of hot sunshine.

Their discomfort was to increase by onlookers press-ganged by the Japanese to line the pavements and jeer at their stricken and disgraced masters in their supreme act of losing 'face' - to oriental eyes, the ultimate disaster - and it was clear that this parade of their prisoners in front of the Chinese was designed to inflict the greatest possible humiliation upon their defeated enemy.

It was clear, however, that the sight of the weary staggering under their heavy loads was a source of inexpressible sorrow for many of the onlookers. Roger saw many bedraggled men, faces with tears running down them and some when the guards were not looking, with arms outstretched towards them. However, to show any sign of sympathy or compassion was to invite a jab from a rifle butt or a blow across the face. The crowd had been marshalled to witness the humiliation of the Westerners and the triumph of the victors, who were determined to extract the maximum of advantage from their victory. The Japanese had replaced the British as the master race, and no one must be in any doubt about it.

They had not gone far before some of the elderly began to show signs of exhaustion and distress. Days of hunger, thirst and sleeplessness were taking their toll. One by one, the heavy cases, bags, bedrolls and parcels were abandoned on the roadside to be swooped upon by the onlookers and carried off in triumph, leaving their owners bereft of their treasured possessions and, as it proved, even worse equipped for the ordeal which awaited them.

One kindly coolie pulling a rickshaw slipped into the column unseen by the guards. The little cart was piled high with bags and cases and accompanied the grateful prisoners for a blessed half mile until he was spotted by the Japanese. He and his rickshaw were thrown violently onto the pavement, where he received a brutal punching and kicking as his reward for his plucky action.

By now, Jack Wood, who was by no means a young man, was showing signs of real distress and, although he did not complain and stuck doggedly to his case, was clearly not going to stay the course. To have abandoned him at this critical moment was unthinkable, and even to have left him resting at the side of the road would have been to invite savage retribution or even, as they learned later, a sword thrust into the body, leaving the victim bleeding to death at the pavement's edge.

Much younger and fitter, Roger grabbed the case, and together, they staggered on. Jack, in a state of near collapse, stumbled to his knees from time to time. To avoid his condition being spotted by the guards, they got him into the centre of the rank where there was less chance of his being seen and beaten as so many of the others had been.

At long last, more dead than alive, and with aching legs and drooping shoulders, the weary column made their way through the gates and past the guard room onto the parade ground in front of Jubilee Buildings, which had been Roger's home for his first miserable weeks in Hong Kong.

Utterly exhausted and caring for nothing except that their ordeal was over, they collapsed onto the ground and, in spite of their acute hunger and thirst, fell asleep.

It was approaching evening, and he sat up to take stock of the situation. Clearly, the Japanese had made no preparation to receive their prisoners, and, in this initial stage at least, it was going to be a case of every man for himself.

As there seemed no prospect of food, the first priority was to find some sort of shelter for the night and, recollecting the old maxim that time spent in reconnaissance is never wasted, he got to his feet and started off to survey the possibilities, leaving Jack Wood still unconscious on the ground.

His first area of search was his old home in Jubilee Buildings, but he drew a complete blank here. The building had been badly bombed, and half of the roof and much of the upper floors had been destroyed. As he found to his dismay, the remainder had already been occupied by groups who had been quicker off the mark than he, and he cursed himself for having slept so long on the parade ground.

Having drawn a blank at Jubilee Buildings, he turned his attention to the huts on the other side of the entrance roadway. Here, a terrible sight confronted him. During the battle for Hong Kong Island, the local Chinese had descended on the camp like a swarm of locusts and every movable object - doors, windows, window frames, light fittings, taps, toilets, even, in some cases, roof timbers had been looted. The buildings were no more than empty shells standing on their bare concrete floors.

Uninhabitable though these were, they were already fully occupied by his fellow prisoners, many of whom, far more resourceful than he, were already collecting bits of timber, scraps of metal sheeting and even bent and rusty nails in an attempt to block up the gaping holes where the doors and windows had been and make some sort of living space.

He went over towards the former 5th/7th Rajput lines in a part of the barracks which he had never been in before. To his great joy, here he found an empty cell in what had obviously once been the officers' quarters.

It was a tiny room measuring no more than ten feet square in a compound which formed a sort of quadrangle under a verandah with a grass area in the middle, on the opposite side of which was a long building stripped of every item capable of being moved. It stood on the western extremity of the camp. It backed on to Typhoon Anchorage, where the sea-going junks took shelter in bad weather and formed an inlet between the main harbour and the mainland.

Although far from ideal as a residence, the little concrete cell seemed to offer the best of a very bad job, and he decided that a small room was likely to be more suitable than a larger area which would put them in company with a large number of inmates even if this were available.

His only problem was to ensure that it remained unoccupied until he could collect Major Wood from the parade ground since it was unthinkable that he should be left there to fend for himself.

Luckily, at that moment, he came across Ned Curran, a Major in the R.A.M.C whom he had met at one of Jack Wood's soirees and, although he had not taken to the man, who had a rather supercilious manner and had tended to treat a mere 2nd Lieutenant as something unworthy of his notice, was, nevertheless, like himself, in need of shelter. He agreed to hold the fort at the cell while Roger went in search of Major Wood, whom he found still on the parade ground and gazing around him with an expression of bewilderment and dismay.

"Thank God you've come back, laddie," he said. "I thought you had abandoned me, and I didn't know what I was going to do."

Roger looked down at his Commanding Officer, and a great surge of pity swept through him. Here was this educated and cultured man with his plump ruddy cheeks, long upper lip and deeply cleft chin, self-assured and competent, now gaunt and pale, completely exhausted and obviously quite incapable of coping with the situation or of looking after himself and desperately in need of help and reassurance.

"Don't worry," said Roger. "Things could be worse. I've found us a place of sorts and a friend of yours to share it with." And, picking up their loads, he took him by the arm and led him across the parade ground towards their new home.

When they arrived at the cell, they found that Major Curran had been joined by two more of his friends. Both were majors like himself, known to Jack Wood and the Royal Army Veterinary Corps members.

Pat Simpson was a big, round-faced man with a cheery grin and his companion, 'Wapas' Heane, was tall, thin and gaunt. Roger was to learn that his nickname came from his word of command to the Bombay Mule Corps, which had come under his care - 'Wapas' being the Urdu for 'About turn!', which he had used when inspecting his mules.

As they came into the tiny room, Roger detected disapproval on the faces of the three occupants. All three were large, and it was obvious that fitting five bodies into such a small space was going to stretch its accommodation to the limits. However, they spread their meagre possessions on the concrete floor as best they could, and Roger went off to see what he could forage. This was little enough, but he found a large empty can, and over at Jubilee Buildings, he came across a tap which was still running.

He also collected an armful of wood and returned in triumph. At least they could light a fire and boil the water, which no one in his right mind would have drunk otherwise, thirsty as they were. All five severely needed a wash and a drink when the water had cooled.

As he approached the room, he heard voices raised in apparent dispute: "There just isn't room for five," said one, and: "We are all senior officers, and he is just a bloody little subaltern," said another, whom he made out to be Wapas Heane.

Then came the angry voice of Jack Wood: "I don't give a damn what rank he is. Surely to God, rank doesn't count any more in this situation. In any case, he may have saved my life today. He is staying; if you don't like it, you can bloody well get out. He found the damned place and is more entitled to it than any of us. He stays!"

Roger came into the cell, and the discussion came to an abrupt end, no more being said about his occupancy of the room. Still, he sensed that, at the slightest opportunity, they would get rid of him.

The day was to come when he was to find that he had not been mistaken.

However, the fire was lit, the water boiled, and they washed, drank and hungrily shared a small bar of chocolate which Pat Simpson had found in his kit. By now, it was completely dark and, spreading out what coverings they had, they settled down for the night.

Roger lay on his sleeping bag and looked at the stars through the entrance. Tomorrow would be New Year's Eve, and he wondered what 1942 held in store, if they would survive to see another New Year in and how many more would pass before he was home once again with his wife, who, no doubt, was at this moment sharing the same thought. There was a bright moon well past its zenith. Before it set, it would be rising over Eridge, and somehow, the belief they would both be looking at it at the same time seemed to bring her closer to him.

He fumbled among his possessions in his case, found her photo and, holding it close, drifted off into an uneasy sleep.

Chapter 18

Shamshuipo

The days which followed their arrival in Shamshuipo were ones which they would never forget.

It would be nice to record that everyone reacted to their adversity with high-spirited courage and gallantry with self-denial, true comradeship and unselfishness. However, this would be very far from the truth.

These were a collection of weary, wretched, hungry, desperate men, many of whom had lost all feelings of self-esteem and were totally demoralised, much as he had seen survivors from Dunkirk whom he had helped to care for and organise back in the Aldershot days. Their first consideration was for their personal survival and welfare. They had been utterly defeated and humiliated, and it showed.

Nor, to be fair, could they be blamed for this. The Japanese had made no sort of provision for their welfare as demanded by civilised convention. Their captors had turned them loose into their prison without any facilities. There were no beds or bedding, no cooking facilities, no fuel, no toilet or sanitary provision, no protection from the weather other than the windowless and doorless huts and, worst of all, nothing to eat for the first few days. Seldom had Westerners been forced to endure such deprivation and hardship.

In vain did General Maltby, supported by his senior staff officers, plead with Colonel 'Fat Pig' Tokanaga, the camp commandant, for provision and facilities under the terms of the Geneva Convention. Such protests were brushed aside with the comment that although the Japanese government had signed the Geneva Convention, their parliament did not ratify it, and it did not apply to their prisoners.

Their view of the matter was that those responsible for the conduct of the battle had committed the unforgivable crime of allowing their men to surrender in the face of the enemy and, having done so, had failed to do the honourable thing by committing suicide as any right-minded officer should have done. They had lost 'face' in the most culpable fashion. Therefore, they were worthy of nothing but contempt and degradation; the more senior the rank, the greater their guilt and the humiliation they deserved. In any case, they argued, the prisoners were now subject to Japanese military law and could expect no more consideration than was accorded to their own troops.

For the first two days, no food of any kind was brought into the camp, and only those who had had the presence of mind to bring food with them were able to eat. When sacks of rice were brought in at last, there was no way of cooking it, and each group within the camp to whom it was issued were left to solve the problem as best they could.

In the case of their own compound, they were lucky to find an empty oil drum from which they were able to wrench off the top and wash it out as far as it was possible to do so. This was then filled with water and set on bricks over a fire made from scrap timber. No one had the slightest idea about how the stuff should be cooked. They took it in turns, stirring it around with a long pole until it resembled a sort of grey mud, which they wolfed down, trying to overcome the nausea caused by the lingering flavour of the petroleum oil.

The toilet facilities in the compound were non-existent. Still, by common consent, it was made an unacceptable misdemeanour to defecate or urinate on the ground. For this purpose, an old bucket was found and installed in the corner of the quadrangle and, when overflowing, was emptied through the wire fencing into the harbour.

It was all inexpressibly squalid, and even though the lack of solid food restricted bodily functions principally to urination, it needed little imagination to foresee that, unless there was a dramatic improvement in the situation, it would not be long before significant diseases beset them.

General Maltby and his senior officers did their best to improve the lot of their men and to restore their vanished morale. Meat, they argued, was an essential element of a Western diet and pleaded for a supply. The cynical response of Tokanaga and his henchmen was to drive a tiny piglet into the camp and watch with gleeful satisfaction the capers of their prisoners in trying to catch and kill it.

The poor little beast, screaming with terror, raced around the camp whilst its hungry pursuers chased and finally cornered it and, having done so, cut its throat and chopped it into tiny pieces, skin and all, after which it was boiled in a huge metal container with a vast quantity of water and shared out as fairly as possible.

Roger's portion was a tinful of the resulting liquid, which was floating a scrap of skin attached to a long black hair. He drank the hot liquid that retained some of the flavour of its owner's flesh and sucked the skin holding it by the piece of hair which, when the last vestige of taste had disappeared, he swallowed with the last unchewable fragment of the skin to which it was attached. It was not much of a meal, but it was the last piece of fresh meat he was to taste for more than three years.

Having had their fun, the Japanese sent no further supplies of meat into the camp.

All was not lost, however, because, after several days, the rumour spread that a sampan loaded with food would steal its way at dawn into the little boat slipway at the north-west corner of the camp and would accept Hong Kong dollars or items of value in payment.

Roger cursed his generosity in off-loading all his cash onto the luckless Ah Sing but, fortunately, all four of the majors still had a considerable amount of money with them and, as the trip to the boat slip was fraught with extreme danger since anyone seen by a sentry moving through the camp would most certainly receive a bullet for his pains, it was agreed that in exchange for his taking the risk, Roger should receive an equal share of the goodies.

Fortunately, the little compound was quite close to the slipway. By dawn, the moon had set so that the approach was in complete darkness since the Japanese had not yet installed the perimeter lights and barbed-wire fencing which later surrounded the camp and which would have made the safe approach to the place impossible.

The journey to the slipway was a most eerie experience. When he arrived, he found it already crowded with a dozen or so of his fellow prisoners standing in deathly silence.

Standing close to him, he recognised the dim shape of Captain Douglas Scriven, the doctor whom he had seen deliver the baby in Ice-House Street only a couple of months previously and who, although a civilian, was a member of the Hong Kong Volunteer Defence Corps and therefore, like all the remainder, had been taken into captivity.

To his surprise, Scriven seemed to be carrying a bulky bundle. Roger wondered vaguely why he had thought this necessary on such a risky mission. Any sort of communication being quite impossible, however, he was obliged to restrain his curiosity.

At last and in total silence, the sampan edged its way around into the slipway. One by one, the bargains were made in hushed whispers while a lookout for any approaching sentry was kept.

Roger's turn came, and he was able to buy a tin of corned beef, a packet of tea, some sugar, several tins of fruit and a tin of bamboo shoots. It seemed precious little to risk one's life for, and it had taken nearly two hours and most of the available cash, but at least it would keep them going for a day or so.

He had been almost the last in line at the sampan, and as he turned to go, he saw Scriven, who had lagged behind the rest, slip into the sampan without a word with his bundle and be rowed away noiselessly into the darkness. Roger, his mind now turned to the possibilities of escape, crept back on hands and knees to his little concrete cell and its still-sleeping occupants.

Although this tricky excursion was not the last of his visits to the sampan, slipping away silently into the night without a word of farewell, a handshake, or a gesture of good luck from anyone made a deep and lasting impression on his mind. He scribbled down on a grubby fragment of paper the following scrap of verse, which he entitled "Dawn Market":

'Down in the slipway, closely crammed, as lost souls wait in the docks of the damned
For Charon to ferry them over to hell
We wait, and the hours are as slow as the swell
On the face of the sea in a tropical calm,
As dead as the dirge of a funeral psalm.
We stand, and we wait while the stars grow dim
And the sampan steals under the breakwater's rim.
No sound as the packets are handed ashore
No market was ever as silent before –
It is done; creep away now, each one with his hoard
And the boat slips away with strange cargo aboard.'

The possibility of escaping was reinforced even more strongly a few days later when, one evening towards dusk, Colonel Ride, who, like Scriven, had been a civilian doctor in the colony and a friend of Jack Wood, appeared in the doorway of their cell.

They stared at him in disbelief. This was no ragged and dishevelled prisoner but an immaculately dressed civilian, his trousers smartly creased, the cut of his jacket faultless as were his collar and tie. He was wearing a new trilby hat, and in his hand, he carried a new leather briefcase, a well-turned-out city businessman.

"Just thought I'd drop in chaps to say goodbye," he said.

"And where the hell do you think you are going?" Simpson asked him.

"Why, back to England, of course. Any messages for the folks at home?" came the casual reply.

Obviously, the man was mad. "Poor chap," thought Roger. "He's obviously gone off his rocker." But, whatever the situation, he decided to humour him.

"Yes," he said, "you can give my love to my wife and tell her I'm O.K."

"Certainly, old chap," returned Ride. "You're Rothwell of the Middlesex, aren't you? Well," he continued, "I must be getting along. Aren't you going to wish me luck?"

"Of course!" they said, going along with what was so obviously a joke. They shook hands solemnly, wished him a safe journey and went along with him to the start of the roadway leading down to the camp entrance.

"I wouldn't come any farther," said Ride, "just stand and see the fun and, for God's sake, don't say a word or make a gesture or movement."

With that, he walked jauntily the two hundred yards or so down the middle of the road and with their hearts beginning to race, they watched him stroll casually down to the gateway, past the two sentries sitting on a bench in front of the guard room, who took not the slightest notice of this smartly dressed civilian - so clearly not one of the prisoners - leaving Roger and the others staring in utter disbelief as he disappeared into the dusk still walking calmly, his head up and looking straight in front of him marched unhesitatingly along Nathan Road to freedom.

The only explanation for this remarkable escape, which must surely rank as a supreme example of cold courage, was that Portuguese traders who, because of their neutrality, had visited the camp to organise business contacts and that the sentries had mistaken him for one of these because of his immaculate appearance or, just possibly, had not noticed him in the gloom of the evening.

Whatever the explanation, this daring exploit was rewarded with total success. Ride was smuggled aboard a junk which sailed him up the coast and into territory not occupied by the Japanese. Here, they learned after the war, he met up with his colleague Scriven, and together they established a centre at Kukong to pass through anyone lucky enough to escape through the underground of Chinese agents to Chungking and, from there, by air, home.

Ride was as good as his word. On 20th June, Daisy received a telegram from the War Office: "Information received that 2nd/Lt. R.S.Rothwell, the Middlesex Regiment, previously reported missing, is a Prisoner of War in Japanese hands."

Now their thoughts turned seriously to the possibility of escape. In the first instance, any attempt must be made before the Japanese had organised a reliable counting of their prisoners, which could now be delayed only for a few more days. General Maltby had already been warned that anyone caught attempting to escape would be brought back to camp and executed in front of his comrades. And anyone assisting would be similarly dealt with, and the whole camp would be severely punished.

The nearest safe haven was Chungking - some 850 miles away through country held by the Japanese or roving guerilla bands who were just as likely to murder the escapee for his boots. All this must be accomplished through an unknown country without money, maps or knowledge of the language and where the colour of their skins must immediately mark them out for attention.

Roger's doubts about the practicability of escaping were reinforced by the sudden and unexpected appearance of Ken Sawyer, his clerk at headquarters who had collected his seventeen copies of 'Lady Chatterley.'

At first, Sawyer was unrecognisable. Gone was the dapper, well-turned-out Corporal and, in his place, was a gaunt, ragged individual with a week's growth of beard who pumped his hand up and down, happy to have found him safe and uninjured. Roger was equally delighted to see him, having given him up for lost after the 'Odds and Sods' had dispersed following the incident at the time of the surrender. Sawyer, it appeared, had made a spirited attempt to escape the island immediately following the resignation. He went with two companions to the western end, and after some difficulty on the way, they had got hold of a small boat which, almost immediately after setting off, had developed a leak.

Unable to fix the boat and without a map, they were carried by the current away from the mainland, which they had hoped to reach. They landed on the island of Lantau, a large piece of land three times the size of Hong Kong.

On the way across in the darkness, they were joined by another boat, also leaking, manned by two American sailors, survivors from a cargo ship which had been sunk in the harbour. These two additional companions were something less than welcome since their only possessions appeared to be a large quantity of whisky and two revolvers.

They came ashore in total darkness, trying to suppress the Americans, who by this time were singing lustily and flourishing their revolvers.

Sawyer and his two companions had managed to get clear of them and made for the hills without too much time to spare since the rumpus caused by the drunken sailors attracted the attention of a local fishing village. The locals, fearful of being found harbouring escapees, handed them over to the Japanese, who, finding them in possession of revolvers, promptly executed them. A friendly Chinese with a few words of English told them: "Americans him caught", and drew his finger across his throat in a manner that left no doubt about their fate.

By now, the famished and weary Sawyer and the other two made their way down to a fishing village where they tried to negotiate the use of a sampan but merely succeeded in drawing attention to themselves, with the result that a passing gunboat was alerted. They were handed over and returned to Shamshuipo camp with nothing worse than a good deal of physical violence in traditional Japanese fashion.

Reflecting on all this, it became abundantly clear that unless one had substantial help from outside or a great deal of stamina, the chances of a successful escape bid were extraordinarily remote and that, on balance, one's chances of survival would be greater if one stayed put and hoped that release would come before death.

This philosophy was firmly endorsed by General Maltby, who let it be known that because of the likely retribution from the Japanese, who would regard escape as a severe loss of 'face' their side, and the very slim chances of success, an attempted escape should be discouraged even though it was the duty of every serving soldier to do so if possible.

However, despite all this, at the beginning of April, a group of four Hong Kong volunteers made the most daring and successful attempt three months into their captivity. This mission was led by Sergeant David Bosanquet together with three comrades: Douglas Clague, Lynton White and John Pearce. It was against all the odds and at a time when the Japanese were taking a careful count of numbers at a morning and evening parade, which usually lasted for a couple of hours and at which any discrepancy in numbers would be immediately discovered.

Their escape resulted from several weeks of careful planning, during which General Maltby and his Staff Officers, fearing repercussions on those left behind, did their best, without success, to dissuade them from making.

The escape was through a manhole at the western end of the parade ground, hidden by a patch of long grass and leading down into a stormwater drain which emptied into the harbour and was, at low tide, above water level.

Through their contacts on the other side of the wire, the party assembled a quantity of rations. These, together with clothing and other essentials, were sewn into groundsheets which they sledged along the tunnel provided by the underground drain and floated on a Li-lo mattress which they towed across the harbour to the mainland.

On the evening of the escape, groups of prisoners, few of whom knew exactly what was afoot since strict secrecy was an essential part of any escape plan but who were not averse to having a bit of fun at their captors' expense, were recruited to set up diversions in various parts of the camp to engage the attention of the patrolling sentries and keep them away from the manhole.

One group into which Roger was enlisted sat around on the parade ground at some distance from the manhole but close enough so that their noise could be heard by those in the drain and set up a sing-song which was accompanied by a piano accordion operated by Bosanquet's Battery Commander while an accomplice, lying flat and hidden by the long grass, held a piece of string attached to a brick which could be lowered into the drain.

The piano accordion striking up the tune 'Stormy Weather' and accompanied by the 'choir' singing lustily was a signal that danger was near. The brick would be lowered into the drain three times and knocked against the side. If all was well, the singers would give a raucous rendering of 'It's a Lovely Day Tomorrow' when the brick would be lowered once only, and the escapees knew that it was safe to go ahead.

The operation went like clockwork, and by the time darkness fell and the diversion parties were obliged to go back to their huts, the intrepid quartet were swimming across the narrow stretch of water which separated the camp from the mainland with the reassuring sounds of 'It's a Lovely Day' ringing in their ears.

Against all the odds, the likelihood of betrayal by Chinese agents of the Japanese, the colour of their skins which marked them out as Europeans, their rudimentary knowledge of Cantonese, the possibility of capture by guerilla bands, and the vast distance to be crossed, they succeeded in making contact with Scriven and Ride, who had now set up their escape organisation up-country and who passed them through friendly connections to Chungking and, eventually, home via India.

Although the four courageous men made good their escape, the sequel, as Maltby had predicted, had tragic consequences for those left behind.

The parade next morning revealed the discrepancy, and the entire camp was forced to stand to attention for twelve hours hatless in the oppressive heat while the Japanese made an inch-by-inch search to find either the missing men or some clue as to their escape route. The parades went on for days until, eventually, a groundsheet that had inadvertently been left behind in the drain was discovered, resulting in more punishment parades and interrogations.

John Pearce's brother, Alec, who was, of course, in on the conspiracy, was the immediate suspect and was taken out for interrogation, but despite his solitary confinement in a tiny, dark, filthy cell, torture, threats and vicious beatings had the courage and fortitude to hold his tongue and was eventually returned to the camp in a terrible physical state.

However, the discovery of initials on the groundsheet led to the rearrest of Alec and nine of his companions, none of whom had been positively implicated in the escape but who were apparently chosen at random.

What then happened was typical of the treatment meted out to those whom the Japanese suspected of involvement in some forbidden activity. The unfortunate men were stripped and thrown naked into tiny cells without light, ventilation, water or toilet facilities. Their imprisonment was punctuated by brutal interrogations during which they were forced to kneel naked on the concrete floor while they were made to study maps of possible escape routes in the hope that they would be tricked or frightened into giving helpful information. The fact that they had no notion of where the escapees had gone only made matters worse since, had they known, they would undoubtedly have given the information required since, under torture such as this, there comes a limit to what the human frame can stand. It is not a matter of courage or cowardice. A man can only endure so much, and ultimately, he has to break. One would betray one's closest friends to bring the agony to an end, and the victim can only pray that death will intervene before this point is reached.

By the end of January, the worst of the initial misery was over, and things began to become somewhat better organised and to improve a little. A ramshackle kitchen was set up in Jubilee Buildings, and the addition of a little vegetable, mainly slimy lettuce, chrysanthemum stalks and the green tops of sweet potato, which turned black when boiled and tasted bitter and totally unpalatable. This was added to the meagre ration of rice boiled into a grey, soggy mush.

Those who fared best were the Hong Kong volunteers, particularly the Portuguese who had friends or family still at large and those regular soldiers, mainly NCOs, who had had Chinese girlfriends in the town. Many of these were 'down-homers' and had been installed in flats where they kept house and faithfully looked after their benefactors during their off-duty periods.

The Portuguese wives were allowed to leave parcels of food and clothing for their husbands or sons at the guard room, although they, themselves, were no doubt suffering great hardship.

Many of the Chinese women showing great devotion and courage would walk up and down the roadway which ran along the eastern edge of the camp and, when the patrolling sentries were not looking, would dash across the road and throw little parcels to their men waiting by the wire.

To be caught doing so was to invite immediate arrest and, in some cases, execution. The roadway along which they walked led across the end of Nathan Road and down to the water's edge. There were occasions when the unfortunate benefactors would be driven at the point of the bayonet down to the water's edge and despatched with a thrust of the weapon into the stomach and toppled into the harbour, where they drowned. It was a common sight along the waterfront behind Jubilee Buildings to see their bloated corpses washing to and fro with the tide.

Most of these corpses disappeared within a day or so, but two men, their hands tied behind their backs, used to float every day into the slipway from where they were pushed back with poles into the harbour, their blackened bodies becoming increasingly bloated. In a ghoulish way, they became old friends and were christened Mutt and Jeff. One day, the pole pushing them out into the harbour penetrated their brittle skin, and the gas filling them and keeping them afloat came hissing out. They sank into the murky water and were not seen again.

Roger, fascinated by the courage of these Chinese, would go along to the camp's edge to watch the little dramas taking place and, with some of the other spectators, help to distract the attention of the patrolling sentries by creating a noisy diversion when it was obvious that a parcel was about to be thrown over the barbed wire.

On one occasion, however, a woman standing on the pavement held up a tiny baby towards the father standing behind the wire. A Japanese officer passing by seized the little scrap, and everyone held his breath, expecting to witness yet another atrocity. Looking around to ensure he was alone, the officer took the baby across the road and held it out for the father to hold for a few seconds before delivering it back to its mother. This was the first, but by no means the last, act of kindness they were to see from this particular little man.

Once, someone had managed to lift up the wire fencing and one of the Chinese members of the H.K.V.D.C., profiting from a diversion created by his friends, slipped under the wire, dashed across the road and disappeared among the blocks of tenement flats on the other side.

David Bosanquet, who was, even in those early days, making preparations for his escape and was anxious to have a good pair of boots, asked his friend Victor Nunes, who had a Portuguese wife still at liberty, to throw the boots over the wire to have them repaired. The same process returned the boots, perfectly restored three weeks later.

All this meant that some in the camp fared much better than others, and Roger remarked somewhat bitterly to Jack Wood as they stared at their unappetising tin of soggy grey rice that the wages of sin appeared to be tins of bully beef.

This state of affairs was, however, very short-lived. The fences were reinforced, lights installed at seventy-yard intervals around the entire perimeter, and the patrolling sentries reinforced so that the little dramas at the fence became increasingly infrequent.

His last visit to the perimeter came towards the end of January when he saw two Japanese Sergeants strolling along the road, obviously engaged in an argument about the techniques of swordplay. One drew his weapon and slashed it through the air in a sort of forehand sweep, while the other countered this manoeuvre with a powerful backhand drive.

An old Chinese woman was approaching them along the pavement, trying to make herself as inconspicuous as possible when the Sergeant grabbed her and, forcing her to her knees, swept her head from her shoulders in a single backhand sweep and, wiping the blood from the blade, sheathed his sword and, with a gesture which clearly said, "Well, you see what I mean," went on down the road, leaving the headless body on the pavement while the prisoners clawed at the wire screaming out their horror at this butchery.

Roger never went back to the eastern perimeter fence again.

Within days of their captivity, a regular muster was held twice a day at 8 a.m. and again in the evening, at which they were obliged to stand to attention in ranks of five while they were counted, any movement as the inspecting camp staff passed by being rewarded by a savage kick or a blow to the face.

These parades never lasted less than an hour and, frequently, as after Bosanquet's escape, lasted much longer and were extremely exhausting. Many would collapse as, hatless in the hot sun, they could no longer stand upright. They would then be smuggled into the middle rank, where they were less conspicuous and would be dragged up on their feet by their comrades when the inspecting party passed by.

They soon found that, under these conditions, it was better to come barefoot on parade; this seemed to insulate their bodies in some curious way from the worst effects of the heat.

By the beginning of February, the first effects of their extreme deprivation were beginning to show themselves. Dysentery was undoubtedly brought on by the vegetable matter they were forced to eat and began to spread through the camp from the polluted water supply. The first signs of Beri Beri, the swollen limbs and painful extremities, became apparent. What was cynically termed a hospital was opened in what had been the Rajput Officers' mess on the other side of the quadrangle from Roger's cell.

The 'hospital' consisted of a long bare room with a concrete floor on which the sick were stretched with no beds or coverings other than what they were lucky enough to have with them.

As someone ruefully commented, it was helpful as all the dying could be put together in one place, making it easier for them to be collected.

It was presided over by a Japanese medical officer – a sadistic devil named Saito, who, after the war, was hanged as a war criminal – who visited the place once a day and noted those likely to die before his next visit.

It was not long before Roger was to make a closer acquaintance with the hospital and its 'Doctor' Saito.

Chapter 19

Valley of the Shadow

One afternoon towards the end of the first week in February, Roger was sitting outside the little cell swallowing his ration of rice and fishing the bits of vegetable from the watery 'soup' in his tin when he started to feel a chill in his back despite the heat of the day. He moved out into the sunlight to get warm, but although the bright sun beat down on him, it seemed to have no power. He clambered to his feet, the coldness increased, and as he started to shiver, he beat his arms against his body without success. He was icy cold all over.

Then a dull throbbing started in the back of his skull; he felt his muscles contract into a spasm, and he began to shake uncontrollably. He recognised the symptoms from his experience of the previous June and guessed at the cause. He was starting an attack of malaria.

That night things got very much worse, and he realised that he was seriously ill and was sinking into a black pit of pain with his head bursting and his limbs beating a tattoo on the concrete floor.

Major Ned Curran, the doctor, examined him and, producing a thermometer, announced that his temperature was 105, that he had most likely got malaria and a bad attack at that.

"That settles it," he said, "he can't stay here. We must get him across to the hospital straight away."

It was useless for Jack Wood to plead for him to be left where he was and that he would look after him. Curran was adamant: "We've got no mosquito nets," he argued, "and we can't afford to risk getting infected ourselves, especially in our state of health."

And so Roger was carried across the quadrangle and dumped on the bare concrete floor of the hospital along with the rest, many of whom were suffering from dysentery and vomiting. Others, badly injured and in great pain from a working party which had been sent to Kai Tak to extend the airfield and who had been buried by a falling rock which had crushed their limbs and had killed others whose broken bodies, their eyes already glazing over, he had seen brought back into the camp the previous day.

That evening Saito, accompanied by his orderly and with one or two of the British doctors, who were allowed to accompany him but not permitted to take any action or volunteer any comment, followed disconsolately behind. The medics, although they did their best during the day, were without any drugs or equipment, not even an aspirin tablet, and so were powerless to do anything except diagnose the various complaints and give what reassurance they could.

The Japanese orderly was holding a thermometer which, as he went along the line of prostrate bodies on the floor, he pushed first into one mouth and then another without wiping the saliva from the bulb. Roger was still conscious enough to push the thermometer away when it was his turn and shut his mouth tightly. Still, all he received for his pains was a savage kick and a blow on the head, and so was forced to submit and allow the instrument to be thrust into his mouth.

Gradually he began to lose all sense of time or to know the difference between night and day, lapsing into a deep black well of discomfort and misery, too ill even to swallow the daily dose of Epsom salts, which was the only form of medication provided by the Japanese and which was not entirely appropriate for those suffering from dysentery.

Every so often, roughly on alternate days, as is the case with malignant tertian malaria, there would be an intermission following a violent outpouring of perspiration which left the body limp and dripping and such bedding as there was soaked with sweat. This gave a brief respite from the rigours which cramped the limbs and allowed a return to full consciousness.

On one such occasion, he was aware of further and even more sinister problems. He had been violently sick and had had acute diarrhoea.

The inside of his sleeping bag into which he had huddled was a stinking mess of the excrement which, he realised, was plastered all over his body. He had contracted dysentery on top of his malaria due to the infection on the thermometer bulb. His stomach was gripped by agonising pain, and he had lost control of his bowels.

He found, also, that he was no longer in the main room of the building but had been moved into a small back room no more than ten feet square, which, he was to learn later, was reserved for those expected to die and which was occupied by six or seven other bodies, all as ill as himself, packed so closely together that they had to crawl over each other to get to the doorway.

He clambered out of his sleeping bag with a vague idea of finding some water to wash himself down and to reach the lavatory bucket, which, he was told, was in the adjoining cell. Too weak to stand upright, he crawled on hands and knees across the recumbent forms that cursed him for disturbing them and reached the bucket in the next room.

The bucket was covered by two pieces of board separated from each other to allow an opening in the middle, but as he reached it, he found it to be occupied by a fellow sufferer who was slumped forward, his head on his knees. Roger waited in agony, his stomach cramped by the spasms of dysentery and the mess running uncontrollably from him.

At last, he could stand it no longer: "For Christ's sake, get off," he pleaded, "and let someone else have a turn!" The man neither replied nor moved, and, at last, in desperation, Roger gave him a weak shove. The man toppled over onto the concrete floor, stone dead.

One evening during one of his more lucid spells, the little Scottish doctor who, before the war had worked in a missionary station up-country and who did what he could to help with the aid of a bucket of water and a piece of rag, produced a red-coloured leaflet closely printed with Chinese writing, which had been dropped with many others from aircraft flying over the town. He knew a little about the characters and told them it was a leaflet claiming the capture of Singapore and victories in Java and Sumatra, which had given them complete mastery of Southeast Asia.

Up to this time, however faint the hope, they had tried to believe that, despite the absence of a viable American fleet following the disaster at Pearl Harbour and the sinking of the British battleships Prince of Wales and Repulse, there was a remote possibility that the invaders would be driven out of Malaya and that a rescue bid would be made to recapture Hong Kong.

Now even this last slender thread of hope had vanished, and, ill though he was, he realised that his imprisonment was likely to go on for years and that, in his present state, it was very unlikely that he would survive it. He turned his face to the wall against which he was lying and realised that death could not be far away.

There seemed to be no point in continuing the struggle for survival, and he found himself slipping once more into unconsciousness. As he did so, despite his illness, he felt a strange sensation of utter peace come over him; his mind seemed clear, and with a sensation akin to happiness, Roger felt that if this was the approach of death, he had nothing to fear from it. He sank into a calm and peaceful sleep.

He was aroused by a rough shaking, and, looking up, he found himself looking into the repulsive face of 'Doctor' Saito, bending over him and holding what seemed to be some sort of tape measure. He was speaking to the little missionary doctor.

"Tonight, this man will die," he said. He ran the tape over Roger's body, for what purpose he never knew since the dead were not provided with coffins by their captors, nor was it likely that he would have been accorded the dignity of a separate grave. However, this action may have saved his life since there arose a deep anger and a strong determination to survive.

"You bastard," he heard himself saying, "you won't bloody well get me. I'll cheat you yet."

Fortunately, perhaps, Saito either did not hear or understand what he was saying and, with a shrug, he moved on to the next body. The effort had taken the last of Roger's strength, and he sank back into unconsciousness.

Then, something happened that he would never be able to explain for the rest of his life. Opening his eyes, he saw with great clarity Daisy, his wife, leaning over him, her eyes filled with tears. "It's alright, love," she said, "I'm here, and I'll look after you. Please get well again and come home to me. For my sake, don't give up." And it seemed that he felt her hand on his forehead and her kiss on his lips.

Not for one moment doubting that this vision was a reality, he felt a deep peace settle upon him, and he sank once more into a calm and untroubled sleep. Once or twice more that night, he seemed to wake up to find her still standing there.

No doubt, he has often told himself since, logic and commonsense demand that this was just a part of his delirium and yet the vision was so clear, the face was her dear face and the voice he knew and loved so well that, deep down inside his consciousness, he believed and still believes that she was there and that she fought with Death and pulled him back from its grasp that night.

The strange thing was, as she has told him since, during the third week in February that year, she found herself overwhelmed by deep despair and a belief that she would never see him again. She prayed in desperation, as she had never prayed before, for his safe return to her.

Be it as it may, when he woke up the following day, although he was still very weak, the fever had left him, and he saw, standing by him, not Daisy but the little missionary doctor who had been brought down from inland China.

"Well, young man," he said, "I never expected to see you alive this morning. What's happened to you? It's a blessed miracle." Roger did not argue with him. He knew that the little man was right.

The doctor was holding a couple of little white pills in his hand.

"I got these from a Japanese officer who speaks English and, I believe, is a Christian," he said. "I think he is an interpreter. These are called M and B tablets, and they are magic. I don't know how he came by them, but if you can keep them down, I think they may well do the trick. Now swallow them, and if you bring them up, I might as well kill you now. They are the only ones I have left, and they mustn't be wasted."

Picking up a piece of an iron bar from the floor, with a grin, he flourished it over Roger's head. Roger did as he was told. He had had nothing to eat for more than a week, and the effort not to vomit was almost superhuman, but he managed it and settled down again to sleep.

The little doctor had been right, and as day followed, Roger's condition improved so much that, after two or three days, he could take food and was moved back into the central "ward". Here he learned that Jack Wood and Colonel Monkey Stewart had taken it in turns to watch over him all through the worst part of his illness and had given him up for lost.

It was now the beginning of March, and Roger, still weak and able to walk only with difficulty, was sent back to join the others in the cell, but here a rude shock awaited him. He found Jack and the other three in an angry dispute.

"I tell you he can't come back here," Curran said. "Good God, he's had malaria and dysentery, and heaven knows what else besides. It would be bloody suicide to let him back in here. I'm sorry for the lad, but we've got ourselves to think of. He's got to go." And taking Roger's bits of kit, he put them out on the verandah.

Now Jack Wood intervened. "He can't just be thrown out like this. Haven't you got any Christian heart in you? The lad's sick. He nearly died there, and we can't put him out without shelter. If he goes, then I go and be damned to you." And, so saying, he put his arm around Roger's shoulder. "It's alright, laddie," he said, "you just sit here on the verandah, don't worry, and I'll go and find us somewhere to live." And he went off towards Jubilee Buildings.

At that moment, someone came across from the hospital with a green bag on his arm. "I think this is yours, old man," he said. "I'm afraid it's in a bit of a state. We washed it out as best we could and put it over the wire to dry. Sorry, but we forgot it was there, and it's got a bit damaged."

Roger looked at his sleeping bag in dismay. It was snagged into a hundred little triangular slits where the tines of the barbed wire had torn it, and out of each hole poked a wisp of feathers.

"I say, you still look a bit peaky, old chap," commented his visitor. "Have you seen yourself recently?" He produced a bit of looking glass and handed it to him.

Roger looked into the glass and saw, staring back at him, a gaunt parchment-yellow face framed in a ragged black beard, the skin drawn tightly over the cheekbones and the eyes sunk deep into the skull. He handed the mirror back, filled with horror at what he had seen, and set about trying to push the little feathers back through the holes in the sleeping bag. Groping into the recesses of his kit where Ah Sing had thoughtfully packed a needle and some black thread, he set about the near-impossible task of repairing the bag. After a few fruitless attempts, the enormity of the undertaking overwhelmed him. For the first time in many years, he burst into tears.

After a while, Jack Wood returned: "It's alright, lad," he said, "I've found somewhere for us. It's not much of a place, I'm afraid, but it's better than nothing."

He picked up Roger's kit and his own valise and led the way across the parade ground to Jubilee Buildings. They climbed up to the top floor and into a room that had received a direct hit from a bomb. The floor was littered with debris from the explosion, and it was about as undesirable a residence as one could wish. The floor at one end was non-existent, and a gaping hole led down to the ground floor. The roof at this end was also missing, leaving the room open to the sky but with enough left on the other side to afford some protection from the elements.

It had, however, one important saving grace. Through the gaping hole where the window had been, there was a magnificent view over the harbour and the island; provided one did not look down, there was no sight of barbed wire or patrolling sentries.

In early October 1942, 1,800 of his fellow prisoners set sail in a Japanese cargo ship, the 'Lisbon Maru', bound for work camps in Japan.

The ship, which was also transporting some 2,000 Japanese troops, had no indication, in direct contravention of the Geneva Convention, that it was carrying Prisoners of War. It was torpedoed by an American submarine about a quarter of a mile away from a small island off the Chinese coast.

The prisoners were crammed so tightly into the hold of the vessel that they were not able to all lie down at the same time. Following a violent explosion, the lights went out, and they were all in pitch darkness.

Orders were given by Nimori, the Japanese officer in charge, for the hatch covers to be fastened down and covered with tarpaulins. The heat was intense, and the men were in danger of suffocation. Many were suffering from dysentery, and there was no water available. Their situation was desperate.

Colonel 'Monkey' Stewart, Roger's Commanding Officer who had watched over him during his illness, was among the prisoners and, as the senior British officer, he pleaded with Namori to allow the hatch covers to be opened to give his men a chance of escaping. Namori's response was to pour a bucket of urine down into the hold onto their heads. The ship was clearly sinking rapidly, and 'Monkey' called for volunteers to smash a way through the hatch.

Lieutenant Potter, together with Lieutenant Hamilton of the Royal Scots standing on the backs of their comrades, succeeded in breaking through and making an opening for the rest to clamber onto the deck.

They were immediately shot and killed by the guards, who also fired down onto the prisoners below. Undeterred, the survivors rushed the gap and, climbing over their dead comrades, made their way onto the deck and leapt into the sea, where many drowned or were machine-gunned in the water. The gallant Potter had found his longed-for passage to the sea.

Two of his Sergeants seized Colonel Stewart, despite his orders to let him stay and perish with his men, who, like him, could not swim. They succeeded in keeping him afloat until they reached the island. Those strong enough swam to the island, where they were picked up and taken on to Japan.

He was taken to a prison camp where, typically, he informed the camp commandant that he would see that those responsible for the atrocity - one of the worst of the war - would be hanged when the war was over!

He was immediately taken away to a prison 'hospital' where, six weeks later, he was reported to have 'died from pneumonia'. 'Monkey' Stewart was a true Diehard, and he died like one.

Jack Wood and Roger lived in their airy accommodation with a sea view for the next two months. Although there was no improvement either in food or in the brutality of their guards, they managed to cope reasonably well.

It was to be several weeks before Roger's strength returned, and he was able to walk any distance. His recovery was not helped by the interminable muster parades, often lasting for four or five hours at a time, which sapped what remained of his energy.

Once, when the parade had lasted most of the day, his legs would no longer support him, and he was dragged back into the middle row by his friends, who pulled him to his feet and held him upright when the inspecting party walked down the line.

One of the British officers, a Major in the RASC, known to his comrades as 'Queenie', had allowed himself to be persuaded by the camp commandant, much to the disgust of his fellow prisoners, to act as a liaison officer and had been provided with an arm-band bearing Japanese characters as a badge of rank. He also enjoyed many other privileges, such as accommodation in the prison staff building where he shared their food and, it was rumoured, the services of their 'comfort' women.

Part of his duty was to keep his ear to the ground and pass on any scraps of information concerning plans or pieces of conversation which might come his way, a duty which he performed with zeal and which resulted in the death of a number of his comrades. He was also expected to accompany the inspecting officer on muster parades.

'Queenie', observing the apparent ease with which the Japanese had captured Hong Kong, Malaya and the East Indies, had come to the conclusion, not altogether unreasonable at the time, that Britain was facing defeat in the Far East as well as in Europe and that it would be well for him to come out on the winning side.

On one occasion, during one of the 'punishment' parades not long after Roger's return from the hospital, as the inspecting party passed by Roger's part of the line, this gallant officer pointed out to the guard commander that Roger, still very weak and being supported in the middle rank by his friends, was not standing to attention as required and obligingly held the inspecting officer's sword whilst the statutory beating was administered with the buckle end of the commander's belt. Although this was a minor example of Queenie's treachery, it bred in him a deep loathing of this cowardly man willing to sell his comrades in exchange for the enemy's favours.

Needless to say, at the end of their incarceration, 'Queenie' was immediately placed under close arrest and, on his return to England, was tried by court martial for treason.

Unfortunately, all the specimen charges carelessly selected by the Judge Advocate General's department had occurred more than three years before the date of the trial and were not, therefore, admissible as evidence. He walked from the court a free man leaving those who had suffered at his hands and who, like Roger, had been part of the guard mounted by the officers at the end of the war to prevent the other ranks, who had suffered most at his hands, from gaining access to him, regretting that they had obeyed their senior officer's orders to let justice take its course and not to put the rope which they had prepared for him to its appropriate use.

Although Roger's recovery was progressing slowly, Jack Wood's condition was steadily deteriorating. He had developed a painful fistula which made any bowel motion an excruciating agony, and this was further increased by his lying on the concrete floor. Jack also found that drinking hot liquid eased the pain. It was clear that if some means of boiling water could be found, it would not only ease his pain but also enable him to bring relief to the affected parts.

It was then that, for the first time, luck was on their side. Rummaging through the rubble in the adjoining room from which the entire roof was missing, Roger came across a rusty old army wire mattress with all its springs still intact. This was an absolute godsend, and he was able to prop it up on square pieces of rubble and make something approaching a real bed for his friend. There is no doubt that this lucky find, which Jack used for the remaining three years of his imprisonment, saved his reason and, so Jack believed, his life.

A second piece of good luck occurred when he spotted two pieces of electric cable poking through the wall where there had been a power point. He was absolutely sure that all the electricity supply to the building had been destroyed during the battle, so he joined the two wires together.

There was immediately a brilliant blue flash, a bang, and he was thrown backwards across the room. When the Japanese installed the perimeter lights, electricity was restored to the building. Clearly, Jubilee Buildings had remained connected to the main supply.

He remembered reading in a book entitled 'A Hundred Things a Boy Can Make' how to construct a primitive immersion heater. It consisted of a metal container to the rim of which the neutral wire was attached and, from a piece of wood laid across the top of the tin, a piece of metal connected to the live wire was suspended into the water. When all this had been achieved, the current switched on, and the water was boiled.

He found a large tin, a piece of wood and a rusty nail with which he secured another sliver of tin to the wooden cross-piece.

The next part involved stripping enough of the insulated cable from the wall to allow him to fix one wire to the tin and hold the other against the central piece of metal by means of its insulating cover without electrocuting himself. Holding the wire gingerly with a dry rag, he held his breath and waited.

Almost immediately, tiny bubbles moved across from the metal to the side of the tin and within less than two minutes, the water was bubbling away merrily. They were in business!

All of a sudden, life took on a much brighter aspect. They could now wash and shave in hot water, and this made life infinitely more bearable. Roger's clandestine visits to the slipway had also resulted in the acquisition of a quantity of Chinese tea - useless up to that moment, but now manna from heaven. They were able to enjoy the luxury of hot tea at the end of a dreary day, and, most important of all, Jack Wood was able to apply the treatment to ease the pain of his fistula.

Their new facility was not without its problems. The manufacture of water heaters became a cottage industry, and the proliferation of them caused frequent disruption of the supply resulting from blown fuses. This was overcome through the kindly offices of the Royal Engineers, who located the fuse boxes and equipped them with fuses of stout wire which not even a lightning flash would have melted.

The consequent blowing of the main fuses in the Japanese Headquarters persuaded them that all was not well. A sudden raid uncovered the cause, resulting in a series of beatings and extremely long muster parades by way of general retribution, and the heaters disappeared for good.

By now, it was the middle of April, and although life was beginning to settle down to a more organised routine, their days at Shamshuipo were drawing to a close. A new chapter was about to begin.

Chapter 20

Argyle Street

Whether as a direct result of the discovery of the water heaters or the escape of Bosanquet and his friends in the middle of April, or because the Japanese felt that there was an advantage to be gained by segregating the officers from the other ranks was not clear but, at the beginning of May, the occupants of Jubilee Buildings, by now mainly officers, were transferred to a new camp at Argyle Street on the other side of Kowloon and close to the Kai Tak airfield.

This haphazard method of selection resulted in many officers, including the renegade 'Queenie', being left behind in Shamshuipo while a number of other ranks were included in the party, which numbered some 600.

On this occasion, the Japanese provided a lorry to carry any heavy possessions and, in the scramble which then ensued to pile as much as possible onto the ramshackle vehicle, Roger was lucky enough to load on Jack Wood's wire mattress.

The long march of some three and a half miles with only one short break proved extremely exhausting for many who were now suffering from malnutrition and beri-beri. All were weak and emaciated, and what would, under other circumstances, have been no more than a typical route march proved a well-nigh intolerable burden.

Argyle Street Camp, styled by the Japanese as "Camp N", was on a square platform of land raised above the level of Argyle Street, which was a main east-west thoroughfare to the north of the town terminating at Kai Tak and occupying a roughly rectangular area of some 800 square yards overlooking barren stony ground to the south and west, a built-up area to the north and dominated from the east by a tall tenement block which housed the Japanese headquarters, the verandah of which was on a level with the camp parade ground.

The camp, which had initially housed refugees from mainland China, contained a collection of fifteen wooden huts arranged in three rows of five. As with the buildings in Shamshuipo, they had concrete floors and had been stripped of doors, windows and fittings so that physical conditions were no better than their previous quarters and were even more cramped.

Two of the huts, at the end of the outer rows, had housed the original camp staff and were separated from the others by wire fences, and each had a little garden with a lawn. One, which they christened 'Flagstaff House', was used to accommodate General Maltby and his senior officers. The other, nicknamed 'The Aquarium', was occupied by Captain Collinson, the Naval Commodore, and his senior officers.

One hut served as a cookhouse and another as a hospital so that the remainder of the prisoners were crowded into twelve huts with about fifty in each, packed so close together that their room for movement was practically nil. Life was very uncomfortable indeed, particularly as the former occupants had been less than particular over sanitation and hygiene, leaving the huts infested with bed bugs, which lived in the roof by day and on the prisoners by night.

The camp was surrounded by a ten-foot wire-mesh fence, inside of which were a triple layer of dannert barbed wire and a high-voltage electric fence so that escape through this barrier would have been well-nigh impossible and, indeed, throughout the time of its occupation, no one attempted to get away.

'Fat Pig' Tokunaga was determined that there would be no further escapes. The compound was guarded by seven watch towers occupied night and day by armed sentries. It was flood-lit at night, so the prisoners were under constant observation.

The approach road to the camp was up a steep incline with double wire-mesh gates and protected by the guard room in the space between them.

On the other side of Argyle Street was a camp housing the Indian prisoners with whom any form of communication was forbidden on pain of instant execution, but since it was in earshot, the Muslim Mulveh conducting evening prayers was able to relay a daily bulletin in a loud voice in Urdu, of which the Japanese were ignorant, to their 'Sahibs' across the road, who were thus able to keep an accurate track of their illness, suffering and ill-treatment. However, they were not able to respond even by sign language.

The Indian troops were equally as malnourished and disease-ridden as their British comrades but were regarded by their captors as possible fodder for the renegade Indian army being assembled in Burma under the command of a former native Indian Army officer, Subhas Chandra Bose, and were, in consequence, wooed by promises of good food and treatment if they would agree to be transferred.

Similar pressure was exerted on the Indian Army officers. It is greatly to the credit of both these and their men that, despite lavish promises of brutal torture, very few were tempted away when these failed.

One officer in particular, Lieutenant Ansari of the Rajput Regiment, whom the Japanese tried to recruit as leader of a break-away group, endured indescribable torture and, when this failed to break his resolve, was tied to a wire army mattress and slowly roasted alive, his death coming as a merciful release.

Although neither food, accommodation, nor general brutality were any improvement on Shamshuipo, Argyle Street had one tremendous advantage in that it had two Asiatic-type 'squat' toilets connected to a sewer and also a primitive shower-bath so that, although these had to be shared between 600 men, the problem of keeping clean was very much more manageable. As a result, the incidence of dirt-related disease was considerably less than it had previously been. Although serious illness was frequent, the camp escaped the great diphtheria epidemic that struck Shamshuipo in August 1942 and killed more than two hundred men in a couple of weeks.

The bodies of these victims were either buried or cremated on open funeral pyres on the rough ground west of the camp over which the sickening sweet stench of the burning flesh wafted in great waves.

The great advantage of Argyle Street, however, was that being on a much smaller scale than Shamshuipo, it was possible to develop a better-organised community. Although officially, no group larger than five in number was allowed to congregate during the daytime, a quite remarkable organisation of classes and activities was able to develop.

At one time in early 1943, Roger recorded a total of sixty-three classes in operation in the week, covering no less than thirty-seven different subjects ranging from English literature and Oriental philosophy and a variety of European and Oriental languages - French, Spanish, German, Portuguese, Russian, Cantonese, Urdu and Japanese - engineering, economics and medicine, to Science and mathematics.

The 'Argyle University' had forty 'lecturers' and covered a total of 135 'sessions' each week. The groups were necessarily small, and lessons were frequently interrupted by the activities of the sentries. Still, their vital role was that they helped to avoid the soul-searing boredom which, with the perpetual hunger, was almost the greatest enemy of all. Achievement was of no importance; it was the effort which mattered.

Roger was responsible for four of these 'classes': one in elementary, one in intermediate and two in advanced French. He included among his students a Major General, two Brigadiers and a Colonel, along with a selection of lesser ranks, including Corporals and Privates. Rank had ceased to matter.

The lessons were, of necessity, oral, although the 'acquisition' of a considerable quantity of official Japanese paper and writing materials resulting from the activities of various working parties in the Japanese headquarters building enabled a certain amount of written work to be done.

By no means all the attainment was at a high academic level. One of Roger's 'students', George Gray, was well advanced in years and had the watery pale blue eyes of an old man. As far as Roger could ascertain, he was a regular attendee at the elementary French class and never retained anything from his previous lessons. George did, however, know the French for seventy-seven. So, at the end of each lesson, Roger, from the kindness of his heart, would say: "Well, George - seventy-seven?", at which a happy smile would spread across George's wrinkled old face, and he would reply promptly: "Soixante dix-sept," which signalled the end of the session for that day.

After several weeks of this, Roger was prompted to ask: "Why is it that the only word of French I have ever taught you is soixante dix-sept?" A twinkle came into George's eye: "Ah well, you see," he said, "you didn't. I served in a battery of French 77-millimetre guns during the First World War, and that's how I know it, couldn't ever forget it, see?" Roger was suitably humbled.

As a concession, the Japanese allowed a weekly service taken by Padre Gordon Bennett. This was an event to which everyone looked forward as the high spot of the week, and the tiny garden by the 'Aquarium' was always crowded. The service consisted of little more than a couple of prayers and a few words from the padre. Still, it brought the whole camp closer to each other and to their loved ones who were never far from their thoughts, especially as no news of them had been received since their captivity and, even then, his first letter from Daisy posted in July 1942 did not arrive until the end of March the following year.

Curiously enough, permission was given for plays to be produced, always provided that, during rehearsals, no more than five met at the same time, which demanded great ingenuity on the part of the producer with the cast divided into separate groups, each at a discreet distance from the others.

The first of these extraordinary performances 'staged' on September 19th, 1942 consisted of the murder scene from Julius Caesar and two scenes from 'A Midsummer Night's Dream', which, as there was only Roger's copy of Shakespeare available, resulted in a not inconsiderable amount of 'ad libbing' and this, together with a bizarre array of 'costumes' scrounged from the limited wardrobes of the prisoners, contributed to what must rank as the most unorthodox rendering of the Bard ever staged. What the performance lacked in professionalism was more than compensated by its enthusiastic reception from its captive audience, and even the camp staff, who did not understand a word of what it was all about and who sat with mouths agape, seemed to sense that this was an occasion worthy of note and, quite exceptionally, a small ration of sweet potatoes was added to the menu the following day as a reward.

Thus encouraged, the 'Argyle Dramatic Society' launched a more ambitious production, which was a performance of John Masefield's dramatic poem 'Good

Friday', of which someone had a copy, which was passed from hand to hand among the cast. The moving piece was performed in a space between the huts by the full moon's light on Good Friday evening, 1943.

The capture of the remains of the garrison as a whole rather than piecemeal during a long campaign proved to have been another advantage since all the experience and skills of all branches of the Service Padres, Doctors, Engineers, and Signals were all together in the same place. This gave them a much greater chance of survival than those unfortunates who were sent into the jungles to build the notorious Burma Railway and who, being constantly on the move, were not able to get themselves organised in anything like the same way as those in Hong Kong or in the Changi prison in Singapore.

Between them, they represented an amazing range of experience and expertise. Major, the Lord Merthyr, was skilled at boot repair and the manufacture of wooden clogs. Stanley Jarvis, with the aid of thread and some mysterious sticky concoction, transformed purloined paper into books of such strength that they were still in serviceable condition fifty years after their manufacture, whilst others patched, renovated and adapted tattered clothing into practical garments, carved chessmen from scrap wood or manufactured playing cards.

These craftsmen were a godsend to Roger, who contributed the tattered remains of his shirt to cover a scrapbook and diary for Daisy and others. Stanley's books were used to record lectures given and a dictionary of French idiomatic usage, which he compiled over a period of two years in collaboration with an accomplished linguist and new-found buddy, Albert Haines, who was responsible for the Spanish classes in the Argyle Street University.

The possession of written matter was strictly forbidden, and their discovery would undoubtedly have led to violent retribution, so their concealment was a matter of absolute necessity.

The only topic never written down was the news of the outside world, which came from the radio skilfully built by the signals people from components stolen from the Japanese Headquarters and buried in a biscuit tin between the huts. The radio was tuned to New Delhi, and they received the news of the war's progress, comparing this with the bulletins issued by the Japanese in an English language propaganda publication, 'The Hong Kong News', and by their readers as 'Comic Cuts'.

The enthusiasm of its editor occasionally ran away with him as when, on November 13th, 1943, an "attempted raid by 200 American planes on Rabaul" was reported as "resulting in 201 of the enemy being destroyed by our ground and fighter defence forces".

Occasionally the paper's delighted readers were regaled by Japanese jokes, of which the following was typical: "An elephant was standing on a bridge when it was joined by a flea. The elephant said to the flea: 'Please get off the bridge; it will not stand the weight of both of us.'" Just in case the stupid British were unable to grasp the oriental of the story, the editor added the footnote: "The humour of this story will be better appreciated if the relative sizes of an elephant and a flea are taken into account", which did, indeed, make the whole joke genuinely hilarious.

All in all, the Hong Kong News was a great asset, and its appearance was eagerly awaited. Quite apart from anything else, it was beneficial as much-needed toilet paper.

The couple of days' respite between the surrender and the move into captivity proved to have been a tremendous advantage to them since they had been able to bring with them into camp an extraordinary variety of personal possessions, including books, musical instruments, pens, ink and pencils, even a couple of portable typewriters. Most of these had to be concealed except that books were allowed, provided they had been vetted and stamped as 'harmless' by the camp staff. Roger often wondered what the interpreters had made of his copies of 'Winnie the Pooh' and 'Wind in the Willows'.

Playing cards were also available, although these were very limited and, despite careful handling, eventually became almost indecipherable. A good deal of ingenuity and artistic expertise was expended in manufacturing new packs.

On one memorable occasion, a tin of bully beef was 'found' by a working party in the headquarters. After a solemn conference about its fate, a knock-out bridge contest was ordained to decide on the winners.

The competition, which involved the whole camp, lasted for more than three weeks, and as it drew towards its close, excitement was at a fever pitch. Although Roger had no real skill at the game, his luck did not desert him. The great day arrived when he and his partner, Jack Wood, sat in the middle of the parade ground surrounded by the entire camp and a ring of armed sentries to play the final of the contest.

Having lost the first of the three rubbers, they scraped home by a handful of points to win the second. Honours in the third were even, and all depended on the final hand. The silence was electric. Roger picked up his cards from the dusty surface and, unable to believe his luck, saw the entire suit of diamonds in his hand. He will never forget the moment of triumph when following his bid of "seven diamonds", which was promptly doubled by his opponents and redoubled by Jack, he put the cards face upwards on the parade ground, and the coveted tin of 'bully' was theirs.

Following this extraordinary piece of luck, the odds against which were several million to one, Roger took an oath that he would never again play contract bridge, and he has never done so through the fifty years which now separate him from that memorable day.

Never has bully beef tasted so good, nor when he eats it now does he fail to recall that moment and which, apart from his reunion with Daisy, if given the opportunity to have one moment of life to live over again, he would choose without hesitation.

Sharing their prison with them was a collection of four or five dogs who eked out a meagre existence on scraps of rice and vegetable supplemented by what vermin they could catch. These dogs were worshipped by everyone since they represented a link with a previous life and a hope that one day this could be resumed.

Two of the dogs were thoroughbred Sidney Silkies and belonged to the General, having been brought into captivity with him at the time of the surrender, and lived in splendid isolation in 'Flagstaff House', having little to do with their less well-bred companions.

Bo'sun was a tremendous black lollopy thing with more than a hint of Labrador about him. He was as daft as a brush and would fraternise with the enemy as eagerly as with his companions, although on one occasion, a sentry, mistaking his friendly approaches as a prelude to an attack, thrust his bayonet into his vitals, which, had it not been for the prompt intervention of Doctor 'Woody' Woodward and the sacrifice of some carefully husbanded suture, would have been the end of him.

But by far and away, the star of the tiny pack was Peter Flood's dog, Judy. She was a scruffy little thing, more Yorkshire Terrier than anything else, and was exclusively a one-man dog. Her arrival in camp was an event that no one will ever forget. Peter, a Captain in the Diehards, had been obliged to abandon her during the battle and had given up all hope of ever finding her.

On one never-to-be-forgotten afternoon, however, after they had been in Argyle Street for two or three weeks, a tiny, bedraggled creature limped whimpering into the camp and made straight for Peter's hut.

The reunion was something that will never be forgotten by those who saw it. If it is possible for a dog to laugh, Judy was laughing. She rolled on her back with her little paws beating the air, cuddled against Peter's legs worshipping him and licking the hand stretched down to pick her up, making queer little squeaking noises of pure happiness. She had found her master and asked for nothing else.

Peter was in tears.

How Judy had found him, no one will ever know. She had been left behind on the island, and to get to Argyle Street would either have had to swim the half mile or so across the harbour or, more probably, have hitched a lift on a ferry. Perhaps the most remarkable thing was that nearly four months had elapsed since her abandonment, and yet some unerring instinct urged on by blind devotion had led her back to her beloved master.

Not that Judy was a cuddlesome creature by any means. On the contrary, she had a deeply ingrained hatred of all mankind, with the sole exception of Peter. It was a very reckless man who would lean in to stroke her silky coat while she was lying on Peter's floor space, as she always did.

And yet everyone loved her and would bring what few scraps they could spare and lay them on the floor at a respectful distance from her.

Above all, she could smell a sentry from fifty yards, and when the inmates of Hut Number 1 were engaged in such nefarious activities as writing diaries or passing on the latest snippets of news from the secret radio, a low snarl from Judy would result in a scurry of activity; books and slips of paper and any other contraband would disappear into their hiding places as if by magic. When the little man strode into the hut, it presented a picture of utter calm, the prisoners lying silent and motionless on their bed spaces, models of well-behaved and submissive captives in whose mouths butter, if by some miracle such a thing had been available, would have remained unmelted. The sentry, with a grunt, would retreat while Peter released Judy's snarling jaws, and the hut returned to normal.

As well as providing some sort of link, however fragile, with their previous existence, the dogs performed two useful functions, one of which arose from the other. Not only did they keep down the rat population, but when, as not infrequently happened, they chased one into the drainpipe under the entrance to one of the huts, their only means of escape was into an ingenious trap devised by one of the engineers. This was conveyed to the edge of the parade ground; the dogs were lined up behind, and the creature was released and invariably made for the fence on the other side of the square. The dogs were released, and bets were taken on which would get the rat before it reached the wire. It rarely did.

This happy state of affairs, however, was not to last. At the beginning of November 1943, after they had been in Argyle Street for eighteen months, the camp commandant issued an order that, because of their under-nourished condition, all the dogs must be handed over for humanitarian reasons and to improve their standard of living.

Everyone was appalled and produced a hurried referendum, the unanimous conviction, supported without hesitation by their owners, that the dogs must be destroyed forthwith, and the doctors were consulted as to the speediest and least painful way of implementing this terrible decision.

Doctor Woodward still had a small supply of spinal anaesthetic, which he husbanded jealously for the not infrequent operations on organs below the level of the heart for which it was suitable, but he had no doubt that the situation fully justified the sacrifice, and so, on November 6th, which all those who survived their captivity will count as one of the blackest days of their prison life, the dogs were led into the hospital compound, and the injections were given.

At that time, Roger was seriously ill in the hospital hut suffering from a nasty bout of malaria and amoebic dysentery. He was too weak to walk, and as he crawled on hands and knees towards the latrine, he passed by the pathetic row of little bodies.

The daft old Bo'sun had succumbed immediately, and the others had died within a few minutes. As he passed the inert body of Judy, he saw that her limbs were still twitching.

Overcome with an unutterable sadness, he reached out his hand to stroke her head.

Judy roused at his touch and, with a final faint spasm, tried to snap at his hand. The effort was too much, and she fell back dead. She had been faithful to her nature until the end.

For the second time in his prison life, Roger wept.

Following the death of the dogs, there was some discussion as to their disposal. There were those who argued that the dog's flesh was meat and that as they had had none for nearly two years, the bodies of their dead friends should be put to good account. However, the great majority opposed the suggestion, and the little mounds stayed in the hospital compound behind the guard room until the Argyle Street camp was closed.

Chapter 21

Stormy Weather

The putting to sleep of the dogs was judged a flagrant disobedience of a direct order from their captors, which had caused the camp commandant and, through him, his Imperial Majesty a severe loss of face that could only be redeemed by the punishment of the whole camp.

As with other similar incidents, this consisted of a week or so of long punishment parades which dragged out for several hours, during which the guilty prisoners were obliged to stand smartly to attention while they were harangued and abused by Panama Pete, who took great pleasure in the exercise. These diatribes were received with impassivity by his victims. His inability to detect any reaction to his performance excited him to a frenzy of rage which made him even more comic until some wretch, who should have known better, could endure it no longer and burst into a snigger, which provided the trigger for physical assault.

Much worse than the punishment parades was the reduction in the already meagre rice ration, which, in their emaciated state, was a grave matter indeed.

Compared with other similar punishments, however, the retribution for the incident of the dogs was a mild affair.

They had had worse, and much worse was to come.

Towards the end of November 1942, the camp commandant announced that, as proof of his Imperial Majesty's divine clemency, all prisoners were to receive a gift for Christmas and, in recognition of this, they were required, following the announcement, to shout "Banzai," which they did with enthusiasm - at least, they bellowed out several words beginning with the letter 'B', and the general volume and confusion of sound which cloaked the required words was such that even Panama Pete could not fault the performance.

This promise of a Christmas present aroused tremendous speculation among the prospective recipients ranging from the distribution of Red Cross parcels on which they knew their captors were living to the possibility of an issue of cigarettes or chocolate, both of which featured prominently in their list of priorities, to a ration of sugar or soap or razor blades or even fruit of some kind. Almost anything would be most acceptable, and the anticipation provided a valuable new topic of conversation.

Now it happened that, at this time and as frequently occurred, fuel for cooking the daily ration of rice was in very short supply and consisted either of dry grass gathered by the working parties from outside the camp or of knotted chunks of wood – often gnarled tree roots which took all their strength to dismember and which was a daily and most unwelcome chore but essential if they were to eat.

When the great day arrived, excitement was at a fever pitch. The long-awaited lorry was driven into the camp, and everyone gathered round to witness the unveiling of the emperor's largesse.

The covers were thrown back, and there, lying on the floor of the lorry, were three young fir trees.

Panama Pete leered benignly: "Christmas trees," he said. "Gift of His Imperial Majesty."

Roger and his fellow prisoners fell upon the trees and, dragging them to the chopping area, reduced them to a supply of sufficient fuel for a couple of days.

Had they wished to display their contempt for the generosity of His Divine Majesty, they could not have done so more effectively. Since this was a mass misdemeanour, the resultant series of punishment parades and reduction of rations was such that the insult to the emperor was eventually adjudged to have been expiated. Everyone agreed, however, that the gesture had been very much worthwhile.

Towards the middle of 1943, possibly as the result of the reports on conditions in Shamshuipo received in England from Bosanquet and his comrades who had succeeded in reaching home, all prisoners were ordered to make a written declaration that they would not attempt to escape.

This was a very serious matter since giving it would have been directly contrary to British military law, which made it the duty of every prisoner to escape if possible. A committee of senior officers was convened to come up with an official policy since it was unthinkable that they should not be of one mind on the matter.

In the end, the official instruction from their senior officers was that the requirements of military law and the Geneva Convention would be satisfied if every officer, before signing the document, were to declare that, as the signature was being obtained under duress, it did not bind him to keep the promise and that he proposed to attempt to escape if at all possible.

The day for the signing had arrived, and the whole camp was marshalled in single file across the parade ground and marched, one at a time, into the hospital hut.

Here a table had been set up, behind which sat the camp commandant and an interpreter flanked by armed sentries. At the open door on the other side of the hut stood two massive Korean guards at least twice the size of the squat Japanese.

The prisoners were marched in, one by one, and each stood smartly to attention in front of the table. Clearly and in an expressionless monotone, they chanted the agreed form of words, which were then translated into Japanese. A piece of paper bearing the undertaking printed in English and Japanese was thrust before them and signed. The camp commandant bowed, the prisoner saluted, made an extremely military right turn and marched through the opposite door. Here, each of the guards delivered a mighty clout to each side of his head, and he staggered out into the sunshine.

The performance had all the elements of comic opera, and it would have delighted the hearts of Gilbert and Sullivan to have seen the long line of gaunt, ragged prisoners chuckling as they went into the hut to receive their beating and emerging from the other side still chuckling albeit somewhat ruefully. In fact, such episodes were not entirely unwelcome since they provided fresh topics for conversation, which were in very short supply after nearly two years, during which every minutest detail of their personal lives had been told and retold a dozen times.

Despite the verbal declaration making it invalid, the Japanese were quite content. They had ordered their prisoners to sign a document, and they had signed. "Face" had been saved, and that was what mattered.

A much more vivid and sinister incident occurred on September 21st, 1943. The secret radio buried in its biscuit tin between two of the huts had kept them in touch with the outside world and, in particular, with the progress of the war for more than a year and put the excesses of the Hong Kong News with its wild claims of the defeat and destruction of the Allied forces into perspective. Although everyone knew of its existence, its exact location was closely guarded.

On that particular morning, however, the camp was turned out onto the parade ground while the Japanese swarmed through the huts like ants turning over every item of kit in a minute search. Roger, guessing that something very dangerous was afoot, gathered up his diary, the existence of which would have resulted in a severe beating at best since the keeping of any sort of record was strictly forbidden, put on his tattered shorts instead of his fundoshi and hid the incriminating document in the region of his posterior.

After two or three hours of waiting on the parade ground, there came a shout of triumph from the searchers. They emerged from between the huts brandishing the biscuit tin with its contraband contents. The game was up with a vengeance.

Now there followed a period of great tension while the Japanese carried out their usual routine of investigation. This consisted of identifying a suspect and submitting him to the most excruciating torture until he revealed the name of an accomplice who would then be arrested and subjected to the same treatment until he broke down and gave the information they demanded.

This process would continue until either the Japanese tired of the exercise or came to the conclusion that there was no further information to be obtained.

This betrayal of one's comrades was not a question of disloyalty or cowardice - usually, those involved in clandestine activities tended to be more courageous than most - it was that the human body can stand only so much and, in the end, the ordinary man must break and would betray his own mother to bring the mental and physical torture to an end. Even so, as in the case of Bosanquet's escape, not all the victims by any means survived the interrogation.

On this occasion, the immediate suspects were arrested. The following day, four officers, Commander Craven, whose greatcoat Roger had borrowed on the night his teeth had been knocked out, Lieutenant Commander Young, Lieutenant Commander Chattock and Lieutenant Dixon, were taken out. These were followed two days later by Lieutenant Colonel Levett of the Royal Signals, and on September 26th, by Colonel Field of the Royal Engineers. Major Boxer of Intelligence, Captain Woodward and Captain Godfrey Bird followed the next day. Of those who survived, Boxer was driven insane, and Craven suffered a complete mental breakdown and was temporarily paralysed from the waist down, having been forced upright into a fuse cupboard so small that the door pressed him against the back wall, making it impossible for him to sit down while he was fed with balls of rice rolled in salt over seven days and given nothing to drink.

Godfrey Bird, the last to be interrogated, was, like the remainder, the victim of fiendish torture and held out until he could take no more. Now Godfrey was a devout Roman Catholic and finally, in his agony, did the only thing left to him by calling on his Saints to help him.

"Peter and John," he cried, "blessed Peter and John save me!"

By this time, the Japanese had begun to lose interest in the proceedings and were concerned only with saving face and were trying, without much hope, to force him to reveal more names. As soon as they heard Godfrey's cry, they stopped the torture, gave him a cigarette and brought him back into the camp. He had done as they had asked. Two names had been given, and although they were without meaning for them, they had had their way. Face had been saved, and that was the end of the matter, but it would have been very difficult to persuade Godfrey that his prayers had not been answered or that a miracle had not occurred.

But the loss of the radio was a severe blow, as things were improving abroad. North Africa had been cleared, Sicily had been occupied, landings had succeeded in Southern Italy, and Mussolini had resigned. The Russians were making steady progress and had reoccupied Kharkhov. At last, hopes for release had begun to seem no longer an impossible dream.

Bad though the radio incident was, however, much worse had preceded it.

Throughout the early part of 1943, contact had been established with the camp at Shamshuipo and, more important, with Allied forces operating in China from the American base in Chungking. By this means, an efficient spy system had been established, and the movement of shipping in and out of the harbour, work on the enlargement of Kai Tak airfield and the construction of defences had all been accurately located and reported and were dealt with appropriately by the American planes, whose attacks had become a matter of almost a daily routine.

Eventually, the Japanese came to the conclusion that in one or other of the camps, there must be a short-wave transmitter working.

They were wrong, and the solution was much more straightforward. The former chief of the Chinese intelligence branch of the Hong Kong police had succeeded in getting himself appointed as the driver of the food lorry which deposited its load of rice and vegetable at the camps each Monday morning, and in both Shamshuipo and Argyle Street rota was established to pass messages between them and, from him, through the grapevine into China where agents passed notes through to the Americans at their base in Chungking.

The lorry would pull up as close as possible to the ablutions hut leaving only enough room for a man to squeeze through. The driver would nonchalantly dangle his arm out of the cab window, and the man on duty would slip the messages into his outstretched palm as he passed through.

The system worked admirably. Not only were they able to keep in touch and make a contribution, however slight, to the conduct of the war but even to lay plans for a simultaneous break-out from both camps to take place in the autumn and to make contact with guerilla forces in Kwang Tung Province to the north. Although, if it had been put into effect, the chances of success were highly problematical and would, no doubt, involve very heavy casualties and took no account of the civilian internees in Stanley Camp or of the fate of those too sick or feeble who would have had to be left behind.

The lorry pulled up as usual on Monday, 28th June. The two men on duty, Lieutenants Haddock and Prata, one collecting a note from the driver's hand and the other walking behind, slipping the message into it, failing to notice that the driver had been changed.

Instantaneously the canvas tarpaulin on the back of the lorry erupted, and a dozen or more armed Japanese leapt down, seized the unlucky couple and bundled them off to the guard room.

They were never seen again.

Later, after the Japanese surrender, they learned that Prata, whose wife was in Hong Kong, was made to watch while she was raped in front of him. Then he was torn to pieces by Alsatian dogs while she was forced to look on and was allowed to crawl away. Haddock was blinded as a result of the terrible beatings he received.

During the days of interrogation that followed, the now familiar ones and twos separated by pattern, agonising days of suspense took place, none of those involved ever returning. The waiting was excruciating for those team members not yet arrested. Sure that his turn would come, Roger wrote a last letter to Daisy, wondering how long he could hold out when he was tested.

He never was.

The last to be taken out was Colonel Newnham, formerly Commanding Officer of the Middlesex Regiment before he was appointed Commander of Operations at Headquarters, who was the plan's architect, and, after him, there were no more arrests.

As the days went by without further incident, it became clear that, like the man of supreme courage that he was, he had endured without breaking and that the rest of the team had been saved.

They learned later that, after fiendish torture had failed to break him, he had been hung upside down in searing agony whilst his torturers slashed the calves of his legs over three days until he was at the point of death.

Still unable to break his spirit, they took him over to the civilian internment camp at Stanley, where his wife was imprisoned with the other wives and non-combatants.

Here they tied him to a stake in front of her and ordered her, if she wished him to live, to plead with him to give the information they required and so save what was left of his life.

The poor lady, knowing the courage and resolve of her husband and seeing the wreck of his body, limp and bleeding, pleaded with them for God's mercy to end his suffering. A bullet brought him a merciful release.

Colonel Newnham was a true Diehard whose death was in the very highest traditions of the regiment which he had served so well and, at the end of the war, was awarded the George Cross for supreme courage, indeed, never more deservedly given.

The fate of some of the others interrogated can only be guessed at. Still, it is known that Flight Lieutenant Gray of the Royal Air Force, with two companions who had remained behind at Shamshuipo after the move to Argyle Street and who had masterminded the operation from that end and had supplied much valuable information about Kai Tak airfield, endured many months of starvation and torture. Finally, on the afternoon of December 18th, 1943, they were taken to the beach at Big Wave Bay, where they were beheaded. He also was awarded the George Cross, and after the war, his comrades brought his R.A.F. Wings back to England and presented them to his father.

One unfortunate sequel to this whole unhappy affair was the transfer away from the camp, initially to Formosa, of every officer above the rank of Lieutenant Colonel who, although they could not be proved to have taken any part in the affair, were no doubt considered as providing undesirable leadership for the prisoners and were, therefore, thought to be better out of the way. This included General Maltby, whose calm commonsense and example were stabilising factors throughout their incarceration. He and the Commodore were sadly missed by them all.

Roger, himself, had had a most lucky escape and, indeed, apart from the loss of his front teeth and the agony of his punishment following the incident of the stolen pot-scourer, he managed, not counting the usual run of kicks and punches, to steer clear of significant trouble during the remainder of his time in Argyle Street.

In fact, significant events such as these, terrible though they were, stood out like jagged peaks from a dreary plateau of monotony which seemed to stretch endlessly away into the future. It was essential to find some occupation or interest, however pointless, to relieve the dreary monotony of life. Until the discovery of the radio, 'Argyle University' had been a blessing. However, the classes and lectures were restricted to one hour per day as a punishment. So the 'University' was virtually destroyed. As far as Roger was concerned, however, this sanction had little practical effect since, from that time onwards, his long illness confined him to the hospital hut for the remainder of his stay in Argyle Street.

He had, since his move from Shashuipo to Argyle Street, kept a diary of events on the tattered pages of a pad of old NAAFI order forms which he had come across among the debris in Jubilee Buildings and which was a treasured possession since paper was difficult to come by during those early days.

The keeping of a written record of any sort was strictly forbidden, and the diary had to be carefully concealed. Roger had to be extremely careful over its contents because for it to be discovered would have been bad enough but had it contained information which could have been traced to any source other than the Hong Kong

News or, if it had recorded details of any atrocities or of criticism of his captors, the discovery could well have cost him his life. Such information was consigned to an undecipherable code which he and Frank Austen, the Cipher Officer, had worked out and which they were sure could not possibly be cracked. Unfortunately, by the time of his release, when the information would have provided valuable evidence for war crimes trials, the key to the cipher which they carried in their heads had been forgotten, and the diary was never decoded.

Now its only use, apart from its value in passing the time, was to keep a record of American air raids, which were an almost daily event in the second half of 1943 and of such progress of the war as could be gleaned from reading between the lines of the Hong Kong News. This invariably reported sweeping victories by the Germans and Japanese. Still, it was not difficult to conclude that a smashing defeat of the Russians at Kharkhov, followed by a disaster of equal proportions at Kiev, 200 miles to the west, represented a significant victory for the Allies. Roger, using a tattered atlas which he had come across among the debris and which was in great demand, kept a careful tally of the advances in Africa where, according to the Hong Kong News, the British had been heavily defeated at El Alamein before suffering equally heavy reverses in Tunis, Sicily and Italy and, similarly, of the westward advance of the Russians on the Eastern Front.

The air raids during this period were on a comparatively small scale. Usually, they consisted of half a dozen or so bombers with fighter escorts against which the Japanese appeared to have little response apart from poorly aimed anti-aircraft fire.

The raids concentrated mainly on Kai Tak airfield, the dock area and the oil storage depot at Lai Chi Kok to the south of Shamshuipo.

The position of the Argyle Street camp on its elevated platform overlooking the eastern end of the harbour often brought it uncomfortably close to some of the areas under attack. The entry in Roger's diary for November 16th, 1943, is typical of many such:

"Very heavy air raid by American planes last night. Many bombs were dropped. One stick of bombs I should judge nearest was along the line of the waterfronts very close to camp, just over 200 yards away, 50 yards from Commandant's house. The hospital was badly shaken, and things were thrown off shelves. Glass in Daisy's photo smashed. All clear midnight. In an air raid by 11 American 2 engined bombers at 12.40 p.m., 9 planes flew over from North to South at about 6,000 ft and dropped a large number of bombs. Two other planes carried out a low-level bombing attack on a ship in Kowloon Bay. The planes glided in at a

height of 100 feet, the first one scoring a direct hit with a small bomb. We had a grandstand view of this attack. The two planes did not seem to be in any hurry. Quite a lot of A.A. fire no planes were hit. All clear at 1 p.m."

Whilst the men were accorded the privilege of carrying out dignified tasks such as quarrying, extending the Kai Tak airfield and constructing anti-aircraft and other defensive positions, their officers were only worthy of doing work usually performed by the lowest-grade coolies. Hence the scrubbing out of toilets at the Japanese Headquarters, the cutting and carrying of grass which they much preferred to heavy manual work for which they would not have had the strength.

The Japanese needed not to understand that they had no objection to their 'humiliation' since, if they did, it was inevitable that these activities would have been brought to an abrupt end and substituted by something more unpalatable.

Consequently, from time to time, dignified representations were made to the Camp Commandant to release them from these degrading tasks. Never, it was urged, would they be able to face their wives and families on their return home if they had to confess to such a loss of face and would be obliged, henceforth, to lead a life of celibacy.

The ploy worked admirably, and not until early 1944 were the inmates of Argyle Street made to carry out any form of strenuous labour.

One outcome of their visits to the Headquarters was proof that the Japanese were systematically looting the food parcels sent through the International Red Cross, which they desperately needed. From their captivity at the end of 1941 until the end of August 1944, they had received only one parcel.

Although the International Red Cross had appointed a representative in Hong Kong, a Swiss national by the name of Zindall, he was able to make a maximum of only two visits per year to the camps, none of which lasted for more than ten minutes in all and during which the prisoners were strictly forbidden from speaking to him or making any movement or gesture as he was whisked at high speed through one or two of the many huts.

On one of his tours of duty in the Japanese Headquarters building, where he had scrubbed out their toilets and swept their rooms, Roger discovered to his delight that his G.E.C. Overseas 6 radio, which had, obviously, been looted from his room in the Courtland Hotel, had been installed in the bedroom which he was cleaning. Scarcely able to believe his good fortune, he took a close look at the back of the set, and there, sure enough, was his name which he had scratched into the casing some two years previously as some sort of protection against theft.

It so happened that working with him in the building was a radio expert from the Royal Signals who, as soon as the opportunity offered, removed various components required for the secret camp radio and carried out certain adjustments to the wiring of the set to ensure that the next time it was switched on, there would be an entertaining firework display and, hopefully, substantial injury to the operator. His radio would have played its own small part in the conduct of the war and would have perished in an excellent cause.

In pursuance of their policy of humiliating their cowardly prisoners, the Japanese insisted that they should all have their heads closely cropped like the criminals they were and even provided scissors for the operation. Again, their instructions, which were faithfully observed, had the reverse effect from what they had intended and the opportunity of keeping themselves free from dirt and, particularly, lice was most welcome. Of course, strenuous protests had to be made for the sake of appearances.

The order that all prisoners should salute the sentries whenever they passed by was less well-received until Colonel Simon White of the Royal Scots came up with the brilliant idea of a special type of salute which, the camp commandant was assured, was reserved for persons of the highest rank. From then on, the special 'salute' involving the display of two fingers was received with a slight inclination of the head from the sentries, and so everyone was happy. This unexpected gesture on the part of their prisoners was received with enthusiasm as a sign that, at last, their captives were learning true humility.

However, not every act of humiliation was insignificant.

During the early summer of 1943, shortly before the cholera outbreak in which Roger was involved, all the prisoners were paraded and forced to suffer the indignity of receiving a glass rod thrust into their nether portions. Whether this was in pursuance of some medical experiment or a deliberate attempt to spread infection in the camp will never be known, but dysentery was already commonplace. The fact remains that dysentery became more widespread and was supplemented by cholera in early June.

One apparent attempt to upset the morale of their prisoners was a bizarre display staged one evening for the benefit of their guests.

The headquarters building was set on ground below the eastern edge of the camp; the first-floor balcony was on a level with the parade ground only a few yards from it and formed a useful vantage point for off-duty staff to survey the movements of their captives.

As in all establishments of its kind, the Japanese kept a posse of "comfort women" whose services were of value in whiling away off-duty hours. One evening, just before dusk, strollers on the parade ground were amazed to see the entire team of these wretched women being paraded stark naked along the balcony and being forced to display the more intimate parts of their feminine charms to their astonished audience while their lords and masters sniggered and cavorted in the background.

If this was an attempt, as it undoubtedly was, to cause mental anguish and frustration to their celibate captives, it was a dismal failure. Hunger and malnutrition had long since nullified any sexual urges which they may have had, and, as someone put it, they were no longer capable of raising even a smile.

The incident provided, however, a most welcome opportunity of turning the tables on their captors and everyone on the parade ground promptly turned their backs on the display and went back in silence to their huts.

The following day a deputation of senior officers sought an audience with the Camp Commandant and explained, with great dignity, that, whereas such practices might be acceptable here, the western races regarded them with contempt as being a token of depravity and the prisoners, who were used to treating their womenfolk with much greater respect, would be grateful if no more such regrettable displays took place in future.

The expected reaction to this protest, which, as intended, caused them a massive loss of face, followed, but there were no more nude parades after that.

And so the long empty days passed into weeks, and the weeks into months without any real hope that things would improve or that their release was any nearer, and, although it would have invited total social ostracism to give voice to their thoughts, many wondered if they would ever see home again or even for how long they would be able to survive.

Chapter 22

Hungry Days

A backdrop to prison life was the constant nagging emptiness in their stomachs, which sapped their strength and resolve. Although it was not socially acceptable to refer to hunger as such, food was, nevertheless, a constant topic of conversation. Menus were planned, discussed and disputed; considerable heat could be engendered over cooking methods and the presentation of the various dishes. League tables of restaurants were drawn up and bickered over. A whole evening could be spent listing the merits of different brands of liqueurs, wines, spirits, cigarettes, tobacco and cigars.

Life was, indeed, particularly hard on those who had been heavy smokers and drinkers. The total absence of alcohol, however, and the impossibility of the manufacture of a substitute for it was a problem which soon disappeared as blood systems were cleansed from its effects. Still, tobacco was a completely different matter, and the addicts developed alternatives which were as foul as they were anti-social.

However, one thing that was not in short supply was tea, which consisted of brittle black stalks rather than leaves but which, when infused, made a weak and somewhat bitter brew which was, nevertheless, most welcome. When dried, the remains of the mess were, however, greatly sought after as a substitute for tobacco, although the smoking of it resulted in sore throats and a vile stench. Dried papaya leaves were also used for the same purpose and, although not quite as socially offensive, were, no doubt, equally damaging to health.

The food ration consisted almost exclusively of rice, the daily issue varying according to the state of their disgrace vis-a-vis the enemy but averaging out at about eight ounces per man per day. This was served in two meals, although one had the option of foregoing one of these to have a bumper evening feed of the whole day's ration.

In pursuance of their policy of treating their captives as low-grade coolies, the Japanese had provided two primitive hand-querns for grinding the rice into flour. These consisted of a circular platform of granite about eighteen inches across with a small raised boss in the centre to act as a hub and a shallow trough around the circumference towards which a number of grooves were let into the surface as in an old-fashioned mill wheel. Onto this was placed a heavy solid cylinder also of granite which engaged in the hub and sunken at the top with a small hole bored down through to the base and turned by a wooden handle set into the rim.

The dry rice was tipped into the depression and swept by degrees through the hole while the whole cylinder was rotated slowly. The ground rice was swept by the rotation along the grooves and into the trough from which it was retrieved with great care so as not to waste a single speck of the precious dust. Mixed with water, the rice dust formed into a stiffish paste, the resultant mess being poured into a tin which could be placed among the ashes of the fire in the cookhouse, resulting in a sort of baked pudding which was no more palatable than the regular cooked rice but made a change of routine diet. On the rare occasions when dried soya beans were issued, they were also ground and mixed with the rice flour, and this, combined with the dirty brown rock salt, if one had any, formed a sumptuous meal.

As might be expected, the rice itself was of the poorest quality, frequently consisting of the sweepings from the warehouse floor where it gained bulk from fragments of grit, which could only be separated from it at the time of eating and caused dental problems.

Much of it had been left lying about so long that it had become a home for numerous little black weevils and, even more unpleasantly, soft white maggots - presumably the grubs of the weevils. These spun tiny silken cocoons which bound the grains of rice together into little white spherical webs.

At first, working parties were appointed to sift these unwelcome guests from the rice before it was cooked. However, this was found to be very time-consuming and tended to be wasteful of precious rice grains. In any case, the doctors pointed out that the weevils and maggots were a valuable source of protein which, in their malnourished condition, ought not to be wasted. So they were cooked and eaten along with the rest of the rice and neither added to nor detracted from its taste.

There was, however, some advantage to be gained from the poor-quality rice as it still had its husk and germ, which was valuable as it provided a little vitamin B and, no doubt if the regular polished rice had been provided, their state of Vitamin B deficiency, which was responsible for beri-beri, pellagra and deterioration of eyesight, would have been even worse than it was.

Their supply of Vitamin B was also significantly increased by the brilliant discovery of one of the cooks who had managed to lay his hands on a small supply of live yeast, which he persuaded with great patience over many weeks to grow on a culture of cooked rice to the extent that, eventually, there was sufficient for a tiny weekly hand-out to everyone in the camp. Although it was insufficient to eradicate it, the essential vitamin acted like magic in controlling beri-beri. Gradually the swollen limbs, the acute pins and needles in the feet and the failing eyesight began to disappear under its benign influence. No one grudged the small deduction from his rice ration for the production of this minor miracle.

The remainder of the food provision consisted of vegetable matter, which was pitched steaming onto the parade ground on a Monday morning and had to suffice for the whole week and which was calculated to work out to about one ounce per man per day.

As often as not, it consisted of lettuce leaves already limp and slimy when they arrived. These were transformed into a weak, watery stew with a vaguely unpleasant taste.

Other similar delicacies were chrysanthemum leaves and stalks, which had a faintly aromatic flavour, and the green haulm of the yam, which consisted of a hollow stem and small ivy-shaped leaves and which, when boiled, produced a black liquid which was as unappetising as it was unattractive. Very occasionally, root vegetables took the place of these delicacies. The least favoured of these was the daikon which had the appearance and texture of parsnip and was entirely without flavour, with no amount of cooking ever succeeding in softening it. Less unpleasant and resembling a beetroot was the taro, which had a starchy purple root and leaves which gave out an acrid smell which, luckily, disappeared when cooked, the root itself having a floury consistency with a not unpleasant taste except when as frequently happened, it had been left lying about for too long when it became slimy and tasteless.

Pak Choi, or swamp cabbage, whose thick white stalk had a buttery flavour, was much more popular, as was the sporadic appearance of sweet potatoes. However, on one occasion, the gang responsible for washing and dismembering its thick roots spotted that, instead of its normal starchy consistency, the flesh consisted of tiny clear globules and Roger, remembering his geography teaching, pronounced that these were the roots, not of yams but of the cassava plant, which in its raw state is very poisonous and must be thoroughly washed, dried and shredded to reduce it to tapioca before cooking. This process was duly carried out, and a message was sent to the camp commandant thanking him for providing the delicious tapioca. This was sufficient to ensure that there would be no repetition of this dangerous provision.

Although they were constantly hungry, the diet was just sufficient to keep body and soul together, and, with the exception of Captain Lewis of the Pay Corps, who lost his reason in Bowen Road Hospital and refused to eat, no one in camp actually died from starvation.

A number of the Canadians fared a little better than their British counterparts thanks to the large numbers of Japanese living on the West coast of Canada who were interned at the outbreak of hostilities and who, by agreement between the two governments, were allowed to receive parcels from home.

In return, Canadian prisoners were given the same facility and, from time to time, received parcels of clothing, tinned food, chocolate and cigarettes from home, all of which could be bartered with the sentries for essential food like sugar, fat and eggs. The result of this was that the hungry British had the occasional chagrin of seeing their comrades, sometimes in the same hut, enjoying a fragrant meal of bacon and eggs finished off with a Sweet Caporal cigarette while they made do with their rice and greens.

The Canadians were as generous as they could afford to be, but there was simply not enough to go around, and, in any case, personal survival was an essential feature of everyone's life. No one really expected them to share their good fortune.

Some very slight relief was provided by an allowance of 40 Military Yen per month to each prisoner on the understanding that the British government would reimburse the Japanese at the rate of 4 Yen to the pound, this payment to be deducted from the prisoner's accumulated pay on his return to Britain.

As he had made an allowance from his pay to Daisy, Roger was worried that a deduction of £10 from his total monthly income of £16 might leave her in financial straits. However, in the event, no such deduction was ever made, and, indeed, on his return home, he was to find that the dear girl had saved a handsome nest egg with which to start their new home.

Following the introduction of 'pay' in July 1942, an enterprising Japanese corporal opened a 'canteen' for an hour each week where, in theory, it was possible to supplement the diet by the purchase of such delicacies as dried beans, rice bran, rock salt and peanut oil. Most important of all, however, were cigarettes, a packet of which engulfed almost a month's pay for ten, which looked like, smelled like, tasted like, and probably were mainly dried grass. Nevertheless, they offered some relief to those who craved for them and reduced the number of those, on one occasion a Colonel and a brigadier, who were observed to follow a sentry round on the parade ground in the hope that he might drop his dog-end, which could then be pounced on to add to the collection until it was large enough to roll into a cigarette with the aid of a scrap from the Hong Kong News or any other piece of paper which might be handy.

The real problem, however, was not only that of hunger but also that the diet, which was almost totally lacking in vitamins, fat and protein, reduced their resistance to disease and, once ill, recovery was painfully slow. Infection spread like wildfire unless strict precautions against it were taken.

The Japanese, whether from cynicism or, more probably, from sheer ignorance, responding, on one occasion, to a plea for an issue of animal fat, produced tins of dubbin from the looted British Army stores and which had been used for preserving the leather of the army boots.

This dubbin consisted of goose grease liberally mixed with paraffin. In spite of this, it was mixed with the rice for as long as it lasted and, notwithstanding the unpalatable paraffin flavour, was eaten with relish.

The Japanese response to the outbreak of disease was to place a trough of whitewash into which everyone was obliged to tread on entering the camp and to insist on the wearing of cotton face masks, which were as uncomfortable and irritating as they were useless.

June 1943 saw an outbreak of cholera which demanded drastic action if its spread was to be checked. Under the direction of Captain Woodward, known to everyone as Woody, a hard-swearing, hard-working and totally dedicated Australian doctor, a hut was cleared, and its occupants distributed among the others to the general discomfort of everyone.

Hut No. 5 was selected as the quarantine hut as it was nearest to the perimeter fence, with sufficient space between it and the wire for digging a pit to serve as a latrine, thus isolating its contents from the remainder of the camp. This quarantine was of the strictest kind, with no one except the doctor and the orderlies being allowed in or near the hut or to leave it except into the space between it and the electric fence.

Food for such of its inmates as were capable of eating was left in its bucket outside the doorway, and an interval of a minute had to be allowed before its collection. In this way, the dreaded disease was contained, and undoubtedly, the lives of many men were saved.

Since the nature of the disease demanded constant nursing attention, Woody appealed to anyone who had been inoculated against cholera within the last two years to volunteer for the job. Roger just qualified, having received his jab in the stomach soon after his transfer to headquarters, as he became a volunteer medical orderly.

The job, although unpleasant, had some advantages since the sentries who were terrified of infection gave the hut a very wide berth, and, of course, none of the orderlies were allowed out into the camp or to go on morning roll call.

Cholera is a foul disease, worse even than dysentery and far more deadly. The sufferer, as well as having a high fever and constant diarrhoea, vomits until all the contents of his stomach are exhausted, and he is finally sicking up nothing but black blood from his stomach lining, after which his body becomes completely dehydrated. Death comes as a merciful relief.

Woody was tireless in his efforts to save the lives of his patients, and he was very appreciative of the risks which his assistants were taking in helping him. He had a most extraordinary bedside manner, which, under the circumstances, was ideal:

"Well now, you poxy bastard," he would say to the recumbent body, "still haven't bloody snuffed it, I see. Never mind, old cocker, there's still plenty of time. See what you can do today!", and the patient would screw up a faint grin and with a touch on his forehead as gentle as any woman's Woody would pass on to the next. The man was completely without fear as Roger was to find some months later when, due to this, his life was undoubtedly saved.

One afternoon, a few days after he had started in his new role, Roger was suddenly overcome with violent nausea and a black, blinding headache. At first, he thought that his stomach had been turned at the sight of some of the messes which he had to clear up, but after violent vomiting, he told Woody what had happened.

The doctor thrust a thermometer into his mouth, and for a moment, his usually cheerful face screwed up in dismay: "I'll tell you what, you stupid bastard," he said, "you've been and got a dose of the poxy cholera. Sorry about that, old son," he went on, "it's all my fault, but I'll do what I can. Keep the bloody pecker up, and you'll be all right. You've had the jab, and it shouldn't go too hard with you."

Roger had only very confused recollections of the next few days. Sometimes he was vaguely aware that he was on his hands and knees vomiting black slime into the makeshift latrine. Sometimes he was cursing in the most lurid terms as Woody bathed his naked fevered body in cold water but, in the main, he seemed to be lying at the bottom of a deep black pit from which there was no escape. Then the day came when he was once more aware of what was going on around him. Woody was leaning over him.

"Well, you old bastard," he said, "you aren't going to poxy well snuff it after all. You're bloody lucky, and you've got your inoculation to thank for that, but that'll teach you not to be a stupid bastard and try to be so bloody noble again!", and he let his hand rest on Roger's forehead for an instant. "Still," he went on, "thanks for trying old son."

After that, he never failed to address him as "The noble Knocker".

After a couple of weeks, Roger and the epidemic survivors were strong enough to return to circulation and resume the regular dreary routine of camp life.

Shortly after this, an incident occurred to change the whole course of medical care in the camp, revealing Woody as a skilled negotiator.

One afternoon two sentries came to him and, in their limited English, asked him to examine them, indicating where the trouble was. With their trousers down, Woody looked at them and, with delight, exclaimed: "Well, my lads, you've both got a good dose of the Clap and the best of luck." He went on: "I no can help. You want special medicine. I no have got."

The two Japanese turned pale. Venereal disease was absolutely forbidden in the Japanese army, and to be found suffering from it was as good as a death sentence.

"Can get medicine," they replied, "You tell what medicine we get."

"Where from?" demanded Woodward.

"We take from medical store," came the reply.

"Very good," replied Woody

Writing in capital letters on a scrap of paper, "You get Sulphanilamide in a tube. You bring a syringe." And he drew a sketch to make sure that there was no mistake. The two departed and returned the next day with a phial of the precious liquid and the syringe. Woody inspected it and grunted approval.

"Good," he said. "You write your names on paper and the words 'Venereal disease'."

The two men did as they were told.

"Right, you little bastards," said Woody pocketing the evidence, "I inject medicine, and tomorrow you bring me these other medicines."

He presented them with a long list of drugs, including disinfectants, quinine, Emetine and Rivenol, which were vital in the treatment of amoebic dysentery, along with vitamin tablets and much more.

"Now," he said, "if you not bring this medicine and more when I say, I show paper to your officer and tell you have venereal disease!"

And so the bargain was struck, and there are many still alive, fifty years later, including Roger himself, who owe their lives to Japanese VD and Doctor Woodward's presence of mind and low cunning.

Luckily, the need for surgical operations was limited. The most common requirement for surgery was the rupture of stomach ulcers caused by their contaminated food.

Occasionally, as in the case of Roger's former colleague Frank Austen, who developed a ruptured duodenal ulcer, the Japanese allowed the patient to be carried by stretcher to the makeshift operating theatre in the Indian camp. On these occasions, only the surgeon and his assistant were allowed out of the camp. They were obliged to carry the patient between them before performing the operation.

Other, less serious operations were carried out in the hospital hut in the camp. When these occurred at night when the only illumination available was from the lights on the perimeter fence, the surgeon worked by the flickering light of a bean oil lamp using a safety razor blade and, in the case of Woody, addressing his assistant in the most expressive and lurid terms.

"Hold the poxy light still, you stupid bastard," he snarled when, on one occasion, Roger was acting as his orderly. "How, for Christ's sake, can I see the poor sod's entrails with you waving the bloody lamp all over the place?"

Dental problems caused further complications as there was no cocaine available, nor could Woodward's contacts find any in the medical stores.

The only qualified dentist in the camp was Colonel McCurdy, a charming old Belfast Irishman who had been the Commanding Officer of the Army Dental Corps in the colony and who had not personally practised dentistry for many years. He was getting on in years and, like Jack Wood, had been an enthusiastic drinker so that his old hands, holding his instruments of torture, shook a little as he set about his task.

Roger's first encounter with camp dentistry occurred soon after the unfortunate episode of the sentry's rifle butt, which had snapped off two of his front teeth, leaving the nerves bare to the world with excruciating pain. McCurdy sat him down on the wooden box which served as a dentist's chair and examined the damage.

"Well now, my boy," he said in his broad Belfast accent, "I think we shall have to do a little drilling round here." Producing a hand-operated drill together with a pair of forceps and some tweezers, he went on: "Now open wide, lad, this may hurt just a wee bit." And, with the drill trembling in his old hands, he proceeded to drill out the nerve from the two teeth.

Roger was in agony.

Finally, the old man produced his tweezers and, with a smart tug, triumphantly exhibited two tiny white strands like little pieces of fine cotton.

"There now," he said, "there's the little chaps that have been causing all the trouble!" Sometime later, on September 3rd, Roger's diary for the day recorded:

He would never have a fear of dentists again.

Worse, however, was to come. One blisteringly hot afternoon in September, when he was on wood cleaving duty, trying to dismember a gnarled old root, he was aware that it had suddenly turned freezing. Not suspecting that there was anything seriously wrong, he stopped work and went back into the hut to find his old shirt to put on. Seeing that this had no effect and still shuddering with cold, he wrapped himself in his sleeping bag, the only warm article he possessed.

Jack Wood found him shaking with cold on his bed space and immediately went off to find Woody. The doctor produced his thermometer and shoved it in Roger's mouth.

"You bloody noble old Knocker," he pronounced, "you've got a temperature of 105. It's off to hospital with you, old son!" Roger was escorted to the hospital hut behind the guard room, installed on a sacking bed supported by wooden poles and enjoying the rare luxury of a torn mosquito net. By evening he was very ill and again suffered the agony of cold water compresses on his naked burning body.

He had malaria again, but this time, it was of a different strain known in the trade as 'benign tertian malaria'. However, he never discovered what was kindly about it. The temperature remained high, unlike the malignant type he had previously suffered from. With none of the intermissions that had occurred before, he steadily became weaker; instead of recovering after ten days, the illness dragged on for weeks, and September dragged on into October and November with no sign of improvement.

And so the weeks dragged by with no sign of any real improvement. Woody still kept up his cheerful verbal profanities, but it was clear that he was becoming increasingly anxious.

When Roger had been in hospital for nine weeks at the beginning of November, Woody decided that his only chance of improvement was to be transferred to the hospital at Bowen Road, where the most severe cases were dealt with.

"You've got bloody amoebic hepatitis, old son," he said.

"Is that serious?" asked Roger, alarmed by the thin line of Woodward's lips.

"Well, yes, you can say that," returned the usually cheerful Woody. "It means we can't have you poxy well snuffing it, and I must get that bastard Saito to do something about it."

Indeed, Roger was now feeling very ill and, despite, or perhaps, because of the daily doses of Emmetine, which is pure ipecacuanha, so nauseous that it could only be taken by being wrapped in a screw of paper, he was constantly vomiting and, because of the effect of the drug on his heart, was unable to get out of his bed.

During his visit to the hospital hut on October 12th, Saito refused permission to put him on the Bowen Road list and was again approached on his next visit in December. After a cursory glance at him, he shrugged his shoulders and walked away. Clearly, once again, as during the early days at Shamshuipo, there was to be no help from him, and Roger began to lose hope.

One day, Jack Wood, who was a daily visitor, said: "Do you know what tomorrow is, Laddie?"

Roger shook his head. He neither knew nor cared. "It's Christmas Day," said Jack. "What would you like Santa Claus to bring you?"

Roger thought: "Well, now," he said. "I would like a handkerchief, a tablet of soap, a razor blade, some cigarettes, a pencil, a razor blade, an orange and a single ticket to Eridge. How's that for a list?"

Jack Wood grinned: "It's a bit of a tall order, laddie," he said, "but we'll see what can be done. You'd better hang up your sock and hope for the best!"

The next morning when he woke up, having forgotten all about the day, he saw that the tattered sock hanging at the end of his bed was bulging and, to his astonishment, found that, by some miracle, Jack had managed to find everything he had asked for, even a piece of cardboard on which was inscribed in neat print: "Passenger to Eridge, Sussex. Single Ticket Not available for return." Attached to the sock was a note: "With every good wish for a Happy Christmas and a speedy recovery." Despite the lump in his throat, Roger knew from that moment that, unlikely as it seemed, he would recover and one day be glad of that ticket.

By the middle of January, however, it was clear that his condition was steadily deteriorating. Neither the malaria and its effect on his hepatitis nor the dysentery showed any signs of improvement despite the Emetine and Rivenol, which seemed, if anything, to aggravate the problems.

Woodward had stopped chaffing him. "Look, Knocker old son," he said, "we've bloody well got to get you to Bowen Road. I'm going to have another go at that bastard Saito. He's due to come in soon to agree to the next draft, and you've got to be on it."

Saito's next visit took place on January 29th. Woody took him across to Roger's bed. "This officer is very sick," he said. "He must go to Bowen Road before it is too late."

The little man put his hand contemptuously on Roger's forehead.

"This man not sick," he said. "He pretend only. Tomorrow he go on parade with rest of prisoners." Saito, escorted as always by two armed sentries, walked away.

Woody stepped between Saito and his protecting guards, his face white and his eyes blazing with anger. With his hand gripping the front of Saito's collar, he half-lifted him off the ground: "Listen, you little bastard," he said, "if this man doesn't go to Bowen Road, he will die and when the war is over I will see that you bloody well hang for his murder!"

Roger was appalled and half lifting himself feebly up from his bed: "For Christ's sake, Woody," he pleaded, "leave it."

This could be interpreted as a physical assault on a Japanese officer and an extremely vindictive one at that, and must surely result in Woody's instant arrest and probable death.

What, in fact, happened was so incredible that Roger still thinks of it as a miracle. Saito pushed Woodward away, beckoned to the sentries and marched out of the hut without a word.

The following day Roger was carried out onto a lorry and taken across the harbour with the rest of the draft to Bowen Road Hospital.

Woody had risked his life to save him. He was never to see either Argyle Street or Doctor Woodward again.

Chapter 23

Bowen Road

On Roger's previous acquaintance with it in June 1941, when he had been admitted with his first attack of malaria, Bowen Road Military Hospital had presented a distinctly austere and gloomy appearance. Its dull red brick walls, large bare wards with their unscreened beds, and its male nursing staff seemed to him sadly lacking in comfort and gentleness. He had longed to get back to the cosiness of his room in the Hong Kong Club.

However, even though the paintwork was shabby and uncared-for and the surroundings untended and surrounded by barbed-wire fencing, it now seemed to him, ill though he was, like paradise. There were actual beds with mattresses, pillows and blankets, clean wooden parquet floors, doors which could be opened and shut and windows with real glass in them. Even the patrolling sentries, keeping in the main to the exterior balconies, were less obtrusive. There were real flush toilets, wash-basins and baths - albeit with cold water most of the time - and one had the illusion of returning to civilisation after a long absence.

Although the food was no better either in quality or quantity than it had been at Argyle Street, and indeed not as well prepared, the rice being cooked in shallow metal baking trays from which it was cut out in solid damp unappetising little slabs, was served from trolleys onto real plates and eaten with real knives, forks and spoons such as he had not seen for more than two years. Water and tea, when this was available, were drunk from real china mugs. This was clearly a place where one's chances of survival were going to be vastly improved.

Doctor Anderson, who was in charge of the hospital, had access to their surgical equipment and facilities as well as to anaesthetics. However, these were by no means plentiful and had to be husbanded with the greatest care. Even the most straightforward operation was at the mercy of the wildly erratic electricity supply, as Roger found to his cost when a sigmoidoscopy intended to explore the extent of the damage caused by dysentery to the lining of his bowel had to be suspended to await the resumption of power, leaving him spreadeagled across a vast metal grid for more than an hour. A telescopic tube several inches in diameter embedded in his posterior into which it had been inserted with great difficulty accompanied by considerable agony.

In view of the difficulty in obtaining permission from the Japanese for transfer from the camps to the hospital, one depressing feature was the condition of many of the patients who were far sicker than himself - many terminally - and death was a frequent visitor.

One member of his old platoon, 'Ollie' Taylor, who had travelled out with him to Hong Kong in the 'Empress of Japan', was in the final stages of beri-beri, his limbs swollen to a grotesque size so that his arms and legs resembled huge white barrels. Yet, when Roger was well enough to make his way down the ward to see him, he was greeted with Ollie's customary cheerful grin: "They're going to syphon me off tomorrow, Sir," he said, "and I'll be as slim as a bloody ballet dancer."

Roger saw him again the next day after two and a half gallons of fluid had been drained from his body. He was lying limply on his bed and, in response to Roger's enquiry, raised his thumb and gave a wink.

"I'm O.K., Sir," he said, "thanks for asking". And he laid his head back on his pillow.

Within twenty-four hours, he was dead.

The death of Captain Lewis of the Pay Corps was more than a little macabre. Not only did he die at four minutes past four on April 4th, 1944 - "on all fours" as someone put it - but his death was due to starvation; he not having eaten for several weeks, but when his locker was opened, it was found to be crammed full with tins of meat and fruit, the like of which had not been seen since their captivity, and which he must have amassed and hoarded over the many months of his captivity. However, not allowing sentiment to stand in their way, they all fed royally for the next week.

On the morning of his burial the next day, which, unusually, those who were able to were allowed to attend, the sky was a deep blue with brilliant sunshine. As the body was carried in its white sheet to the shallow grave behind the hospital, there was a tremendous clap of thunder. The guards looked up at the clear blue sky and shuffled uncomfortably.

Again, as the body was lowered into the grave, another clap was even louder, repeated as the earth was shovelled over. Everyone felt a little strange, and when they stood up and looked around, the guards had vanished. Clearly, whatever Gods they worshipped were displeased, and they felt safer out of it.

A few minutes later, it transpired that the strange phenomenon had been due to a storm brewing behind Victoria Peak, which had hidden it from their view. Nevertheless, when the corpse had surfaced for the third time during the next few days owing, no doubt, to the shallowness of the grave due to the thinness of the soil over the underlying hard rock, they all felt a little strange. No one present at the funeral ever forgot it.

Major Benny Carter in Roger's ward was suffering from cancer of the gullet and had been unable to swallow food of any kind for nearly two years. He was fed a gruel made from ground rice through a metal funnel from which a rubber tube led directly into his stomach. Yet, no one ever saw Benny as anything other than cheerful. He would sit propped up against a mound of pillows, happily pouring the stuff down into his funnel, cracking jokes and pulling the legs of the remainder of the ward. He was a good artist and enjoyed nothing better than drawing caricatures of himself at 'feeding time', as he put it. However, he knew only too well what the inevitable end must be.

It was, indeed, even worse than he or anyone else could possibly have imagined. One day, through some lucky chance, someone had got hold of a tin of corned beef – perhaps the remains of Captain Lewis's hoard. Benny watched with envy as the container was peeled open.

"What wouldn't I give," he exclaimed, "for the taste of a bit of bully beef!"

Someone had a bright idea. "Why not?" they said. "Why can't you put it in your mouth and chew it so that you can get the taste and then spit it out?"

"That's brilliant," replied the delighted Benny, "let's have a go!"

He put the bit of meat into his mouth and chewed with a blissful smile on his gaunt face as his tastebuds savoured the unaccustomed flavour of real food. Instead of spitting it out, however, he gave a great gulp and swallowed. The others looked on incredulously. A miracle had taken place.

"Christ!" said the delighted Benny. "I've swallowed it. I can eat!"

His exclamation turned immediately into a cry of agony, and they were aghast to see him writhing on the bed. Someone dashed out of the ward to find Doctor Anderson and tell him what had happened.

The doctor rushed in, his face blanched. It was too late. Benny, his whole body contorted with pain, was in the last throes. The food had dropped right through the gap where his gullet had been and into his body cavity. Within a few hours of unspeakable suffering, he was dead.

Roger's own recovery was unexpectedly rapid. Within a few weeks, both the dysentery and the liver problems had begun to clear up and although there were frequent relapses, the severity and frequency of these began to subside and, in the intervals, he was able to get about and visit other wards to see the members of his regiment. The malaria still persisted, but its high fever was kept at bay by copious draughts of raw quinine – a thick greenish-yellow liquid so foul to the taste that he sometimes felt that the thundering headache and paralysing rigours of the complaint were to be preferred.

The only drug freely available were pills rejoicing in the name of Wakamoto, which the Japanese clearly regarded as a panacea. Whether they had any beneficial effect was debatable. Still, at least they did no harm, and it was alleged that they contained Vitamin B and, indeed, his beri beri seemed to benefit from them. However, the pellagra sores, caused by vitamin B2 deficiency, which dug deep into his legs and feet in seeping ulcers, still continued to resist treatment.

Various appeals to higher powers having failed, including writing a poem to God and pleading for food, the dreary round of rice and tasteless vegetables continued. The Almighty, who he had to admit had so far not done so badly by him, all things considered, clearly did not share his distorted sense of humour or admire the crudeness of his rhyme. Perhaps the greatest bonus of all provided by Bowen Road was that its extensive library had remained intact. They had access to an extremely catholic selection of books ranging from the classics through novels, plays and poetry and even extending, to Roger's great delight, to languages and, improbable as it seemed, to his pet study - an Anglo-Saxon Grammar and Bede's 'Ecclesiastical History of Britain' in the original so that, as soon as he was fit enough, he was able to spend many happy hours reading, translating and making notes.

What was even more fortunate was that his buddy Bert Haines, who shared his enthusiasm for language and literature, had also been a victim of a severe attack of amoebic dysentery even worse than his own and had been transferred to Bowen Road at the same time as himself, and the discovery in the library of a French dictionary enabled them to continue with their project, begun in Argyle Street with the help of Captain Egal a refugee Free Frenchman from Shanghai - of compiling a dictionary of French idiomatic usage.

The hospital's resident dentist, Norman Fraser, a cheerful red-headed Scot, occupied a small room on the top floor, which they were able to use as a study and where Norman, an enthusiastic but most unsuccessful artist, who had managed to keep his mammoth supply of oil paints, spent all his spare time on a picture of an imaginary tropical island which remained unfinished throughout their stay at Bowen Road and which, by the time of their departure, had amassed a formidable depth of paint to the undisguised chagrin of its creator.

Among the books in the library was a collection of short one-act plays from which they devised performance, a given as required by their captors in the presence of their officers and sentries, of 'The Bishop's Candlesticks' and two other sketches, which so pleased everyone that they were emboldened to launch forth on a full-scale production of 'Ten-minute Alibi', of which the Japanese understood not a word but which resulted in a solemn presentation at the end of the performance of a bottle of Guinness to each member of the cast. Remembering lines of his recent address to the Almighty, Roger reflected that God "moves in a mysterious way indeed, His wonders to perform" and was suitably grateful.

The high spot of each day for those who were sufficiently mobile was the evening 'Epilogue' conducted by Padre Squire in the day room, which consisted, invariably, of the same two prayers and hymn: 'Heavenly Father in Thy mercy, hear our humble prayer: Keep our loved ones, now far distant, 'neath Thy Care.'

At these little services, which brought them all great comfort, Roger noticed that a Japanese officer stood reverently at the door and seemed to be joining the prayers. Roger recognised him as the officer who had carried the baby across the road at Shamshuipo and had put it in its father's arms for a few moments – the first act of kindness from a Japanese that he had seen since his imprisonment.

The officer occasionally came into the ward, and he learned that he was an official interpreter by the name of Kyoshi Watanabe. Watanabe always spent time at Benny Carter's bedside. One evening, Roger saw that he had produced an autograph album for Benny to draw his picture of himself at 'Feeding time.' Clearly, here was an outstanding exception to the general run of Japanese and, one day, Watanabe came over to his bed and, with a nervous smile, asked him if Roger would write something in the autograph album. Not knowing what else to do, he wrote down the words of the Sussex prayer: O Lord, support us. Watanabe was delighted.

"I also am a Christian," he said. "Before the war, I was a minister in the Lutheran Church at Hiroshima in Japan. You are very kind. If there is something I can do to help you, please tell me."

Roger had no hesitation. He was desperate for news of Daisy. Roger was back into a severe relapse of malaria and was feeling ill and very down in the mouth. He had had no word from her for many months, although, from the first welcome letter he had received in March 1943 – written in July 1942 – every word of which he knew by heart – it was clear that she was writing every week. It was equally clear that the Japanese were destroying the mail when it arrived from the Red Cross, just as they were feeding off the Red Cross parcels for which, from Daisy's letter, he knew that she and all other relatives were sending regular contributions.

From June 1942, the prisoners were allowed to write a postcard with twenty-five words once a month. The cards had to be written in block capitals and contain no complaints or reference to their prison conditions; any suspected reference, however skilfully concealed, being censored, the writer punished, and the concession cancelled. However, withdrawing this privilege was an effective form of punishment for misdemeanours.

In fact, Roger got one significant message confirming the hardships inflicted on them. He wrote on his card to Daisy: "Love to Luke for his 15th birthday on the 16th."

For several days Daisy, guessing that this was a code of some sort, racked her brains for the solution. Then, suddenly, she reached for her bible and at verse 16 of the 15th chapter of St. Luke, she read: "And he would fain have filled his belly with the husks that the swine did eat, and no man gave unto him." The message had got through.

Although this was of little comfort to her, it proved valuable in confirming to the government through the Hong Kong Wives' Association, whose meetings she attended regularly, the grim conditions being experienced in the camps and may possibly have helped to bring pressure on the International Red Cross to make even more determined efforts to get relief.

Not surprisingly, Roger's request to Watanabe was that he might help to find a letter from her. Watanabe smiled gently: "Then," he said, "I think you should pray."

That night Roger felt a movement of his pillow under his head, and reaching behind it, he found a bundle of letters - all from Daisy. The little interpreter had more than amply repaid his gesture in writing the prayer in his album.

The next time Watanabe passed by his bed, he tried to thank him for this magnificent and, as far as the little interpreter was concerned, hazardous effort. Watanabe said nothing but pointed his finger upwards to heaven, smiled and walked away.

After this, his visits to Roger's bed became more frequent, and he learned that the little man, now aged about 50, had come from a well-to-do family in Nanataki and, although brought up in the Buddhist faith, had been converted to Christianity and had spent two years in the Lutheran seminary in Gettysburg before becoming pastor of the church in Hiroshima.

He had two sons, Shinwa and Shigawo, of whom he was clearly very proud, serving in the Japanese army, and two daughters, Kei and Miwa. His wife, Mitsuko, of whom he spoke with great tenderness and whom he had married after the death of his first wife from dysentery, which had also killed his first two daughters, was the headmistress of a school in Hiroshima.

There was no doubt from the pride and tenderness in his voice that his was a very happy family and that, as a loyal Japanese, he took great satisfaction from his country's victories.

Following the capture of Hong Kong, he had been drafted, at the beginning of February 1942, to Shamshuipo camp where he shared with Inouye, the 'Panama

Pete' of Argyle Street, the job of interpreter. His exaltation at his fellow countrymen's victories was quickly transformed into horror at the sight of the brutal treatment of the prisoners in Shamshuipo, the squalor of their living conditions and their gaunt, disease-ridden bodies.

His pity for the condition of these ill men was soon to be translated into surreptitious attempts, as a devout Christian, even though they were his enemies, to bring what help he could to relieve their sufferings and, in doing so, however careful he was, because of his religion, which they despised, he was held in contempt and hatred by his comrades. He was in constant danger of exposure for his aid to the enemy, which would undoubtedly have resulted in his arrest on a charge of treason, which could have had only one outcome. Moreover, he was, he said, terrified of the consequences of his actions and confessed frankly to being a great physical coward who could not stand the prospect of pain.

Roger was astonished and humbled by these revelations. He had no doubt that it was to Watanabe that he owed the M and B tablets which had saved his life in the early days at Shamshuipo.

Here was a man who, because of his faith and in spite of its perils, was prepared to risk his life and face a terrible death for its sake and wished that he could share the sort of cowardice with which Watanabe professed to be filled. He asked him how he had had the strength to reach his remarkable decision. Watanabe's reply was immediate and unprompted:

"I had no problem," he replied simply. "I asked my God what I should do. He told me, and I did it."

Roger reflected that of such stuff, the saints were made.

The days which followed his first acquaintance with Watanabe, who begged him to use the name he had adopted on his conversion to Christianity of 'Uncle John', saw the arrival of more letters from Daisy, resulting from the interpreter's surreptitious searches through the abandoned sacks of mail. The letters did Roger far more good than any medicines could possibly have done, and he was soon making a steady recovery.

Another great bonus at Bowen Road was that, concealed somewhere in the building, was a radio from which secret daily bulletins of the progress of the allied forces were received. The existence of this was even more fraught with danger than it had been in Argyle Street, for its discovery might well jeopardise the whole existence of the hospital on which so many lives depended.

The war, in fact, was going very well indeed.

Before he had left Argyle Street, news had been gleaned of the successes in North Africa and of the landings in Sicily, which had taken place in August of 1943. Now they learned that Italy had been invaded and had offered unconditional surrender but that this had been offset by stiff German resistance and that desperate battles were in progress to the south of Rome. There were also rumours of increased American naval successes in the Pacific. Although these were invariably reported by Japanese propaganda as sweeping successes by their fleets, it was clear from the location of the battles that the tide was turning inexorably in the Allies' favour.

In the day room at Bowen Road, a loudspeaker poured out an incessant cacophony of music so that it was almost unbearable to stay in the room.

However, at about 4 p.m. on the afternoon of June 5th, the music stopped abruptly. An English voice announced distinctly: "Today, Allied troops entered Rome." Then, just as suddenly, the blare of noise was resumed.

There was a moment of stunned silence, then a great cheer which brought the sentries running along the corridor. This, surely, was the beginning of the end, but the question remained who had engineered this miracle? The radio from which the music came was in the Japanese Headquarters across the road from the hospital. It was unthinkable that anyone could have gained access to it, let alone found the set and manipulated it at that precise moment.

The mystery was never solved, and it would have been indelicate, to say the least, to investigate it any further. Still, they had no doubt that Kyoshi Watanabe had been responsible for the apparent miracle.

Each day which followed brought news of the progress of the invasion. When the breakthrough came, everyone was eager to trace the lines of advance through Normandy. A couple of days later, they learned from the secret radio that the Allies had landed in Normandy on June 6th and that a great battle was in progress for the possession of Caen.

Roger, as the geographer who also had access to the atlas in the hospital library, was deputed by his ward to make a map of northern France on which events could be traced.

Those wishing to look at this secret document had to come to his bed space to see the arrows which, from day to day, advanced farther and farther into France.

News of the existence of the map spread to the adjoining ward, and a deputation arrived asking if it could be borrowed. Roger refused point blank at first, but because of pleading that some of the permanently bedridden would give their eye teeth to see it, he very stupidly gave way and parted with the precious document on the firm understanding that it should not leave their hands.

What happened was that the bearer of the map went into his ward and, at the top of his voice, shouted: "Here we are, chaps, I've got the map. Come and have a look!"

At that moment, a passing sentry, intrigued by the shout, came into the ward and, seeing the map snatched it, looked at it and marched out of the room brandishing it in triumph.

Upon receiving the news, Roger felt a chill of horror course down his spine. Like an idiot, he had put his initials at the bottom of the map, and it was only a matter of time before the author of it was discovered. He recollected the fate of those involved in the betrayal of the secret radio in Argyle Street and had no doubt that he would share the same treatment.

It was, indeed, much worse than this since, no doubt, the interrogation would reveal the source of information; the existence of the radio would be discovered, and the fate of the whole hospital and its inmates would be in jeopardy.

Three days of total mental agony ensued, during which he awaited the inevitable arrest and interrogation.

He wrote a last letter to Daisy, made out a form of will leaving whatever he possessed to her, and entrusted this to Norman Fraser, the dentist.

At last, the dreaded moment arrived, and he was frog-marched between two armed guards to the interrogation room. His head was down, and he scarcely had the strength to look up into the face of his interrogator.

When he did so, he saw, with complete incredulity, that it was none other than Kyoshi Watanabe. The two guards pulled him roughly to attention and took their places behind Watanabe, their bayonets fixed.

The interpreter said something to them in Japanese. With a look of astonishment, they reluctantly left the room and took up a position outside the door.

Roger was dumbfounded, and a significant surge of hope swept through him. He had expected, at least, to be confronted by Inouye or one of the other interpreters who were notorious for their brutal methods of extracting information. By what miracle had Watanabe been chosen for the job?

Watanabe's face looked strained and anxious, and he was clearly apprehensive as to the outcome of the interrogation.

He was a loyal Japanese under orders and might have to betray his friend.

"You make a map?" he said.

Roger nodded. "Yes," he said, "and I would much like it back."

A faint smile came on Watanabe's face. "I am afraid that will not be possible," he said. "The map is of France and has many little arrows on it. The commandant has told me to find out what they mean. Why did you draw it?"

Roger breathed a sigh of relief. Things were going much better than he had feared, and he had been allowed to recite his carefully prepared explanation.

"Yes," he said, "I have a straightforward explanation. You see, I am a teacher and, as I believe you know, I sometimes give lectures to my comrades. Before the war, I used to spend my holidays on cycling tours in Northern France, and my map was going to be used for a talk to my friends to show them the details of my journeys."

He was aware that it was a very thin story, but it had been the best he could come up with during the terrible days before his arrest.

The little man gave a thin wisp of a smile. "That," he said, "is a good explanation, but," he went on, "the commandant thinks it may be a map showing some battles."

"What battles?" asked Roger. "There are no battles in France. The last battle was at Dunkirk, which is not in the part of France shown on my map." Watanabe got up from his chair and put his hand on Roger's shoulder: "This was a perfect answer, and this is what I will tell the commandant. I think, perhaps, it is not true, but you are my friend, and perhaps, when this war is over, which may be quite soon, I hope we shall still be friends. Now, he went on, "perhaps you will help me. The commandant says I must beat you to make you tell the truth. Perhaps you will make noises like I am hurting you and tell your friends I have beaten you."

Roger was happy to oblige and let forth very convincing yells.

Watanabe nodded approval.

"That is good," he said. "Now you can go from the room and pretend to the guards that you are in great pain."

Roger did as he was told and put on the performance of his life, groaning with pain as he was pushed unceremoniously along the verandah by his disappointed guards.

His heart was bursting with gratitude for Watanabe, who, undoubtedly, had saved his life. He reflected not for the first time that his guardian angel had done overtime on his behalf.

However, as the map was still in possession of the Japanese and might yet be used in future evidence of malpractice despite Watanabe's report, it was thought prudent both for his own sake and, more importantly, for that of the hospital for him to be declared wholly recovered from his illness, so he was included in the next draft to return to camp.

Before his departure on August 9th, Richard Medhurst, his old platoon corporal who had travelled out with him from England, presented him with a pair of bookends bearing the regimental crest and Chinese junks which he had painstakingly carved from a piece of oak using only his penknife. They were exquisitely done, and Richard had taken great pride in them, hoping he could one day bring them home to his family.

"I would like you to have these, Sir, to remember me by in case I do not come home," he said.

Roger, greatly moved, accepted them with gratitude and fifty years on, they are still among his most cherished possessions. Richard Medhurst died the week after Roger left Bowen Road.

Chapter 24

Return to Shamshuipo

The flat-decked ferry taking them back to the mainland set off from the Star Ferry pier. Instead of heading straight across the harbour to the dock at the tip of the Kowloon peninsula as they had expected, they veered off to the left. The ferry carried them north-westward towards Stonecutters Island and, tying up at a wharf in the typhoon anchorage, deposited them at the Yau Ma Ti dock.

They were not headed for Argyle Street, which lay on the peninsula's eastern side, but instead returned to Shamshuipo. He was horrified as he had left all his important possessions - his sleeping bag, books and, even more critical, his secret diaries in the care of Major Jack Wood at Argyle Street, who had agreed to keep them hidden while he was away. Had they been discovered, they might have caused severe problems for their guardian.

The forlorn little column found themselves being marched through the familiar gates and past the guard room into the Shamshuipo camp.

Turning to the right from the main approach road, they went past the old Middlesex, now the Camp Commandant's offices, through a gap in a triple dannert barbed-wire fence which now divided the camp into northern and southern sections, past the church hall into which he had marched his platoon on church parade in the olden days. Here they were allowed to disperse to find what accommodation they could in the rows of huts on either side of the road.

All at once, Roger felt a welcoming arm around his shoulder and, with a surge of relief, found that Jack Wood was pumping his arm up and down and with tears running down his cheeks.

"Thank God you are safe, laddie," he said "it is so good to see you again. I have been so worried about you and have wondered if you would survive Bowen Road. You were so ill when you left Argyle Street, and we never thought you would make it."

Jack led him off to his hut near a former cookhouse complex but now did duty as a hospital hut. Outside the cabin was an extraordinary structure consisting of a circular brick tower about ten feet tall with an iron pipe sticking out from the top and which was belching smoke. This, he learned later, had been designed by Lieutenant John Harris of the Royal Engineers and constructed from old bricks held together with dried mud. Harris's ingenious invention served to cook food and heat water. Later, when the Japanese gleefully told them of the devastation being wrought in the south of England by German flying bombs, it was christened 'V2'.

From Jack Wood, he learned that two or three months after his transfer to Bowen Road, a large contingent had been despatched to labour camps in Japan. Among them had been many of Roger's friends, including, to his dismay, Doctor Woodward, to whom he had owed his life. The bizarre selection method of those to be sent to Japan was typical of the mentality of their captors.

Towards the end of February, working parties were sent out to clear the bare, rocky area to the west of Argyle Street. They had been encouraged to move the heavy rocks by the liberal application of bamboo canes on their bare backs.

When the ground had been completely cleared over an area of about 100 square yards, they were informed that the purpose of the work had been to make a sports arena and that a sports day had been arranged for their benefit. Tracks were duly marked out, and a dais was erected to hold the camp staff.

When the great day arrived, all those in any condition to run at more than a snail's pace were lined up to participate in what must have been the most extraordinary sporting event ever witnessed. The times registered for the various events must indeed have qualified for inclusion in the Guinness Book of Records as the slowest ever achieved.

After each race, the first two or three home were segregated and held on one side. Under the impression that they were to be presented with a prize for their prowess, they waited in blissful anticipation of cigarettes, chocolate or some other hoped-for goodies as the reward for their prowess.

When the whole pantomime came to its conclusion, the lucky winners were lined up in front of the dais, where they were harangued by Panama Pete, his face contorted with his usual contempt and hatred.

"You guys," he snarled, "you say you're too weak to work, yet you can win races. Tomorrow you go to Japan to do some real work!"

After receiving the statutory assault, the unfortunate athletes were marched away and despatched forthwith to the Land of the Rising Sun.

This exodus had been followed by the closure of Argyle Street camp and the transfer of its remaining inmates in three batches back to Shamshuipo, the last leaving on May 24th. Here they were segregated from the men's camp by barbed-wire fencing, and communication between the two sections was strictly forbidden.

His departure from Bowen Road had been marked by the kindly Watanabe with a magnificent flood of letters from home, including four from Daisy, so he had returned in excellent spirits.

Jack Wood had turned up trumps and had brought with him the scrapbook that he was making for Daisy and also his precious diary, which would have caused grave problems for Jack if it had been discovered in his possession.

However, the accommodation in their new home was far more cramped than it had been in Argyle Street, and their bed spaces were almost touching, giving no room for movement. Jack had persuaded the inmates of Hut No. 1 to squeeze up still further to make room for the newcomer. Still, understandably, they did move with some reluctance.

To add to their discomfort, it was now the hottest time of the year, and this, added to their close quarters, made life unbearable and sleep in the foetid atmosphere of the hut well-nigh impossible, particularly as, in Roger's case, one of his immediate neighbours suffered badly from body-odour.

But this was, by no means, all. Two weeks before Roger's return to Shamshuipo, Lieutenant Ralph Goodwin of the HKVDC decided that he had had enough and, finding a gap under the wire of the perimeter fence, slipped silently away into the darkness without having breathed a word to anyone. At first, no one was worried, thinking that he had gone to the latrines. When he did not return, there was absolute consternation, particularly as to the probable fate of the unfortunates who had been on duty at the hut entrance and who, if the Japanese carried out their threat, were candidates for immediate execution as punishment for the escape.

Something had to be done without half a moment's delay. They would be on morning muster parade in an hour, and Goodwin's absence would be discovered.

Then someone had a brilliant idea. Leaving it to within a few minutes of the parade to give Ralph the maximum time possible to put distance between himself and the camp, they ran to the office of Lieutenant Tanaka - now the camp commandant - and hammered on his door.

Something terrible had happened, they told him; one of their comrades, a very powerful man, had been insane for a long time and had threatened to kill a member of the Japanese army when an opportunity arose. They had managed to keep him under control with great difficulty to prevent him from doing this dreadful thing. But now they could not find him and were very frightened that he might be hiding somewhere waiting to carry out his threat. Wiping imaginary tears from their eyes, they pleaded for help to find him so that they could look after him and keep him under their control. He must be somewhere in the camp as, of course, no one could escape from such a closely guarded prison.

Tanaka looked suspiciously at the deputation. Was this some sort of trick, he wondered, but the looks of desperation on their faces convinced him that their concern was genuine. Tanaka reflected that for him to have allowed a prisoner to escape would, later, require an explanation to his superior officers. He decided to take a chance and, abandoning the muster parade for the time being – which was just what they had hoped for as it gave Goodwin even more time to make himself scarce – ordered a thorough search of both camps.

Goodwin had, mercifully, patched up the hole under the fence after making his getaway and by the time that no trace of the missing prisoner could be found in either camp, they reckoned that he had had at least twelve hours to get clear of the town and time to hide up safely for the remaining daylight hours before making his way across country and, provided that he did not fall into the hands of bandits, he should be clear away.

As a matter of routine, when something had gone wrong, the whole camp was placed under a punishment diet for several weeks with extended parades and general beastliness.

On August 10th, the day after his return to Shamshuipo, they were astonished to see a large lorry pull up outside the rice store and off-load sides of beef, sacks of flour and sugar, the like of which they had not seen since their captivity. The goodies were carried into the shed, and an armed guard placed around it.

The announcement that the camp was to be inspected by Zindall, the Red Cross representative, soon explained the mystery that afternoon. They were to stand to attention by their bed spaces and make no gesture or attempt to communicate with the inspector.

Roger's next-door neighbour in the hut was a gaunt Intelligence Officer named Ken Barnett, who had been a member of the HKVDC with the Hong Kong government before the battle. He was a man of almost frightening intellect. He had invented a game of three-dimensional chess in camp using three boards – one on top of the other – a game so complicated that only a very few, which did not include Roger, could understand, let alone play. He was fluent in both spoken and written Cantonese and Mandarin and was, in fact, an extraordinary character who neither enjoyed nor sought popularity or the company of his fellow prisoners, some of whom were unkind enough to comment on his aloofness and lack of hygiene. However, Roger got on with him well enough and, indeed, had considerable respect for his intellect.

This respect was to increase a hundred-fold on the day of the Red Cross inspection.

Zindall arrived at the camp.

The prisoners were marshalled into their huts and stood by their bed spaces as ordered, smartly to attention and with faces devoid of any expression. The Red

Cross man came into the hut escorted by Tanaka, an interpreter and half a dozen armed sentries.

As the posse was being ushered through the hut at a brisk pace, Ken Barnett stepped out and barred the way and said in a loud, clear voice: "Mr Zindall, for God's sake, help us. We are being starved, beaten and treated with great brutality by these wicked men. We have no medicines and..."

He got no further.

Three of the guard leapt on him and dragged him from the hut screaming at him whilst Zindall was practically frog-marched through the door at the other end of the hut and out of the camp without ceremony.

Roger had heard of cold courage; now, he had seen it in action. This man, who had seemed to have little regard for his fellow sufferers, knowing full well what the consequences of his actions were likely to be, had sacrificed himself for the benefit of his fellow prisoners.

For three days, they listened to the agonised screams from the guard room as he was made to pay the price for his disobedience.

When he eventually returned, he was clearly broken in both mind and in body, although neither he nor anyone else spoke of or attempted to discuss what had gone on in that room during those terrible days. No one attempted to praise or even thank him for what he had done but everyone from then on regarded him with the most profound respect and admiration.

On August 27th, just seventeen days after Ken Barnett's magnificent protest, lorries drove into the camp laden with hundreds of Red Cross parcels, the first they had seen for more than two years. Each contained goodies the like of which they had only dreamed about - milk powder, chocolate, butter, biscuits, corned beef, meat roll, tinned salmon, sardines, cheese, sugar, coffee, jam, raisins, prunes and a tablet of toilet soap.

Ken Barnett's sacrifice had paid handsome dividends, and everyone knew that it was to his protest to Zindall that they owed this magnificent stroke of fortune. By September 22nd, the carefully husbanded supplies were exhausted. Nevertheless, the general health of the camp had improved dramatically, and the diary recorded that he had gained 10½ lbs since they arrived.

From the news of the war, gleaned from the Hong Kong News and through the working parties from the neighbouring camp who had established contact with sources outside the wire, it was clear that things in Europe were going splendidly. The Russians were in East Prussia and Bulgaria. Romania had surrendered unconditionally, and the British and Americans had occupied Paris and were streaming across the Belgian frontier. There was next to no news obtainable of the American offensive in the Pacific. However, rumours put them within striking distance of the Philippines, so there was a spirit of great optimism. They began to talk of the possibility of freedom by Christmas.

With the exhaustion of the Red Cross parcels, the tightening of the American blockade in the Philippines area, and their ability to overfly Japan and the South China Sea, the food supply was becoming even more sparse. Not infrequently, there was only sufficient for one ration of rice per day, sometimes mixed with a bit of bran or half a cupful of watery vegetable, as often as not a sort of green pumpkin which was all but inedible, as it was the vegetable from which loofahs are made and consisted of a mass of fibre which could be swallowed only with difficulty.

Added to this was the fact that prices in the canteen were now astronomical - a pound of beans costing more than three months' pay and, since anything of value had long since been sold through the RASC entrepreneurs, there was no possibility of supplementing the near starvation diet.

Their situation was, however, marginally improved by their own resources.

When their part of the camp had been occupied in Argyle Street, a piece of waste ground at the northern end of the camp had been cultivated for vegetables, tomatoes and aubergines. Although it was now officially out of bounds, the seeds from the remaining plants were collected and planted in the trenches between the huts where the contents of the lavatory buckets had to be emptied. These proved, not surprisingly, to be highly fertile. The seeds planted there grew so rapidly that crops could be gathered within a few weeks of planting. From these, an issue of one or two tomatoes and an aubergine could be issued to each man once a week.

Also, a few scrawny hens purchased clandestinely from their comrades across the wire and fed on rice and vegetable scraps yielded one or two eggs per week, which were reserved exclusively for the hospital hut, although one notable on returning from the occasion, an officer of an elevated rank, was seen to lift the wire of the compound latrine at night and creep away with one of the precious eggs, thereby earning for himself a very considerable degree of unpopularity and contempt.

The Hong Kong News now appeared only when there was some major reverse for the Allies as, for example, the disaster at Arnhem, the effect of the V1 and, later, the V2 rockets, said to have reduced the whole of south-eastern England to rubble, with the civilian population living in caves and foxholes. And the Germans' counter-offensive in the Ardennes was all reported with gusto as signalling the beginning of the final defeat of the Allies. No mention of the progress of the war in the Pacific was ever made, which everyone regarded as an encouraging sign. The only indication of improvement came from rumours of Japanese reverses gleaned from the working parties from the neighbouring camp, which were, no doubt, as unreliable as the reports in the paper.

One unexpected and most welcome bonus which followed Ken Barnett's gallant appeal to Zindall was the arrival in the camp of a collection of musical instruments in various stages of dilapidation, which, when repaired, formed the makings of a tolerable little orchestra in which Roger, who had a little skill as a violinist, was lucky enough to be a member. Orchestra practices and an occasional performance in which extemporisation and memory played an essential role were conducted by Roger's friend and former colleague at the cipher office, Frank Austin. Frank, skilled in composition and harmony, produced some quite reasonable performances and, even more important, occupied some more of their spare time.

Their great moment came when they provided a splendid musical revue complete with an 'orchestra' – perhaps the most extraordinary 'chorus line' ever seen – lyrics and a typically frivolous Whitehall-type plot which they entitled 'Nuts and Mayhem'.

The theme song was based on the pre-war ditty 'A Tisket, a Tasket my little yellow basket' and the audience was delighted as the whole cast, in their weird variety of costumes on which many weeks of ingenuity and skill had been expended, faced the front line of the audience, which consisted exclusively of the camp staff, and, with their fingers pointing at the camp commandant, chanted: "A Tisket. A Tasket. You little yellow basket!"

Tanaka, who had not understood a word of it, smiled and bowed and presented the cast with a most welcome five cigarettes each. Life had its compensations.

Perhaps the most worthwhile project of this stage of their life in the camp was the "Exhibition of Arts and Crafts", in which an incredible variety of products was displayed to raise money for the war widows and children in the civilian internment camp at Stanley. Roger's map of Sussex, copied from E.V. Lucas's book on which he had laboured happily for several weeks, was bought for the princely sum of 200 Yen – a fortnight's pay – and Roger's diary records: "The excellence of the things on display was unbelievable; wood-carvings (I lent my bookends carved in Bowen Road), paintings, knitted things – waistcoats, gloves, socks etc. etc. It was a tremendous success. Even Colonel Tokanaga, who visited the exhibition, said, most graciously, that it was 'commendable'."

The air raids, which had been an almost daily occurrence during the second half of 1943, now no longer took place except for the occasional reconnaissance flight by a four-engined bomber at high altitude, and this had added to their depression. However, the optimists, possibly correctly, deduced from this that the Americans no longer relied on their base in Chungking but were operating from the Pacific islands they had reoccupied and concentrated their efforts on the Philippines and, hopefully, Japan itself.

However, this state of affairs was to change dramatically and, at the beginning of October 1944, the first of a series of raids, far heavier than those which had preceded them, brought tidings of great joy. Instead of small-scale affairs with a handful of planes, they involved low-level attacks by waves of fighter bombers and torpedo-carrying planes concentrating on dock facilities, shipping and Kai Tak airfield.

These were all most exciting since, as Shamshuipo was the only low-lying area of any size, the planes invariably carried out their attacks at an almost roof-top level over the camp itself, frequently so low that the pilot could clearly be seen as he made his run-in for the target and often, returning by the same route, he would bank over and give a cheery wave to the deliriously excited prisoners as he passed overhead.

There were strict orders that all prisoners should remain inside their huts during a raid. Still, since the sentries were similarly ordered to stay in the shelters at the same time, few bothered to do so. In three years, this was the first time they had felt on the winning side, and they made the most of it.

Not that they were entirely free from danger at such times since, because of the low altitude of the attacking planes, the anti-aircraft fire directed against them frequently raked the camp itself. Since these were mainly small-calibre explosive bullets, the thin-boarded huts provided little protection, and there were several severe casualties. In Roger's hut, Henry Eardley lost a leg during a raid on December 2nd. 'Pixie' Stansfield and Lieutenant Richards, his hut companions, were wounded during the great air raid of January 16th, 1945, which lasted more than twelve hours and involved nearly 400 planes, leaving the prisoners excitedly worn out.

This raid, which had concentrated on shipping and the airfield, was the last for more than three months. It was clear that, as a threat to American shipping and air attacks, Hong Kong was regarded as having been eliminated. Life returned to its regular dreary routine of monotonous, empty days.

Roger's attacks of malaria were, once again, on the increase. After several minor relapses of 'benign' tertian, he was struck down on 13th November by a vicious return of the malignant variety, which had nearly killed him way back in February 1942.

This attack kept him on his back for more than a fortnight and left him as weak as a kitten for several weeks. Further, less severe attacks occurred during the early months of 1945. Early in April, he was once more in the hospital hut, this time a victim of pneumonia resulting from the shock of an injury to his knee.

This happened during a barrel-throwing session in the former church building, which the Japanese used as a storage depot for empty oil drums. These had to be thrown onto a stack that grew steadily higher and higher. The work was so exhausting that they had to work in shifts, two to each barrel, and could only last for thirty minutes at a time before being relieved by the next gang.

He had reached the end of his shift and was about to hand over to the new team. One of these was Major Hedgecoe, now commanding the Middlesex Regiment since Monkey Stewart had been sent to Japan on the ill-fated 'Lisbon Maru' back in October 1942. Hedgecoe, a big and powerful man, seized his end of the barrel: "Come on, Rothwell," he said, "just this last one before you fall out," and, with a mighty swing, slewed the sharp rim of the drum round into Roger's leg, shattering the knee-cap and leaving him writhing in agony on the floor of the building.

This injury and its resulting illness put him out of action for several weeks, by which time the hot weather had set in, bringing with it the misery of prickly heat, and this was aggravated by a return of beri beri, which the Red Cross parcels had helped to clear up. At the same time, an epidemic of cerebral meningitis put the hut in quarantine and killed his Canadian friend Major Hook.

On May 27th, as so often happened when they were feeling that things had got almost as bad as they could, came confirmation of the fantastic news that the war in Europe was over, that Hitler had died in Berlin on May 1st and that the surrender had been signed on May 7th.

Chapter 25

Towards Freedom

When the first euphoria, which followed the collapse of Germany and the ending of the war in Europe, with its surge of thankfulness that loved ones at home were no longer in danger, had died away, came the chilling realisation that release might still be very distant.

If, as seemed likely, the Japanese were determined to stand and fight, their defeat in Burma, Malaya and French Indo-China might take many months or even years. It was quite possible, also, that if the Allies were to invade Japan itself, it would make sense, from a strategic point of view, for them to keep clear of the Chinese mainland and not get bogged down in what would undoubtedly be a very long-drawn-out campaign over vast areas of territory, so that Hong Kong could well be the last occupied country to be freed.

There were also even grimmer possibilities.

Supposing Japan itself was invaded with massive military and civilian casualties, what sort of revenge might be taken on the prisoners in Hong Kong? Indeed, dark hints had already been dropped by their captors that in the event of an attack on the colony, the first casualties were likely to be the inmates of the prison camps. They were well aware from their previous inhuman treatment that the Japanese might attempt a massacre of their captives. Should this occur, plans were formulated accordingly for a mass break-out - it would be better to go down fighting than to submit to being slaughtered.

Reliable news of the progress of the war was now virtually impossible to obtain, the Hong Kong News having long since ceased to appear, so that all they had to go on were garbled rumours picked up by outside working parties, which had been proved false so many times in the past as to make them scarcely worthwhile to repeat, let alone to believe.

Similarly, no letters from home had been received for months and on August 13th, Roger's diary recorded that he had had no news of Daisy since February 27th and that that letter had been more than a year old and written in the worst of the V1 and V2 attacks, and as he knew that the Kent and East Sussex areas must be in the direct line of these there was no certainty that, even though the war was now over, she was still safe and well.

Time now hung very heavily on their hands. Only the orchestra practices served to occupy the time. The few scores available from Frank Austin's fertile memory, which included the Andante from 'The New World Symphony' and 'Manhattan Moonlight', limited the purpose of these. Their rehearsals became monotonous both for themselves and even more for their unfortunate comrades who commented appropriately on them.

The quality and quantity of food was also steadily deteriorating. The average ration of rice per day was now less than 10 ounces. The tiny amount of vegetables served only to give a cupful each of watery soup, the pips and peel from the Loofahs being dried, ground and added to the rice "porridge" to provide a little more body. However, in July, a ration of 12 lbs per man of beans and bran sent in by Zindall provided a couple of better meals. However, things were now about as bad as they had ever been.

And so July dragged its way through to August.

A week later, however, as if in answer to prayer, came a rumour from a reliable source that Russia had declared war on Japan, and this was followed, the next day, by a story said to have come from one of the sentries that the Japanese armies in Manchuria had offered to surrender. The news was that the Russians had refused this and insisted that only a complete and unconditional surrender by all Japanese forces on all fronts would be acceptable.

Rumours flew thick and fast around the camp – peace had been declared at 10 p.m. on the 11th. At 7 p.m. on the 13th, word spread that fifteen Allied warships would arrive on the 15th, that Tokanagi would visit the camp for a conference and that special tea had been brought in for the occasion. Still, no one was really surprised when nothing happened, and it was not long before everyone became weary of speculation.

But it was impossible not to be eager to hear the latest rumour, however unlikely it was. The working parties from the camp next door continued to bring in stories gleaned from the places where they were working – a shop-keeper in Lai Chi Kok had been told on August 14th by the gendarmerie that peace had been signed and that he had been warned against making a disturbance – Japan had been raided by 1,500 planes on August 13th – Chiang Rai Shek had ordered all Chinese troops to maintain their positions until further orders that all food shops in the town had been closed and manned by marines and so on and on.

As if in contradiction to the rumours, tar was brought in to repair the roof of the hospital hut. The canteen opened in the usual way, although with peanut oil at 810

Yen per lb and salted fish at 420 Yen per lb; this was an indication that the rumours of the end of the war were unlikely to be true.

Clearly, it was time to take some positive action to bring matters to a head and establish the truth. He decided to make his own contribution.

Having written his gloomy diary entry for August 15th, Roger decided to stroll into the guard room without saluting and demand a light for a cigarette he had come by.

Instead of the attack with a fist or rifle butt, which such effrontery would typically have been greeted, the Formosan sentry approached him affably and, showing him a pair of battle dress pants, said:

"You wanchee buy trousers?"

"My no wanchee buy, my wanchee sell - you buy," replied the astonished Roger.

The sentry insisted: "No can my wanchee sell, you buy."

Roger decided to press his luck: "More better you go Hong Kong side, Kowloon side. Can sell that place," he replied in his best pidgin English.

The sentry looked depressed: "No can go," he said sadly.

Things were now looking up. "What for no can go?" demanded Roger.

"My no savvy. Sunday can go. Monday can go. Today no can," came the answer.

This was becoming really promising, and Roger decided to put the definitive question: "Perhaps war finish soon?" he asked.

The sentry's face immediately became impassive. "You have seen paper?" he replied guardedly.

"No. No have seen paper, one two three month no see paper," replied Roger with perfect truth, his heart beating almost audibly. "My no savvy about war. You think war finish soon?"

The sentry gave him a searching look: "My no savvy - perhaps tomorrow, perhaps one year", and it was clear that he would not be drawn any further on the subject. But the exercise had been well worthwhile, and Roger's excitement grew.

That evening they decided to break all the rules to test the temperature. Instead of shutting themselves up in their huts at dusk as required by regulations, they sat around in groups outside, talking, laughing and singing and awaiting the retribution which would usually have resulted from such defiance.

None came.

From beyond the wire came the extraordinary and totally unaccustomed sound of singing and chanting as the Chinese celebrated in the streets against a background of exploding fire-crackers.

Emboldened still further, they tore down planks of wood from the walls and empty window frames of the huts and lit bonfires in reckless defiance, inviting what should have been a violent attack.

When this did not come, they were finally convinced that it was all over and, by common consent, agreed that they would not go out on the morning parade when the call came.

When the bugle sounded as usual for the eight o'clock muster, they sat tight on their beds, waiting for the response to this ultimate act of disobedience. After a while, a sentry stamped into the hut and shouted some guttural commands, thumping the butt of his rifle on the floor in an attempt to move them by force but making no impact whatsoever. They all stood their ground, giving him a cheery greeting and inviting him explicitly to go forth and multiply in any fashion he saw fit.

The sentry grunted, thumped the floor once more, and retreated.

This, then, was really it.

All day long, they lounged around the camp, tore down the barbed-wire fencing which separated them from the neighbouring camp, meeting up with comrades they had not seen for years, and planning their next move.

In the afternoon of the 16th came the final confirmation of the news for which they had waited for more than three years, with the arrival in the next camp of a Chinese newspaper carrying the brief statement that Japan had capitulated and had "accepted the terms of the 14th" whatever they were but, it was presumed, an unconditional surrender.

No one at that time knew what had happened to bring about this sudden and dramatic situation. It was not until several days later that they learned of the destruction of Hiroshima and Nagasaki by single bombs of unimaginable power, which had finally broken the Japanese resolve.

While there was no longer any doubt that the war was over, the immediate future was by no means certain. The Japanese were still in control, their flag was still flying over the camp, and they had the weapons to enforce their authority. Moreover, refusing to surrender was an inviolable part of the Japanese military code.

Against these facts was the knowledge that all that was available to the prisoners were odd pieces of iron, which could be converted into crude weapons, and a great deal of determination to give a good account of themselves if the need arose.

The next day Colonel Field of the Royal Engineers, the most senior officer in the camp, took over control and demanded a meeting with Tokanagi, who asserted that he had received no news of any cessation of hostilities and still regarded the captives as his prisoners.

However, with great reluctance, he eventually agreed to remove the sentries from the gates and replace them with Allied military police.

On the morning of the 18th, both camps attended a ceremonial parade and service of thanksgiving. The poached egg was lowered from the flagpole and replaced by the Union Jack and the White Ensign, which had been removed from their hiding place. This was too much for the frustrated Tokanagi, who demanded that his flag be replaced. A very ostentatious closing of the ranks around the pole followed, indicating that if the Japanese wished to exchange the flags, they were free to try. No further protest was made, and the service began.

As it did so, there was a sudden sharp shower of rain, but as the flags were broken out at the masthead, a brilliant shaft of sunlight shone out between the clouds. A great rainbow stretched itself across the sky as if in celebration.

Roger, struggling to control an enormous lump in his throat, heard a strangled noise by his side. It was his friend Pixie Stansfield, and he was weeping unashamedly.

After the service, Roger made his way to the wire crowded with gaunt Chinese bodies supported on matchstick limbs who clung to the fence shouting: "Tai Pan. Tai Pan, cumsaw, cumsaw! Ni shi mo ah! Ni shi mo ah! – Master, master. Charity, charity! Nothing here! Nothing here!"

Although they themselves were unsure of where their next meal was to come from, at the sight of these pinched faces and the plea in the eyes of the little children, they pushed through handfuls of rice and any spare scraps of food, which were grabbed and gulped down like animals.

The question of food supply was a matter of immediate concern as, by now, their former captors seemed to be totally disorganised and raiding parties were formed to break open and loot any Japanese food stores which could be found both inside the compound and in the town beyond the wire.

These raids, some made in a commandeered lorry, were not without considerable danger from snipers still lurking in the upper storeys of buildings and from the hungry Chinese. Still, they were amply rewarded by unearthing quantities of flour, salt, meat, sugar, oil and cigarettes. Another store yielded Red Cross clothing and food parcels, all carefully stocked and rationed as there were still some thousand or more survivors to be fed.

Another urgent matter to be attended to was the arrest of the renegade RASC Major, 'Queenie', who had banked on a Japanese victory and who was not only a very lonely man but in immediate danger of being lynched. Many who had suffered at his hands had secured a rope and prepared a public hanging until Colonel Field reminded the would-be executioners that they were once more subject to British Military Law.

Consequently, 'Queenie' was placed under close arrest in the former guard room and guarded night and day by groups of highly resentful and reluctant officers, of which Roger, himself having suffered at the hands of this despicable creature, was one.

The eventual fate of this gallant Major whose trial for high treason took place so long after his return to England that the specimen charges, each of which would undoubtedly have incurred the death penalty, had been committed more than three years before the date of the trial, and so, under British Military Law, were no longer valid. After a less than five-minute trial, 'Queenie' walked free from the court to the immense chagrin of those whose friends had been murdered due to information he had relayed to his Japanese masters or who, like Roger, had been subjected to beatings or worse.

In contrast to this gentleman, another person to be taken into protective custody for his safety to protect him from the wrath of his own people was the Japanese interpreter Kyoshi Watanabe, who had taken such appalling risks to bring help to the prisoners and who had, quite certainly, saved Roger's life at great risk to his own.

The two were genuinely delighted to meet again.

Roger felt genuine concern for the future of Watanabe, who would undoubtedly share the privations of his defeated colleagues. He assured him he would give him every possible support should the need arise.

Watanabe gave him his customary imperturbable smile.

"Do not be anxious either for me or my country," he said. "As for me, I am in God's hands, and so I have no fear for the future. As for my country, it will rise again, for it is its destiny that one day, perhaps in one hundred, perhaps two hundred years, it will be the world's leading nation - not by war or force of arms but by its own industry and determination."

He spoke quietly and without any hint of bravado, and Roger, who had no wish to enter into any sort of argument, did not seek to argue with him.

The day after his conversation with Roger, this calm and courageous man was to receive the news that the wife whom he adored, together with all of his children, except for his daughter Kei who had gone on a shopping trip to Tokyo, had been obliterated by the atomic bomb which had destroyed the city of Hiroshima and had brought the war to its sudden end.

Watanabe was overwhelmed with grief, yet when Roger tried to offer a few clumsy words of condolence, he managed a gentle smile: "Thank you for your kindness," he said, "but we must not be bitter. It was God's will, and we must have no complaint."

(On his return to Japan, Watanabe became pastor at the Lutheran Church at Beppu in Honshu and lived to a happy old age with Kei, keeping in touch with Roger and Daisy each Christmas.

In 1960 he was flown to London by the producers of the television programme 'This is Your Life', and spent a weekend with Roger, Daisy and their children in their home, proudly showing them the prayer which Roger had written in his autograph album, attending the school carol service in St. Mary's in Rye and, with tears streaming down his wrinkled face, blessed the children from the pulpit.)

The days following their captors' capitulation were ones of a strange emotional mixture. Although their condition regarding food and freedom from brutality was vastly improved, the perils of venturing weaponless into the town made them virtually prisoners inside their camp waiting for the fleet's arrival to take them home. Added to this, supplies were necessarily strictly rationed, and although peanut oil and sugar relieved the monotony of their rice diet, the European food, bread, butter and, curiously enough, potatoes which they all craved, was still unobtainable. The sampans, which crowded along the harbour wall at the western end of the camp, offered for sale the only food available: the little bony fish which swam around the sewage outlets.

To obtain this, one took a piece of unwanted clothing - a battered old shirt or jacket or a screw of sugar and shouted down: "Mai yiu sik - Buy fish eat." Down would go the payment at the end of a piece of string, and up would come a little bag of wriggling fish, which would then be cooked over a campfire made from scraps of wood torn from the huts.

Throughout this strange period, news was constantly filtering through of more and more of the atrocities committed by their captors. Fraser, the defence secretary for the colony, had been tied naked to an iron bedstead and slowly roasted alive. Another poor wretch under interrogation had had holes punched through the palms of his hands and barbed wire drawn to and fro through them, fingernails having been torn out. These and many more served both to depress and to show them how lucky those who had escaped the attention of the interrogators had been.

Roger remembered with gratitude how Watanabe had saved him from a similar fate.

The first contact from the world outside came on the evening of August 18th when seven American fighter planes flew low over the colony and dropped pamphlets containing a message addressed to *"Allied Prisoners of War and Civilian Internees"* and confirming that *"The Japanese Government has accepted the Allied peace terms set forth in the Potsdam Declaration"* and that final negotiations were being concluded.

Only a few of these fell in the camp, most being carried away by a stiff breeze into the harbour. In return for a little packet of sugar, Roger succeeded in persuading a small Chinese boy to swim out into Lai Chi Kok Bay to recover a copy for inclusion in the scrapbook which he had made for Daisy.

And now followed what seemed to be an endless and frustrating period of inactivity when their release appeared as far away as ever. As day followed with no news other than bulletins from the radio sent into the camp and made no mention of relieving forces, tempers became increasingly frayed.

One nagging thought that he tried unsuccessfully to put out of his mind was how Daisy had been faring all this long time. The last he had heard from her was eight months ago, and her letter had been written more than a year previous to that. Much could happen in nearly two years, which had covered the indiscriminate attacks on London and the South East by the V1 and V2 rockets. He knew he would not sleep peacefully until she was safe. Of her complete faithfulness to him through the long years of separation, he had not the slightest doubt. As long as they were both alive, nothing could ever separate them.

Back at Eridge, Daisy was tormented by the same anxieties. Throughout the war, she had kept hope high, but now the moment of truth was at hand; now she had got to know whether he was still alive, and the reports beginning to appear in the press of atrocities committed on the prisoners and of widespread death from disease, malnutrition and cold-blooded murder did nothing to ease her anxieties.

Back in Hong Kong came the first indication of the end of the waiting when a sizeable American transport plane flew over and dropped several canisters of food and medical supplies by parachute onto the parade ground.

The canisters contained chocolate, cigarettes and milk powder, packets labelled "dehydrated meat", "dehydrated vegetables," and "dehydrated fish", the value of which their Rip Van Winkle existence of the past three and half a years away from civilisation left them a trifle mystified. These parcels, however unappetising they appeared, were transformed into a massive stew, the most gorgeous meal they had tasted since their captivity.

It also resulted in the most spectacular bilious attacks, their stomachs long accustomed to tiny quantities of food of the lowest possible nutritional value.

One of the canisters, however, caused them significant uncertainty. It was labelled "Dried blood plasma", and serious discussion took place in the messing committee, some of whose members asserted that it was most likely a new form of seasoning and should be added to the stew along with the rest. Doctors Strachan and Evans decreed that it must have a medical significance, so reluctantly, the stew was denied this additional attractive and doubtless nutritional component.

The plane returned later in the day with more supplies and, this time, a hammer hurtled down with a label bearing the message: "With the compliments of 11th Combat Cargo Squadron. Good Luck. It won't be long now!" and the signatures of the crew.

The next day, Thursday, August 30th, was one which none of the prisoners will ever forget.

Early in the morning, a shout from a lookout on the flat roof of the Jubilee Buildings brought the whole camp racing across the parade ground towards the water's edge.

Weak though he was from his recent fever, Roger took the bomb-damaged concrete staircase two steps at a time and emerged onto the roof.

Standing speechless among the cheering, jostling crowd, he looked down onto the wide stretch of water which separates the hills of Lantau from Hong Kong island. In that "passage to the sea" down which his murdered friend, Potter, had longed to travel and of which he had written so movingly, Roger saw in the clear light of the new day their grey shapes glinting in the morning sunlight and moving silently, slowly and inexorably towards the harbour, the most extraordinary array of warships he had ever witnessed.

Freedom had come at last.

Chapter 26

Journey's End

The fleet, which dropped anchor in the vast stretch of water between Hong Kong Island and the mainland, their guns manned and their crews at battle stations on that morning of brilliant sunshine, was indeed a formidable one. Its flagship, the battleship 'Anson', under the command of Admiral Harcourt, was escorted by two aircraft carriers, the 'Indomitable' and 'Venerable', two cruisers, six destroyers, eight submarines, seven minesweepers, the submarine depot ship 'Maidstone', an armed merchant cruiser, the Canadian 'Prince Robert' and two hospital ships. All of these, so they learned later, were to have formed part of a much larger force being assembled for the invasion of Japan.

Indeed the two long weeks between the dropping of the atomic bombs on Hiroshima and Nagasaki and this first contact with their approaching freedom had been a time of intense nervous strain for all of them and their unspoken fears that the Japanese garrison, unwilling to accept surrender and isolated from the main theatre of the war, might turn their fury on their defenceless prisoners had never been out of their thoughts.

But now, at last, the long period of waiting and uncertainty was over, and their return home was within reach.

Even so, the ever-present anxiety remained over the safety of those they had left behind for whom they had longed and whose love had sustained them throughout the endless and bitter years.

They had heard from their captors horrific accounts of the death and destruction caused by Hitler's indiscriminate attacks on the civilian population of London and the South East by his V1 and V2 weapons, and it was by no means certain that these were mere propaganda designed for the consumption of their prisoners. It was nearly two years since Roger had had news of Daisy, who he knew must inevitably have been in the direct line of fire of these murderous contraptions, crossing as they would have to do over East Sussex and Kent on their way from Northern France to London. What would have been the point of his survival if she were not to be there to greet him on his return?

For her part, Daisy, who had last heard from him for an equal length of time, must also be haunted by the possibility that he had not survived his captivity. All through the long years, she had had to comfort herself with the thought that somehow he would battle through and come back to her.

But now the moment of truth was at hand, and through all the rejoicing that accompanied the celebrations of victory over Germany and, later, Japan came the chilling thought that now she had got to know. For nearly five long years, she had waited with great patience and unswerving loyalty and devotion while what should have been the best years of her youth drained slowly away.

Throughout this time, she had never lost hope, but now what if it had all been in vain, and she was to be forced to begin a totally new life?

Her anxiety would be relieved much sooner than she had dared to hope.

Immediately after the arrival of the fleet in Hong Kong, a plane load of the fittest of the senior officers were flown back to England to report to the War Office and, among these, was Frank Hedgecoe, the second in command of the Middlesex Regiment who had damaged Roger's knee with the oil drum.

One of his first appointments was to attend a meeting in the Guildhall in London of the Hong Kong Fellowship, which had been formed to exchange what scant news had emerged from the prison camps and to keep the relatives of the captives in touch with each other and which Daisy had attended unfailingly despite the dangers of the V1 and V2 rockets.

At the meeting, Frank stood on a dais surrounded by a milling crowd, hungry for news to give what information he could about the condition of the prisoners.

Looking over the heads of the throng, he saw Daisy. "I recognise you," he said, pointing down at her, "I've seen your picture every day by your husband's bed, and I can tell you that he has come through safely and that he is fit and well."

Daisy wept with delight and knew then, for sure, that prayers are indeed answered when they come from the heart.

Back in the camp, all was a frenzy of excitement and activity.

At 6pm, a convoy of small white vehicles of a type they had never seen before but which they were told were called Jeeps came into the camp headed by Admiral Harcourt with an escort of immaculately dressed British sailors. He told the excited crowd that he was sorry for the delay in the arrival of the fleet but explained that it had inevitably taken time for the necessary redeployment of the naval force to be organised.

"We got here as quickly as we could," he said.

The cheers and the raucous singing of "For he's a jolly good fellow" which greeted him left him in no doubt of the enthusiastic acceptance of his 'apology'!

Perhaps almost as welcome as the arrival of their rescuers was the appearance of copious quantities of provisions, even though these were accompanied by warnings of the perils of loading large amounts of food into stomachs shrunken by starvation – advice cheerfully and wantonly ignored by everyone who subsequently suffered accordingly.

Perhaps the most delicious goodies their eager hands unpacked were real potatoes, the first they had tasted for nearly four years, and freshly baked bread, which possessed an undreamed-of flavour.

Thursday, August 30th, 1945, is a day which will remain forever in the memories of those lucky enough to have survived to see it.

The days which followed were ones of intense activity. The first letters home, promised to be sent by air, took significant priority; the remains of uniform, carefully preserved, brought out and repaired with proper needle and thread; washing with real toilet soap and shaving with new razor blades all were delights to be savoured to the full and even a visit to George the dentist, now equipped with actual anaesthetic, was a welcome activity and relief.

Despite their limited resources, their rescuers did everything possible to bring them pleasure and comfort; an ENSA team, the forces' entertainers, put on a show in the old church hall – now cleared of the stored oil barrels. They laughed uproariously at the not-very-funny jokes of 'Cardew the Cad' and his hard-working colleagues.

Although obviously unable to accommodate the large numbers involved, the navy organised fleets of tenders to carry groups to their ships for entertainment and Roger, now reunited with the remnants of his old platoon, found himself in one of these bound for the battleship 'Anson' where the entire crew welcomed them by lining ship and applauding as they clambered up the gangway.

Once aboard, he was invited to partake of sherry in the admiral's cabin and, after a film show putting them in touch with the events of the war of which they had had little actual knowledge, they were entertained to a real 'afternoon tea' with sliced peaches and cream accompanied by wafer-thin bread and butter. Indian tea was served in thin, delicate bone-china cups, their first contact with the civilisation that had been denied to them for so long, leaving many in tears.

The more senior officers and those who, like Jack Wood, were in a frail state of health had been transferred to the Peninsula Hotel, where they could once more sleep in actual beds and wash in porcelain baths and hot water. The bulk of the men had no option but to live out the remaining days in their old surroundings.

At last, nearly a fortnight after the fleet's arrival, they boarded the 'Empress of Australia', which, with another transport, the 'Aorangi', had followed the fleet. They stowed their meagre possessions into battered suitcases and kitbags and walked out of the camp towards their freedom.

For years, Roger had pictured this moment in his mind and had seen himself and his companions rushing out of the camp with whoops and shouts of delirious joy, but now, when the dreamed-of moment had arrived, and they walked through the barbed-wire gate for the last time towards their freedom, they felt suddenly and quite inexplicably an overwhelming poignancy which caused them to stop and look back soberly at the place where there had been so much suffering and deprivation.

It was where so many of their comrades had perished from disease, starvation and brutality with a sensation which they could not understand either at that moment or, indeed, ever since of something approaching nostalgia. It was as though an important chapter of their lives had closed forever and would remain buried among the squalid and decaying shacks which had been their home for so long.

The strange moment passed almost as suddenly as it had come. The men headed for the Yau Ma Ti anchorage, where the tender was waiting to carry them to the 'Empress of Australia' and home.

By coincidence, the 'Empress' was the sister ship of the 'Empress of Japan', now diplomatically renamed 'Empress of Scotland', which had carried them out to Hong Kong four years previously.

The five years or so since her commissioning as a troopship had taken their toll, and she was in a sorry state of health. Gone were the glittering decor and luxurious furnishings of her former prosperous days as a cruise liner. She presented a drab appearance in her camouflage paintwork and worn and shabby fittings. However, had she been made of solid gold with jewelled accoutrements, the sight of her could not have been more welcome. She was their passage home and their wonderful life ahead.

The following morning, Monday, September 10th, the anchors were weighed, and the 'Empress' nosed her way cautiously between the sampans and junks and headed for the narrow Lyemun Channel at the eastern end of the harbour between Devil's Peak and Saiwan Hill.

Here the impatient passengers waited for a further twenty-four hours while boatloads of civilian internees, mainly women and children, from Stanley Camp were taken aboard and allocated to the available cabin accommodation.

At last, on the morning of September 11th, just over four weeks from the dropping of the nuclear bombs, which had brought the war to its sudden end, they were homeward bound. Roger spent almost his entire day standing, as he had so often dreamed of doing, on the aft boat deck watching Hong Kong and its surrounding islands become blue smudges on the horizon and finally vanish from sight.

He was coming home.

The voyage to Manila was uneventful. Early in the morning of September 13th, Roger went to the railings on the port side of the boat deck to see the island of Corregidor as the ship went through the narrow channel which led to the vast expanse of Manila Bay.

As the grim outline of the island loomed up in the dim light of dawn, the ship slowed to a stop. Roger, leaning down over the rail at the grey mirror of the sea, saw a hatchway from one of the lower decks swing open, and two planks appear from their doors. After a slight pause, a shape wrapped in white slid silently into the water with scarcely a ripple.

There was a sudden swirl of water, and a triangular fin cut the surface and disappeared. The ship gathered speed and headed for the Corregidor Channel. Some poor soul who for nearly four years had fought his way through disease and starvation had, at the last moment, lost his battle for survival.

He was not the last to find a similar grave during that journey home.

Manila Bay was in sharp contrast to the rugged cliffs of Corregidor, shell-torn and devastated from the desperate battle when its gallant garrison had defended it against overwhelming odds. As they learned later, the place was still occupied by remnants of the Japanese army, either grimly determined to fight for their emperor to the last or simply unaware that the war was over.

The bay was a teeming mass of warships and transports with dozens of launches and landing craft weaving their way to and fro between them. So vast was the expanse of water and so slow was the progress of the 'Empress' through the traffic that it was evening before she finally tied up at the dockside.

The women and children were off-loaded and taken away to be accommodated as best they might ashore. It was after eight o'clock, when the daylight had long since faded, that Roger and his companions humped their kit down the gangway and into the open trucks waiting to transport them to their transit camp twenty-five miles inland from Manila City.

The town itself had been all but obliterated by bombs and shell fire. Their truck plunged its way through craters and across banks of debris, throwing them violently from side to side so that when they finally arrived at the camp, they were bruised, hungry and totally exhausted.

It was now long past midnight, and all they craved was somewhere to stretch themselves out and sleep. But this was not to be.

Their American hosts were nothing if not efficient and drooping with tiredness; they were ushered into a medical reception area where they, together with their ragged clothing and possessions, were stripped and sprayed with DDT disinfectant.

Following this procedure, they were marched into more huts where their personal statistics and medical history were noted and detailed interrogations concerning Japanese atrocities painstakingly recorded so that it was long past dawn before they were led away to their tents and allowed to collapse thankfully onto their camp beds.

Roger slept, so they told him, for more than twenty-four hours and awoke to the smell of cigars and the unmistakable and delicious odour of food. His companions were sitting around on their beds or on the floor. Some were smoking; some were eating candy bars; others were drinking from cans with metal tops that looked like the tins of metal polish he had known in his army days, which he discovered contained Australian beer of a daunting potency.

Astonished by this vision, he asked where this had all come from. He was informed that he had only to take himself to the PX building, where all would be freely available. On arriving at this Shangri La, he discovered that he was entitled to nine cans of Australian beer, a quarter bottle of spirits, sixty cigarettes, six cigars and a pound of candy for every day of his residence in the camp.

Like his comrades, he took full advantage of this largesse and, on his arrival home, was the possessor of a great kit bag full of sweets, cigarettes and cigars, not to mention uncounted quantities of soap, toothpaste and razor blades, items which back in England were either strictly rationed or totally unobtainable.

The PX also contained a well-stocked restaurant where food was freely available at any time of the day or night.

Far better than all of this was a wonderful letter from Daisy, safe, well and brimming with happiness, written only a week before. He had no more to ask from life.

He was now given three options for transport home: to accept the opportunity, which was strongly recommended, of a period of recuperation and rehabilitation in Australia; to travel by naval transport via Hawaii and San Francisco; or to return by the 'Empress of Australia' via the Suez Canal. This latter, he was told, would arrive in England three days before the San Francisco option.

Never before or since has he reached a more rapid decision, and so, now kitted in the smart barathea uniform of an officer in the United States army, he boarded the truck for Manila, where the 'Empress of Japan' was waiting.

Now relieved of the Canadians and those who had opted to go home via San Francisco, the journey to Singapore was a little less uncomfortable. However, the open deck was a still much more agreeable alternative to the stifling heat of D Deck.

However, the ageing 'Empress' was in a rather delicate state of health. She limped across the South China Sea, taking more than five days for a journey which should have been done in half that time.

Many were still very far from fit, and Roger, in addition to his pellagra sores, deep suppurating ulcers that penetrated almost to the bone on his legs and groin, which showed no sign of healing, and a dry cough which had plagued him for three weeks. He took himself reluctantly to the ship's Medical Officer. The Medical Officer was clearly unacquainted with tropical diseases and announced that he would paint the ulcers with gentian violet, a powerful antiseptic. Roger, knowing the cause of the problem to be a lack of vitamin B2 and not an infection, refused abruptly, thereby occasioning the wrath of the M.O. who, nevertheless, at Roger's earnest request, reluctantly prescribed the Sulphadiazamine and M. and B., which his friend Woodward had obtained from the venereal sentries in Argyle Street. This not only tackled the ulcers with great effect but also did wonders for the beri-beri, which was still responsible for his swollen legs and electric feet.

At Singapore, a scheduled stop of a few hours was extended to four days while repairs were carried out to the ship's condensers. On September 27th, when the homeward journey had already lasted for more than a fortnight, Lady Louis Mountbatten, who had accompanied her husband to Malaya to take the formal Japanese surrender, came aboard to meet them.

She was informed that the ship had been christened 'Altmark Maru' and represented one of the worst atrocities of the war - which spurred the lady to promise instant action and, as a consequence, within an hour of her departure, the 'Empress' left Singapore at remarkable speed for the Straits of Malacca where it broke a piston and was obliged to limp slowly to Colombo for further repairs.

The three days' stopover in Colombo allowed them ashore. Here Roger met up with a jade merchant by the name of Salinger, whom he had known at Courtland Hotel, who lent him the princely sum of £5, which he invested in the purchase of several yards of fine silk to take home to Daisy.

Hospitality in Colombo was beyond belief and rivalled even that which they had received in Manila. Every time they stepped ashore, the ladies of the Red Cross pressed upon them copious linen bags of soap, toothpaste, razor blades, cigarettes and chocolate, which still further swelled their overflowing store of these good things and which lasted for nearly a year after their return to England. It was impossible to pay for a drink in any of the town's bars and clubs, so their recollections of Colombo were obscured by a blissful alcoholic haze.

The voyage across the Indian Ocean to Aden and from there through the stifling heat of the Red Sea was uneventful. At Adabiyah, the army base south of Suez, they received an issue of scrubby battle dress which, they were told, must henceforth be worn in the place of the elegant barathea with which they had been kitted out in Manila.

The 'Empress' scenting, as did her passengers, the end of the journey gathered up her skirts and took the Suez Canal in her stride, completing the passage in eight hours instead of the statutory twelve and, as they subsequently learned, causing many thousands of pounds worth of damage to its sandy banks in the process.

Cleared of Port Said and out into the Mediterranean, the bit was between their teeth, and the scent of home was in their nostrils. Nothing could stop them now, although a floating mine off the coast of Tunisia passing within a couple of feet of the ship's stern reminded them that there could yet be a slip between cup and lip.

A couple of hours' stop at Gibraltar to take in much-welcomed letters from home, and they were off again to the Bay of Biscay, which welcomed them with a force ten gale which smashed the crockery and filled the casualty department with bruises and damaged limbs.

As dusk was falling in the evening of Wednesday, October 24th, the Wicklow Mountains of Ireland made a smudge of land on the port side and towards midnight, the Holyhead lighthouse flashed out its welcome home.

Only a few more miles to go.

However, the south-westerly gale, which had done its best to speed their journey home, now turned sour on them, and the morning of October 25th found them at anchor in Liverpool Bay under the lee of the Great Orme's Head waiting for the heavy seas to subside and allow them to cross the Mersey Bar into port.

And there they sat for two whole days within sight and smell of the shore and separated from it by a mere mile of frothing water, so near and yet so far. During these two days of acute frustration, many dark plots were hatched to commandeer one of the ship's lifeboats and make for the beach.

It seemed more than a little cruel that after nearly five years away, they were to be denied their homecoming. Waiting impatiently at home, Daisy listened in vain on the radio for the news of their arrival.

But at last, towards the evening of the 27th, the 'Empress' tied up under the towers of the Liver building, and the long wait was at an end.

At least, very nearly so, for they had to wait with such patience as they could muster while the lord mayor, through loudspeakers on the dockside, delivered himself of a long speech of welcome which, although kindly and sincerely meant, was received as ungraciously as any which has ever been made.

At last, however, they clambered down the gangplank and into the great warehouse where they received their final ration of soap and razor blades and piled into the buses which were to take them to the reception camp at Huyton, where they arrived at 10 o'clock in the evening.

Here they were passed through much the same processing as they had experienced at Manila – medical checks, issue of ration cards and travel warrants and interrogations concerning Japanese atrocities – and it was not until 5am that Roger found himself, barely conscious, leaning against a bar in the canteen with a monumental glass of Scotch in his hand. Something was hammering its way into his befuddled brain, something important that he had got to do before anything else.

Suddenly it flashed upon him and brought him entirely to his senses. Of course, he had got to get in touch with Daisy before he did another thing.

Stone cold sober now, he made his way to a solitary telephone box to ring the farm across the road from the school house, which Daisy had told him in her latest letter would bring her to the phone.

Inside the box, he was dismayed to find the coin box so full of money that it was totally impossible to push another penny in. He lifted the receiver. A strong female Liverpool accent greeted him: "Number please," it said and, having been told: "Put two shillings and a sixpence into the box."

"I can't," replied the near-frantic Roger.

"Why not?" said the voice, now with a sharper edge.

"The bloody coin box is full," shouted the exasperated Roger.

The voice now was tinged with acid. "Look, I'm busy," it said. "I can't help with the box. You must find another one. No money, no phone call, lad."

Roger, who knew well that this was the only box available, was in despair.

"Look," he said, "I want to talk to my wife. I've just returned from a Japanese prison camp and haven't spoken to her for five years!" There was complete silence at the other end. Then a curious inarticulate sound. "I'll put you through straight away," said the voice now husky and scarcely audible. "Talk for as long as you like. Forget the money. God bless you, soldier."

At the school house, Daisy was woken by an excited farmer's wife. "Come quickly," she said, 'it's Roger on the phone!"

In her nightdress and bare feet, Daisy rushed across the road. What they said to each other in this magic moment, neither can recall, but she found herself promising to come to Euston Station to meet his train.

How she was to do so, she had no idea. It was a Sunday morning. She had no transport to Tunbridge Wells and did not even know if there would be a train. All she knew was that she would be there whatever the difficulties because that was what he had asked her to do.

The train from Huyton pulled out, and Roger, sharing the carriage with five others, suddenly recollected that in the excitement, he had left the packet of sandwiches provided for his journey in the telephone box and that he was getting hungry.

His companions unwrapped their packets and ate their sandwiches. So conditioned were they all to the ethics of the prison camp that it never occurred to them to share their food, nor did Roger expect them to. Under the circumstances, he would have done precisely the same.

The train shunted from time to time into sidings, made very heavy weather of the journey to London, and the morning drifted into late afternoon.

At Euston, Daisy, who by some miracle had arrived soon after lunch, waited in a milling and increasingly noisy crowd being directed by loudspeakers first to one platform and then to another and wondered how she would ever find him among this mass of humanity and even whether he would have changed so much as to be unrecognisable.

Many of the crowd carried placards on poles bearing their family names, and Daisy wished she had done the same.

A porter's barrow by the main exit seemed to offer the best vantage point, and she climbed up onto it and, without too much hope, looked down on the mass of humanity below.

At last, at five minutes past five, the frantic hooting of a train whistle was heard. The crowd broke out into wild cheering, and the train pulled slowly into the station. Standing in the corridor, Roger was in company with Pontin, the RASC officer who had prospered successfully from his business enterprises in Argyle Street, looking down at the cheering mass.

"However are we going to find anyone in all this crowd?" he asked.

Pontin shrugged. "I expect we shall manage it somehow," he said.

At that moment, the train came to a standstill, and there, face to face with Pontin, on the edge of the platform, was a woman, clearly his wife, and a moon-faced boy, the spitting image of his father.

As one might have expected of him, Pontin's luck had held to the last!

Roger, abandoning his kit on the platform, fought his way through the jostling mass. He did not even know if she had been able to make the journey and, even if she had, how he was to find her.

A woman in a uniform with a Middlesex badge in her lapel stopped him. "You are Middlesex," she said. "Are you looking for someone?"

"Yes, I am," retorted Roger rudely. "I'm looking for my wife and can't find her. Please let me get by."

The woman was unperturbed.

"And what is your wife's name?" she asked. "I am from the Hong Kong Fellowship, and I may know her."

"It's Daisy Rothwell," replied Roger, feeling a little ashamed at his truculence. "Please help me if you can." "Go along to the end of the platform," she replied, "and look for a porter's barrow on the left-hand side."

Scarcely pausing to thank this guardian angel, Roger pushed his way through the jostling, shouting, laughing, weeping crowd.

Then, above all the din, he heard a cry. A body hurtled down, and in an instant, she was in his arms.

How long they stayed like this, holding each other, speechless and silent among all the surrounding noise and tumult, neither can remember. The world went away, leaving them on an island of rapture where there was no need for words, even if they had been capable of uttering them.

At last, Roger spoke.

"Hallo, love," he said.

And kissed her.
